RESEARCH IN
TEACHER EDUCATION

RESEARCH IN TEACHER EDUCATION: INTERNATIONAL PERSPECTIVES

Edited by
Richard P. Tisher
Monash University
and
Marvin F. Wideen
Simon Fraser University

 The Falmer Press

(A member of the Taylor & Francis Group)
London • New York • Philadelphia

UK   The Falmer Press, Rankine Road, Basingstoke, Hampshire, RG24 0PR

USA   The Falmer Press, Taylor & Francis Inc., 1900 Frost Road, Suite 101, Bristol, PA 19007

First published 1990

British Library Cataloguing in Publication Data

Research in teacher education: international perspectives.
1. Teachers. Professional education
I. Tisher, Richard P. II. Wideen, Marvin
370.71
ISBN 1-85000-782-9
ISBN 1-85000-783-7 (pbk.)

Library of Congress Cataloging-in-Publication Data

Research in teacher education: international perspectives / edited by Richard P. Tisher and Marvin F. Wideen.
    Originated from a symposium at the Annual Meeting of the American Educational Research Association in Washington, 1987.
    Includes bibliographical references (p.).
    ISBN 1-85000-782-9 ISBN 1-85000-783-7 (pbk.).
    1. Teachers—Training of—Research. 2. Teachers—In-Service training—Research. 3. Education—Research. I. Tisher, R. P. II. Wideen, Marvin. III. American Educational Research Association. Meeting (1987: Washington, D.C.).
LB1707.R47 1990
370′.71′072—dc20   90-31684
                                 CIP

Jacket design by Caroline Archer

Printed in Great Britain by Burgess Science Press, Basingstoke on paper which has a specified pH value on final paper manufacture of not less than 7.5 and is therefore 'acid free'.

Contents

Contents

Preface

This book originated from a symposium at the annual meeting of the American Educational Research Association in Washington, 1987. The audience response to the presentations from Australia, Canada, Israel, the United States and West Germany prompted us to make plans for a book taking an international perspective on research in teacher education. We approached distinguished scholars from different countries to review the research in pre-service, induction and in-service education.

To gain their international perspective we reasoned it was important to have contributions from different continents or world regions such as Europe, North America, the Middle East, Asia and the Pacific, and to include countries with old and young traditions, large and small populations, and different geographical areas. Talented scholars from twelve countries — Australia, Britain, Canada, China, Germany (FRG), India, Israel, Japan, Netherlands, Singapore, Sweden and the United States — agreed to contribute. They accepted the difficult task of pulling together, for the first time in many instances, the corpus of the research in their country for the last decade. They have also dealt with a moving target during the period of writing as significant national and international events have affected policies, practices and attitudes to education, teacher education and researchers in several countries during the period of review.

The authors have approached their task in their own way, framing their chapters as they deemed appropriate and giving us a flavour of the research in their country. We are particularly grateful to those for whom English is a second language. The contributions constitute a unique volume where scholars from diverse countries have collaborated to produce a volume on research in teacher education. We believe the publication provides a rich, challenging picture of international research to inform and give direction to future action.

The reader is invited to search for comparable themes and issues in the research, noting how it is done, who does it, its influence on practice and policy, what we learned and the directions to be taken in the future.

Richard P. Tisher
Monash University
Marvin F. Wideen
Simon Fraser University

Chapter 1

The Role Played by Research in Teacher Education

Marvin F. Wideen and Richard P. Tisher

The Problem

Public education occupies an important role in most nations. Expectations run high: education should not only provide the engine for economic growth, but also the opportunity for individuals to achieve full access to social and economic participation. Some see schools as the means by which the values and mores of society pass from one generation to the next; others see schools as the hope for a better society through change. Concern over the quality of public education has become an enduring theme as we strive for better schools in the quest for better education of our young.

We can assume that the quality of education our children receive links directly to the knowledge, intelligence and professional skills of teachers. And we can further assume that teacher quality rests in turn on the selection of top candidates for teaching, their pre-service preparation, the support they receive in their induction or first year of teaching, and continued professional education of the teachers themselves through in-service. In short, if we want to give our young people the best education possible, we must first provide the best education and training to those who will teach them. This review looks at the part played by research in the ongoing challenge of providing the best education possible for those who will teach our children. It comes as little surprise that schools, and the colleges and universities which prepare teachers, often fail to fulfil the demanding and sometimes conflicting expectations of the public.

From the general literature of a variety of countries on teacher education, which sets the backdrop for the research reviewed in this book, a rather unhealthy, uneven picture emerges. In some cases we find teacher education under attack from critics. For example, Joyce and Clift (1984) paint a very dismal picture of teacher education in the United

States. Citing various authors, they point out that teacher education draws poor students; institutions that prepare teachers are separated from the knowledge base of education; current practices socialize teachers to a practicality ethic where survival concerns dominate; and current educational processes funnel teaching styles toward the persistence of recitation. Those writing about teacher education in many other countries describe it as badly underfunded, uncomfortable in the universities in which it is housed, and out of touch with the schools for which the teachers are being prepared. Alternative routes to certification are now in place in several states in the United States, and under consideration in Britain. Such alternative routes to certification bypass pre-service teacher education in universities and colleges. Many educators contend this practice will lower both the quality and prestige of teacher education.

Given the picture just described, it is not surprising that most major reports on teacher education call for reform. For example, Fullan and Connelly (1987), who conducted a study of teacher education in Canada for the Ontario Ministry of Education, suggest 'that it is the overall countenance of teacher education, rather than any of its parts, that needs reform' (p. 58). They cite theory and practice, quality of schooling, knowledge and knowing, what it means to be a teacher, and the teacher as a professional, as areas for change. They also recommend that faculties of education become more inquiry-based, both in terms of research and in the reporting of innovative teacher education programs.

While on the one hand the literature paints a dismal picture of teacher education, yet other developments present a more reassuring picture, at least for the future. In fact, the criticisms we have just cited, in themselves, reflect an increased interest in teacher education in many parts of the world, and in some instances the picture of teacher education that emerges looks encouraging.

As a field of study, teacher education is coming of age. In several countries, institutes and centres of study focusing on teacher education have recently been established. An international community of teacher educators is emerging through exchange programs, international conferences and publications. A new interest in research on teacher education has developed, fueled by lively discussion about appropriate methodologies and areas for research. An increased number of research papers are being presented at national and international conferences organized by groups such as the Australian Teacher Education Association, the American Educational Research Association, the European Association of Teacher Educators and the Canadian Association for Teacher Education. The American Educational Research Association has recently created 'Division K' which provides opportunities for teacher educators and researchers to share their knowledge, present research findings and discuss issues pertaining to teacher preparation and professional development. In 1988 Chulalongkorn University, in Thailand, coordinated the First Asia-Pacific Conference on Teacher Education to bring together people from the region, Europe and North America to share perspectives about research and programs in teacher education.

This increased interest in research in teacher education has paralleled an increase in research in education and has produced a much improved knowledge base in education generally. The potential for using this knowledge base as a means to reform presents new opportunities; many now see it as the basis for reform in teacher education (Joyce and Clift, 1984; Fullan and Connelly, 1987). We support this view, but further contend that research-based reform rests on our becoming more self-conscious about the teacher education process and attending more effectively to how research-based knowledge can be brought to bear on the process of teacher education.

This conviction leads us to ask how these issues have been addressed in different countries. It is time to take stock, to examine what we know in teacher education and what we need to know to provide effective teachers for the future. The tasks of attracting top students, preparing them to teach and offering opportunities for their continued professional development are pivotal both to maintaining a high level of instruction in our schools and to bringing about appropriate changes in education.

This book hopes to contribute to the improvement of teacher education through an examination of the research in teacher education taking place in different countries around the world. We take stock of past research, identify what can be learned from it, determine how it can be characterized, assess what contributions have already been made, and in looking toward the future, ask where we should go from here. In the chapters that follow top international scholars review the research on teacher education from twelve countries. The two closing chapters present a framework for examining the results and draw together the emerging themes. Many questions arise throughout the reviews that follow, but we wish to highlight three.

Who undertakes the research being done, and why?

Does the research have any impact on policy and practice?

What does the research tell us about teacher education?

We return to these and other questions in our concluding chapter. As a backdrop to this chapter we highlight these three questions through a discussion of the context for research into teacher education, the pattern of progress in that research, and the value that research can play in teacher education.

The Context for Research into Teacher Education

The context in which any activity occurs determines to some degree the nature of that activity. Research in teacher education is no exception as we see in the chapters that follow. Two contextual factors should be kept in mind in reading them. The first involves the nature of teacher education itself and how people think about it. The second involves how people think about research.

The models guiding the nature of teacher education programs, and the priorities of governments, training institutions, employers and researchers all have an effect on what is done in the name of teacher education. For example, the differences in approaches to teacher preparation described by the authors from West Germany and the Netherlands on the one hand, and Japan and China on the other, provide sharp contrasts in what people consider teacher education to be.

The question as to how such a complex mix of factors influences the research done in teacher education should be considered throughout the reading of these chapters. For instance, when teacher education became a priority in Sweden in the early 1970s, research into the area also became a priority. We are left with the view that research into teacher education has dropped in the last decade, and that it will remain a low priority until the central government makes reform in teacher education a priority once more. Similarly, research into teacher education in Japan had its beginning when the emphasis was placed on teacher preparation. In Britain the changes made in teacher education in the past decade have affected both the quality and quantity of research done in that country. Thus part of the answer to why people undertake research into teacher education in the first place lies in the priorities reflected in the national context.

National issues and their related events also provide a contextual element prompting certain types of research. The national concern for manpower in Israel, for example, is offered by Ben-Peretz as the reason for the heavy emphasis on research on the recruits who enter the teaching profession in that country. Yet in other countries studies of those who enter teaching account for a very small amount of research that occurs.

On the other hand, in countries such as Canada, Australia and the United States, one gains the distinct impression that much research, particularly by individual scholars, occurs out of curiosity or enlightened opportunism (i.e., a sample of beginning teachers happened to be available) that has little to do with national, state or provincial priorities. Perhaps in those countries priorities become more difficult to identify, or perhaps such research occurs simply because people want to engage in it out of their own curiosity. These comments seem naturally to lead to the questions, why do people have a desire to undertake research in the first place? how does that desire impact on the kind of research being done? and how are the results being used?

A further contextual factor which appears to have a strong bearing on the research done in different countries involves the orientation to research in vogue at the time, or the methodological priorities of the day. The role of research in teacher education has progressed through different stages since the Second World War. An examination of the literature of the past twenty-five years reveals that while research occurred throughout this period, its role shifted partly in response to the capability that was available and partly in response to what were viewed as valid claims to knowledge. The role that research is expected to play today is very different from what it was two decades ago because of these changes in both research capability and what appears to be valued in research. To set this context further, we review briefly the patterns of progress in teacher education research since the Second World War.

Early Research Period

In the two decades immediately following the Second World War little research in teacher education was reported, and one might fairly assume that few studies were conducted during this period. In many parts of the world training institutions were responding to a rapidly growing need for teachers to educate the post-war 'baby boom' and resources were devoted primarily to meeting this need. Also, at this time, in many countries teacher education moved from small colleges to university campuses. Teacher education had not yet reached the stage of academic self-consciousness where research was looked at as necessary endeavour.

Beginning of Empirical Research

Peck and Tucker (1973) contend that a quantum leap occurred somewhere between 1963 and 1965 in the design and quality of teacher education research in the United States. In Australia this leap occurred in the early 1970s. These points mark the beginnings of experimental research in particular, and in some cases the rumblings of qualitative studies.

However, the research base developed slowly, and even in the 1970s little research in teacher education itself occurred. Taylor (1978) made the following comment in his work for the Council of Europe:

> The improvement of teacher education is dependent upon... more attention being given to ways in which research-based knowledge from the different disciplines centrally relevant to the preparation of teachers can be brought to bear on the design of programs, the teaching of courses and the organization of practical work (p. 12).

A careful reading of this quotation suggests that at this time the available research base still lay outside teacher education, and that other disciplines were viewed as the primary sources of knowledge upon which teacher education should draw. A knowledge base specific to teacher education was still virtually non-existent. Interestingly by 1983 the same author argues for a research base within teacher education itself.

For much of this beginning period research in education was dominated by an empirical-analytic inquiry orientation. This orientation focused upon identifying specific variables and examining them in the light of dependent variables (Jacknicke and Rowell, 1987). The large number of 'process-product' studies of the 1970s which tried to identify specific teacher behaviours leading to student achievement also reflect this approach. By the late 1970s we saw a greatly increased amount of research in teacher education. Popkewitz, Tabachnick and Zeichner (1979), however, contend that teacher education research based on this notion has not led very far toward understanding the complexity of the enterprise.

Movement toward Pluralism

By the early 1980s the research base in teacher education had begun to develop in two important ways. The accumulation of empirical work, particularly in countries such as Australia, the United States, Sweden, Canada and Britain, had now produced an impressive amount of research. Although much of this knowledge did little to help those who prepare teachers, an important shift had been made: teacher education was now viewed as a valid field of study in its own right. As we mentioned earlier, this interest has led to the establishment of 'Division K' of the American Educational Research Association and the presentation of more research papers at European, Australasian and Asia-

Pacific conferences as teacher educators availed themselves of internationally recognized forums for sharing and discussing research.

During this period teacher education research began to expand in yet another way. Educational researchers in many countries turned their attention to other approaches which might yield further insights into the nature of teacher education. The situational-interpretive inquiry orientation (Jacknicke and Rowell, 1987), taken from the social sciences, became increasingly accepted as a valid approach to educational research. Within this approach meaningful descriptions and interpretations of events and phenomena became the focus. Methodologies within this orientation stress descriptive data collection using observation, interviewing, transcript analysis and direct participation. This growing interest in qualitative research began to be felt in teacher education, paralleling the rise of pluralism in research methodologies, and thereby broadened the scope of research. It appears that at present we are still in the midst of a shift toward a more pluralistic approach, and that fundamental questions about an appropriate paradigm for teacher education research will continue to be debated for some time.

The current literature on education and teacher education contains numerous thought-provoking articles about the relative merits of these different orientations and about what is acceptable as valid knowledge. Some argue that qualitative and quantitative approaches are complementary and should be combined (Howe, 1985; Miles and Huberman, 1984). Others claim that fundamental epistemological differences exist between them, and that educators must continue to examine critically and debate these differences (Barrow, 1988). The influence of these research orientations or ways of knowing upon the research becomes important when examined in different contexts. India and Singapore, for example, continue to pursue research based largely on an empirical-analytic paradigm; yet in Australia the qualitative approach to research within teacher education has had acceptance for well over a decade. The reader must view the research that follows in terms of what appears to be an accepted form of academic inquiry in the contexts in which the research is being done. For the moment arguments in favour of pluralistic or complementary approaches appear to dominate the research scene, providing a rich and varied approach to inquiry into teacher education.

Assuming that research in teacher education has come of age, what contributions might we expect research to make in guiding reform in the field? We have no simple answer to that question. The literature does point to several ways of thinking about it that will be discussed throughout this volume.

Research and Practice

A major issue in education generally and in teacher education specifically remains the link between research and practice. In the chapters that follow several authors take up that issue within their own national contexts. Clearly the issue turns on how one uses the knowledge that results from such research. Does it produce theory, inform decisions, or enlighten one's practice? Should we expect a link between research and practice? As to whether a link exists between research and practice in teacher education, the thrust of Kerlinger's 1977 address to the American Educational Research Association left little ambiguity. He argued that little connection should exist between research and practice in education generally. Research, he claimed, does not solve practical problems related to teaching, and the demand for relevance can often be highly deleterious. What research can do is to develop basic theory to aid our understanding, which does ultimately lead to improved practice, but not in the short term.

This view seeks to evaluate research based on its contribution to theory and ultimately on how that theory might be applied to teacher preparation. However, we suspect that life is not quite like this. Research on teacher education does not simply and easily develop basic theory, or yield findings which can be applied. Such thinking adopts a simplistic model for theory building and educational change which takes little account of political, social and organizational realities. If we are to assess all of its benefits, we must look beyond the ability of research to contribute to theory, or to have its findings applied. The very existence of research, a willingness to allocate resources to it, and the experience people gain by being involved constitute positive 'pay-offs' which, in turn, contribute to the practice of teacher education. In our opinion the view that research has not been able to inform practice comes more in the form of speculative hypothesis than in empirical fact. This important question of the relation between research and practice is addressed in this volume from an international perspective.

One might also argue that Kerlinger's rational-positivist view has now passed us by. Certainly the belief that research develops theory in order to direct practice toward predetermined ends represents the empirical-analytic orientation (Jacknicke and Rowell, 1987). On the other hand, the emergence of other approaches such as those of the situational-interpretive now find acceptance and provide valuable alternatives as to how research can inform practice.

The usefulness of research in aiding the reform of teacher education can be defended on accounts other than its direct links to practice. We invite the reader to consider, among others, three additional possibilities: awareness and understanding; stimulus for reform; and reflection on action. Many educators would argue that the main value of research lies in its identification of issues and problems which need analysis and interpretation so that practice can be modified. From this viewpoint, qualitative research can be useful in helping us see and understand some of the many issues arising from the complexity of teacher education and the contexts in which it occurs. An important value arising from the reviews which follow lies in the problems they identify, not the solutions they propose.

Research not only creates pressure for reform, but also provides some direction as to the nature of that reform. A critical reading — between the lines — of the reviews from the various countries which follow uncovers some critical areas to which all stakeholders must attend if teacher education is to improve in ways that will make it possible to meet the challenges that it faces.

The concept of reflection has received increasing attention in the literature. Many have now built upon Schon's (1983) earlier work. Reflection involves 'a critical examination of one's experience in order to derive new levels of understanding by which to guide future action' (Holborn, 1988, p. 197). Research, as we see it reviewed in the following chapters, can, we submit, provide a basis for such reflection. As such, research can serve to help us examine our assumptions, intentions and motives, sensitize us to the existence of variables and phenomena that might otherwise have gone unnoticed, and provide a forum of people who will debate and share ideas and problems so that reform is more likely to be stimulated and guided by conscious critical analysis rather than by blind faith.

References

BARROW, R. (1988) Contexts, concepts and content: Prescriptions for empirical research. *Canadian Journal of Education*, 13, 1, 1–13.

FULLAN, M. and CONNELLY, F.M. (1987) 'Teacher education in Ontario: Current practice and options for the future.' A position paper written for the Ontario Teacher Education Review. Ontario: Ministry of Education and Ministry of Colleges and Universities.

HOLBORN, P. (1988) Becoming the reflective practitioner. HOLBORN, P., WIDEEN, M. and ANDREWS, I. (Eds) *Becoming a Teacher*, Toronto: Kagan and Woo.

HOWE, K. (1985) Two dogmas of educational research. *Educational Researcher*, 14, 8, 10–18.

JACKNICKE, K.G. and ROWELL, P.M. (1987) Alternative orientations to educational research. *Alberta Journal of Educational Research*, 33, 1, 62–72.

Joyce, B. and Clift, R. (1984) The Phoenix agenda: Essential reform in teacher education. *Educational Researcher*, 13, 4, 5–16.

Kerlinger, F.R. (1977) The influence of research on educational reform. *Educational Researcher*, 6, 8, 5–12.

Marsh, D.D. (1987) 'Research utilization strategies for preservice and inservice teacher educators.' A paper presented at the Annual Meeting of the American Educational Research Association, Washington, DC.

Miles, M. and Huberman, A. (1984) *Qualitative Data Analysis: A Sourcebook of New Methods*. Beverly Hills, Calif.: Sage Publications.

Peck, R.F. and Tucker, J.A. (1973) Research in teacher education, in R.M.W. Travers (Ed.) *Second Handbook of Research on Teaching*. Chicago, Ill.: Rand McNally.

Popkewitz, T.S., Tabachnick, B.R. and Zeichner, K.M. (1979) Dulling the senses: Research in teacher education. *Journal of Teacher Education*, 30, 5, 52–59.

Roth, B.A. (1986) Alternate and alternative certification: Purposes, assumptions, implications. *Action in Teacher Education*, 8, 2, 1–6.

Schon, D.A. (1983) *The Reflective Practitioner*. New York: Basic Books.

Taylor, W.T. (1978) *Research and Reform in Teacher Education*. Windsor: NFER.

Chapter 2

Teacher Education in Canada: A Research Review

Marvin F. Wideen and Patricia Holborn

Context for the Review

Teacher education in Canada is characterized by diversity. Geographical, historical and cultural factors have fostered a decentralized education system in which each of the ten provinces sets its own standards for teacher certification. Levels of funding and policy regulation vary from province to province, and the forty-nine universities which provide pre-service training have a high degree of individual autonomy. In-service for certified teachers is offered by a variety of agencies including universities, teachers' organizations, local school districts, individual schools and special interest organizations. Although attempts are being made to view teacher education as a continuum from selection through pre-servise training, induction and ongoing in-service education, the activities in which teachers engage at different points along the continuum are relatively discrete both conceptually and functionally. While this diversity and changing landscape provide an interesting context for the interpretation of research findings, it also provides difficulty in making generalizations about teacher education in Canada.

During the past few decades the landscape of teacher education in Canada has also undergone significant changes (Wideen and Holborn, 1986). For example, pre-service education has seen the transfer of certification programs from normal schools to universities and the extensive lengthening of pre-service practica, while in-service education has been influenced by the ageing of the teaching force and large fluctuations in the size of the school-age population.

Nature of the Research

This chapter describes and assesses research conducted on pre-service, induction and in-service teacher education in Canada over the past two decades. It comes at a time of increasing research activity and interest in teacher education in Canada. For this review, all Canadian journals of education were surveyed to locate reports focusing on teacher education. We located over 200 published research reports. We believe that a much larger body of research exists in the form of unpublished theses and dissertations, local research reports and in-house documents, but these have proven extremely difficult to locate. This chapter describes typical studies in the areas under which we classified the research.

Until recently, most researchers took what Jacknicke and Rowell (1987) have described as an empirical-analytic approach based on Habermas' tri-paradigmatic framework. This approach isolates variables with an emphasis on quantitative methods, stressing the 'objectivity' of the researcher, frequently without reference to a broader context. Within this approach the studies we reviewed commonly used questionnaires; little true experimental work was reported. The methodological adequacy of individual studies varied considerably and the lack of replication and saturation was problematic, especially given the diversity of the Canadian context. More recently, studies taking a situational-interpretive orientation to research have also begun to appear. This approach seeks insight into human experience by means of clarifying and making explicit the meaning of events and activities, using qualitative methods. We believe this approach holds much promise for enriching our understanding of the teacher education process, although the number of such studies reported remains limited.

Research on Pre-service Teacher Education

The Pre-service Context

Two types of certification programs exist in Canada. On the one hand, most provinces have some form of one-year (or one-year equivalent) professional program in which education courses are interspersed with one or more short practice teaching periods. Campus work typically includes a mix of methodology and foundational courses. These one-year programs exist within four- or five-year degree sequences, or as a separate certification year following degree completion. On the other hand, in almost every province examples of alternative programs exist which provide lengthier field experience and innovative approaches to course-work (Mickelson and Pearce, 1976) and concurrent degree programs where pedagogy and academic work are mixed (Overing, 1973).

General Characteristics of the Research

The studies of pre-service teacher education fell into three broad categories: provincial and national surveys conducted by individuals or provincial teacher organizations; studies originating within institutions carried out by faculty members and graduate students; and studies of program evaluation conducted within institutions.

In terms of content and findings the studies mostly pursued a wide range of unrelated topics and made infrequent references to other studies of teacher education in Canada. Diversity predominated. The bulk of these pre-service research reports addressed the characteristics of students, the practicum and program effectiveness.

Students Who Enter Teaching. These studies, representative of others in this area, suggest that the quality and perspectives of those now entering the profession have shifted. In many Canadian institutions we now draw from a much stronger pool of candidates than in previous decades. In some institutions an 80 per cent average is required to enter teaching. The research also suggests that as the academic quality of students entering the profession improves and as they become more diverse in terms of ages and background experience (McMurray, Hardy and Posluns, 1986), we may see individuals entering the profession with different beliefs about teaching than in past years. However, as with other areas reported here, some strong caveats pertain to these findings. The studies all occurred in different institutions, the questions asked of students differed from study to study, and little or no consultation occurred among the researchers.

Neufeld's (1974) survey of why students select teaching as their profession typifies earlier findings. Prospective elementary teachers entering the profession gave opportunities to work with children as their highest ranking motive, while secondary teachers indicated their primary motive to be interest in subject matter. Prestige, high salary and advancement were less important. Similar results with regard to the split between orientations of elementary and secondary candidates were obtained at the University of Toronto (Martin, Isherwood and Rapagna, 1978) and at the University of Calgary (Unrah, 1981). Unrah noted that most education students said they had enjoyed their previous school experiences, a findings confirmed in part by Sedgwick, Hill and Russell (1981). Their research found that students possess many of the values and attitudes possessed by practising classroom teachers, which they attributed to the students' previous experiences with those teachers. In a more recent study Thom and Klassen (1986) found students at Lakehead University to be highly committed to a personal view of teaching, and concluded their paper with the comment that 'teachers want the opportunity to be creative and have expressed a willingness to take whatever steps are needed in order to ensure a quality educational program for their students' (p. 2).

The Practicum. Several studies deal with the practicum as an entity in itself, and its relationship to campus work. Others focus on the cooperating teachers' role in the practicum.

The nature of the practicum: student viewpoint. The most prevalent means of examining the practicum and determining how it might be improved has been to ask student teachers. A national survey (Bessai and Edmonds, 1977), several studies conducted within institutions (Ratsoy, Babcock and Caldwell, 1978; Housgo and Boldt, 1980; and Montabello, 1989) and in-depth analyses of students' reflective essays (Sanders, Andresino, Isaacs and Irvine, undated) provide a basis of student opinion in different institutions across Canada from which some inferences about the experience can be drawn.

The Bessai and Edmonds study surveyed 907 students in eight faculties of education. The study reported on the learning experiences of the students which prepare them for the practicum, and how student teaching was evaluated. Despite rating 'instruction in disciplinary methods' as essential, less than half the students had received instruction in that area. Preparatory coursework focused on methodology and human development, with much less emphasis on classroom evaluation and micro-teaching. The predominant criteria for evaluation were the students' relationships with pupils, their ability to arouse and sustain interest, and their energy and enthusiasm. Their study typified survey research representative of that period.

Sanders, Andresino, Isaacs and Irvine's study provides a contrasting example. They conducted a content analysis of the reflective essays of ninety-seven students (13 per cent cross-section of the student body) near the end of their one-year program at the University of Western Ontario. The authors expressed surprise at the negative tone of the data, as one-third expressed dissatisfaction with the practicum. The dual role of the student teacher and the sense of gamesmanship which existed centred this criticism. Faculty did not practise what they preached and provided courses that lacked challenge. In contrast, Montabello's (1989) study of students' reflective journal entries at Simon Fraser University indicated that students appreciated their relationships with faculty members and faculty associates who worked closely with them throughout their entire practica as well as in the on–campus portion of the program. The contrast undoubtedly reflects the difference in programs.

From these and other studies it appears that students view practice teaching as an opportunity to adapt to the role of the teacher. They also place considerable importance on learning to interact with children, and see the main criterion of success as the demonstration of interest and enthusiasm. In terms of improving the practicum, students suggest a better selection and preparation of school associates. Students in six–week classroom experiences recommend a lengthening of the practicum period, and more time free from performance evaluation in the classroom.

The practicum up close.   Another group of studies has examined changes in the thinking of student teachers by focusing closely on the development of individual students. All are of a more recent origin than those just described, reflect a situational–interpretive orientation, and used qualitative methods including extensive field notes, interviews and observation data from which to draw conclusions.

Campbell (1985), for example, grounded her work on the notion of student teacher development as conceptualized by Fuller. She observed three students over a sixteen–week internship period, looking for changes in the students' thoughts and actions. She found the process to be developmental, moving through five stages: survival, self–adequacy, instructional task, subject matter focus, and stabilization. She also found the process to vary for each individual. Holborn's (1983) work also supported the highly individualistic nature of development as a student progresses through a practicum. She analyzed the thought patterns of eight students through a sixteen–week practicum, using both observation and journal summaries, and found the integration of theory and practice to be a personal process facilitated by reflective writing and peer feedback.

Tardif (1985) examined the influence of the practicum on the beliefs and attitudes of eight teacher education students. Arguing that socialization has greatly influenced students prior to entering teacher education, she also identified the meanings and assumptions that students brought to the practicum. Student teaching then became a process of learning certain ground rules such as creating a distance, being firm but friendly, and working within the limits. As a result of her study, she argued that teacher educators must work on freeing individuals from these unconscious influences.

One weakness of these studies is the small number of students that were followed. Replication with larger numbers will be necessary before the results can be accepted more generally. However, the strength of these studies lies in their heuristic value, and they also carry with them implications for practice which many others in this review do not.

The role of the cooperating teacher. The importance of the supervising teacher in the student teaching triad is evidenced by the abundance of proposals for improving that role, and the increasing interest that role has received in research. Studies indicate that the role is poorly defined, that cooperating teachers feel unprepared for their supervisory responsibilities, and that they seek more input into the planning process (Ratsoy, Babcock and Caldwell, 1978).

Despite a poorly defined role for the cooperating teacher, a high level of agreement exists among those in the triad of student teacher, cooperating teacher and university supervisor on the expectations for the cooperating teacher's role. Grimmett and Ratzlaff (1986) elicited perceptions from student teachers, university supervisors and cooperating teachers with regard to the cooperating teacher's role and found a high level of consensus on the functions orientation, planning/instruction, evaluation and professional development.

The supervisory assistance provided to cooperating teachers has received a great deal of attention in research and evaluation, particularly within individual institutions. At the University of Alberta nine studies have been conducted to investigate the impact of in-service workshops to assist teachers in the supervision process. Sloan (1981) summarized both the provision of and effects of supervisory training. In response to the findings noted earlier that considerable confusion existed among supervising teachers regarding their role, the faculty provided a cooperating teacher workshop program over a four-year period which was well attended. The findings from a rather extensive evaluation of this program, which included questionnaire and interview data, indicated that teachers perceived the workshops to be highly beneficial in clarifying their role and in providing skills to work better with students. Teachers also felt the need for a continuing program.

In more recent studies at Simon Fraser University (Holburn and Olliver, 1988), evaluation of a comprehensive supervisory training program involving forty-eight hours of credit coursework followed by a semester-long practicum showed positive outcomes in terms of greater role understanding, implementation of skills, and more positive attitudes toward supervisory responsibilities. The two-semester training sequence was based on a broad view of the cooperating teacher's role. A group of fourteen cooperating teachers who participated in the training sequence demonstrated greater understanding of the supervisory cycle, more effective interaction skills, and higher levels of confidence in their supervisory abilities than did a matched group of cooperating teachers without extensive training. In addition, the trained cooperating teachers were rated consistently higher than those in the control group by both student teachers and university supervisors.

The effects of association with a university on the professional growth of cooperating teachers at York University was studied by Wideen and Hopkins (1984). They determined three factors which appeared to maximize professional growth among cooperating teachers: involvement, philosophical compatibility, and source of influence. With regard to the source of influence student teachers were found to be the most powerful. However, data from this study did not support the commonly held myth that teachers necessarily grow professionally during their association with a faculty of education. For many teachers it appeared that supervision of students was simply a chore to be endured.

In summary, it appears that a lack of clarity exists regarding the role of the supervising teachers. Where supervisory training has been provided, teachers have found it useful. In all but one of the studies we reviewed, such training appeared to have an impact on the supervisory process. While some elements of that training were transferred to the classroom, in many cases implementation was somewhat limited. Cooperating teachers see the student as a more important influence in terms of affecting their professional development than other sources such as the principal, university supervisor, or various in-service activities.

Effects of the practicum on students. Increasing emphasis on the practicum has been questioned by Covert (1984) and Clifton and Covert (1980), who found limited empirical evidence to support the extended practicum; they questioned its contribution to the development of beginning teachers' attitudes and values.

Some studies, such as those of Clifton and Covert (1980) and Tattersall (1979), have examined the effect of the practicum on the student teacher. Others, such as those of Mundel-Atherstone (1980) and Harper (1977), sought to use success in the practicum as an outcome measure.

Tattersall (1979), for example, sought to identify patterns of change in student teacher anxiety and self-concept over the course of the extended or thirteen-week practicum. Measures were taken at the beginning of the semester and again at weeks 3, 6, 9 and 12. The randomly selected groups (N = 195) totalled 60 per cent of the students in the professional development extended practicum at the time. While the results supported previous studies in terms of maintained or improved self-concept from pre-test to week 12, they also revealed striking fluctuations within the practicum. For instance, anxiety declined during the early weeks from a high point at pre-test, but rose markedly at the mid-point when self-concept was lowest. Steady improvement occurred only during the latter half of the practicum.

Many unresolved issues related to the conduct of research on the extended practicum and in teacher education as a whole remain. First, the studies reviewed focus on the only one outcome whose relationship to successful teaching has not been defined. Other critical outcomes such as student teachers' instructional and interpersonal competence and their impact on children have not been addressed. Yet even within this narrow framework the evidence suggests that an interaction of variables is at work. Second, these studies illustrate the difficulty of comparing programs from one institution to another, where students may be in completely different contexts and program experiences, so that control of treatment variables is impossible. Third, with the exception of the journal analyses these studies all reflect an empirical-analytic orientation, and do not provide the detailed descriptions and interpretations of events which are needed to provide insight into the complexities of the teacher education process.

Program Effectiveness. The study of program effectiveness which uses components such as the methods course as independent variables and teacher behaviour as dependent variables is largely not in evidence in Canada. Program effectiveness has more frequently been assessed in Canada through the use of follow-up studies in which attempts have been made to relate the total program to the opinions of those who hire teachers, to some measure of teaching effectiveness, or to first-year teacher placement. The opinions of those who hire teachers seem to depend a great deal on who asks the question. Where third parties have been involved in conducting surveys the responses tend to be quite negative (Bessai and Edmonds, 1977; Flanders, 1980). Bessai and Edmonds sum up their results this way: 'Most comments indicated that there was a wide gap between the idealistic teaching situations in university classes and the real world of the classroom' (p. 26).

Flanders used focus-group interviews to probe teachers' perceptions of their roles and various aspects of professional preparation. His research was unusual in its attempt to construct a view of the teacher's role within the current social context and to relate it to both pre-service and in-service programs. Participants in the study were highly critical of their pre-service teacher preparation, but did favour the extended practicum as a more effective introduction to the realities of teaching than shorter student teaching periods.

On the other hand, where institutions themselves have approached those in the field to assess their programs, negative results occur. Unrah (1981) reports on one of the most comprehensive follow-up studies at the University of Calgary where he sought the opinions of forty-three principals in the Calgary area through interview, and four area superintendents in a meeting. In general the author of the report found the results favourable. Among the more favourable aspects of the program was the practicum. The major negative perception was 'that some faculty members are out of touch with the schools — with teachers, pupils, content, methodology, day-to-day problems, etc.' (p. 52). The education courses themselves were not seen to be particularly relevant.

Studies of Pre-service Teacher Education Reported in French

Canada is a bilingual country with two official languages, English and French. Several studies were located dealing with problems in teacher education in faculties where French is the language of instruction. All these studies were conducted in faculties of education in English-speaking Canada. All but one dealt with French immersion.[1] Typical of these were studies by Obadia (1986) and Beauchemin (1985). Because of the newness of these programs the research has focused on supply and demand questions. The demand for French teachers exceeds the supply now and will for several years to come.

Beauchemin (1985) examined the effect of the arrival of French immersion students on French-speaking universities. She argues that faculties of education should be responsible for the promotion of the 'culture' of the minority groups and make this a heavy component of the training of new teachers.

Areas of Limited Attention

Of considerable significance are those areas to which very little or no research attention has been devoted in pre-service teacher education in Canada. One might expect an applied faculty to study very carefully the hiring policies of districts and to conduct follow-up studies to assess the relationship between pre-service training and the teaching careers of graduates. Three surveys were identified which examined the hiring policies of districts (Greene, 1980; Hutcheon, 1972; Randhawa and Kirk-patrick, 1975). A common theme among these was the dissatisfaction among graduates about the lack of matching between preparation and placement.

Apart from works by Clarke and Coutts (1975), Andrews (1986), and Nixon and Bumbarger (1984) one finds very little attention in the literature devoted to the future of teacher education. Clarke and Coutts sought the opinions of key decision-makers about the future of teacher education. However, no follow-up or replication of their work has occurred since publication of their results. Andrews drew on existing research to posit four possible scenarios for teacher education. He offers the excellent conventional model and the creative model as ones to achieve.

Other seemingly important areas have received only minor attention. For example, only one or two studies were located in the areas such as the effects of length of pre-service training (Emerson, 1977); faculties of education as organizations (Wideen and Holborn, 1987); program implementation and change (Friesen and Cooper, 1985; and Hopkins, 1980); and faculty members who teach in faculties of education (Weber, 1986). Further, we found no examination of the relationship between faculties of education and external groups such as the university at large, the department of education, or teacher associations.

Emerging Themes in Pre-service Research

What can one say about pre-service teacher education in Canada, based on the research that has been conducted? The lack of replication, the different programmatic contexts in which research has been conducted, the predominant use of questionnaires, and the examination of variables out of context limit the findings. Within these limitations certain themes emerge from the data, reappearing again and again where certain issues and questions were being addressed.

First, where the practicum and campus input are offered separately, particularly in one-year programs, students are highly critical of most aspects of teacher education. Where attempts have been made to combine campus coursework with practice teaching, students are much more positive toward both campus coursework and the student teaching experience. Campus courses are not held in high esteem by students, teachers or principals. The practicum remains the most favourably viewed component of teacher education. Where follow-up studies have been conducted by third parties, teachers report that the teacher training component occurring on campus had little impact upon their teaching.

Second, while the clients may see the practicum as the most effective component of teacher education, its complexities are poorly understood. The one conclusion emerging from a reading of a number of studies is that the practicum, particularly if extended in length, has a strong socializing influence on students which cancels out the effects of campus input. When one couples this with the finding that students entered teaching because they enjoyed their own experience in classrooms, the tendency to retain the status quo in teaching remains strong.

Third, roles, particularly those of the supervising teacher, are confused. It appears that amid such confusion teachers tend to play a supporting role for students, while faculty supervisors take a more critical position. While differences in perception can be positive in many cases, the different views held by the teachers and the university supervisors do not work to the best interest of students. Training in clinical supervision for supervising teachers is received positively, possibly because it tends to clarify their role.

Research on the Induction Phase of Teacher Education

The Context

Although teacher educators in North America have recently turned increasing attention to the problems of beginning teachers, programs specifically intended to assist beginning teachers have been quite limited in most parts of Canada until recently. Andrews (1984, p. 218), who conducted a comprehensive review of induction efforts in Canada, points out that no comprehensive provincially-based induction programs occurred in Canada prior to 1985. Earlier efforts to assist beginning teachers were undertaken mainly by individual school districts or local teachers' associations, and consisted mostly of orientation sessions and distribution of print materials (p. 219). Since 1985 several projects have been initiated.

Research on Induction to Teaching

Research on this phase of teacher education reflects an overall lack of attention to beginning teachers' professional development needs. The literature is scant, and consists almost entirely of needs assessment surveys and evaluative studies conducted in conjunction with specific projects. We describe five of these reports.

Needs of Beginning Teachers. Two studies look specifically at beginning teachers' needs. Fair (1973) examined beginning teachers' instructional activities in order to identify factors influencing their growth, and determined that their capacity for instructional change was limited by their pupils unless substantial support was provided by experienced colleagues or supervisors. McIntosh (1978) looked at the role of mentors in supporting the socialization of new teachers, and found that experienced and beginning teachers were apprehensive about collaborative activities.

Support Programs. A support program for beginning teachers initiated in the province of Manitoba had support from the Department of Education and the Manitoba Teachers' Society. Reimer (1978) conducted an evaluation and recommended that 'the two year probationary period prior to permanent certification should become a recognized part of the professional preparation of teachers with regular systematic provision for professional growth' (Andrews, 1986, p. 363). With no ongoing funding the project died. In 1978 Ilavsky studied the transitional experiences of nineteen beginning teachers, and found that the work done by the induction project had positively influenced principals' attitudes when working with new teachers (Ilavsky, 1978). But again this study appeared to fall on deaf ears when it came to ongoing support.

The most ambitious induction project in Canada has been the Initiation to Teaching Project, a pilot project of the Alberta government conducted during the 1985–87 school years and evaluated by a team of twelve professors from the province's three faculties of education. It placed beginning teachers in classrooms for one year on two-thirds salary; one purpose of the program was to provide employment for graduates who might otherwise be unemployed. The evaluation included a literature review, surveys, interviews, observation, analysis of reports and a formative evaluation at the end of the first year. The final evaluation report stated that the internship had many positive features which outweighed its few disadvantages, and that virtually all major educational groups in the province expressed strong support for its continuation (Ratsoy, Friesen and Holdaway, 1987, p. vii). As a result of this evaluation, it has been recommended '...that, by September 1990, every beginning teacher — that is, one who has completed the university teacher preparation program and has never been employed on a regular, full-time contract — be required to complete successfully an approved internship, to be known as a "Teacher Residency Program", For "Resident

Teachers".' At the time of writing this chapter the status of these recommendations remains unclear.

The possibility of a province-wide induction program is also being investigated in Ontario. Cole and McNay (1988) recently conducted a survey of inividuals and groups concerned with teacher education in that province by circulating a discussion paper on induction programs to a sample of teachers and representatives of school boards, faculties of education, teachers' federations, the Ministry of Education and the Ministry of Colleges and Universities.

In the pre-service research we noted an emerging trend toward closer examination of participants' experiences through naturalistic qualitative research. Only two studies of a similar nature were found in the induction literature. Turner (1985) studied the first year of teaching as seen through the eyes of three beginning teachers of young children. Using participant observation and interview techniques, she developed descriptive portrayals of each teacher's experiences, and from these identified seven common themes: beginning teacher as stranger, 'I'm a real teacher at last', caring, struggle for control, uncertainty leading to distress, help, and time. The researcher concludes that beginning teachers need help, but only if the helper attempts to know personally and understand the individual and his or her struggles.

Research is required in virtually every aspect of induction. In particular, we know little about the factors which influence teachers' growth at this stage of their careers. Qualitative studies with a developmental perspective would enrich our understanding in this area. Also the large-scale support programs for beginning teachers now emerging will provide a unique opportunity for collaboration among program developers, action researchers and program evaluators in order to examine systematically both the implementation processes and the outcomes of planned induction programs.

Research on In-service Education in Canada

The Context

Most practising teachers in Canada have access to a broad range of opportunities for in-service education. Individually teachers usually choose their own professional development activities, even though goals and guidelines for change may be set by a larger organization such as the provincial Ministry of Education, a school district or a school staff. In the past decade increasing emphasis has been placed on long-term goal-setting and collaborative efforts toward educational change through school staff development projects, district-wide in-service projects and provincially guided curriculum development and implementation programs (Wideen, 1988).

A variety of collaborative in-service projects involving school districts, universities and Ministries of Education has recently developed in several provinces. For example, the University of Toronto has just initiated a Centre for Teacher Development which will work with school boards to provide ongoing in-service in specific target areas. In British Columbia all three universities are working closely with the Ministry of Education and local school districts to deliver regionalized summer institutes and ongoing workshops focusing on curriculum implementation. One interesting feature of these projects is a built-in research component, which should pay off in new research perspectives in the coming years.

Characteristics of the Research

A major difficulty in reviewing this area was to determine the scope of in-service education as a field of research. A broad definition was taken to include any studies in which teachers participated in some form of structured activity for the intended purpose of professional growth. This included self-directed activities and curriculum projects as well as more traditional forms of in-service.

The first characteristic of this body of research is its small size in proportion to the amount of actual activity in the area. The problem of access to research in in-service education is even more pronounced than in pre-service teacher education. Studies are extremely difficult to locate, presumably because the majority are never published. However, their primary purpose is rarely to add to the broader store of knowledge and understanding about in-service education. Those who carry out investigative projects such as school districts do not take writing for publication as a high priority.

Second, diversity marks the research on in-service education. Saturation and replication are almost inconceivable at this stage. Given the number of possible research perspectives and the limited quantity of studies, classification becomes quite arbitrary. For this review we have clustered studies around teachers, curriculum, schools, and classrooms.

Third, the qualitative nature of the in-service research differentiates it substantially from most research on pre-service and induction.

The delicate balance between respecting a teacher's professional autonomy and implementing educational change through in-service education ties together many of the studies and gives meaning to the in-service literature. The challenge of helping teachers accept and embrace educational change remains an ongoing concern. Most agree that effective in-service must go beyond short-term 'quick-fix' approaches, and that teachers must have some ownership over the change process, yet issues of control over educational decision-making and the structuring of professional development opportunities remain problematic for in-service educators. Many of the studies reviewed speak to these issues in some way.

Focus on Teachers. We describe sample studies which relate to teachers' practical knowledge and decision-making, and attitudes towards in-service.

A cluster of studies points to the importance of the practical knowledge of teachers in curriculum decision-making. Typical studies include those of Clandinin (1985) and Manley-Casimir and Wasserman (1988). Clandinin (1985) studied the development of practical knowledge in two primary teachers, using participant observation and interview strategies over more than a year. The key to understanding this knowledge is not found in analyses of teachers' tasks or in the content of workshops or textbooks, but in examination of teachers' classroom practices over time. According to Clandinin, in traditional curriculum implementation teachers have been expected to facilitate someone else's intentions, but this approach has failed. If teachers' practical knowledge could be understood, and if in-service efforts were built on it, change and improvement could be facilitated.

Teacher decision-making was also the focus of a study by Manley-Casimir and Wasserman (1988) who analyzed the ongoing journal entries of practising teachers involved in a university course on educational decision-making which used film as a case study medium. The journal analyses revealed that meaningful decision-making remains deeply rooted in a concurrent process of self-analysis. They conclude that group support can do much to lessen the isolation of teaching and to promote professional respect and openness, and that ongoing participation in individual and group analysis of educational decisions can help teachers engage in intense critical reflection leading to professional growth.

Pansegrau (1984) also examined teachers' perspectives and attitudes on in-service education through in-depth interviews and participant observation involving eighty-six teachers over an eleven-month period. These teachers used the variety of in-service activities they were exposed to to improve their effectiveness. In particular, they considered in-school contacts with colleagues to play a vital role. Most of the learning which had a direct effect on classroom practices was not acquired through formal in-service, although it did serve other worthwhile purposes. Based on her findings, Pansegrau recommends that teachers' own perspectives and needs should determine their choice of in-service activities, and that informal as well as formal experiences should be acknowedged and facilitated.

Focus on Curriculum. The curriculum itself has long been recognized as a potentially powerful device for professional development and has been used for that purpose in some districts. Several studies examined various dimensions of teachers' involvement in curriculum development and implementation as an aspect of in-service education. All pointed toward the need for teacher involvement in both the development and implementation of planned curricular changes.

McRadu, Allison and Gray (1985) found, for example, that while most teacters agree that curriculum guides are important for good teaching, they rarely used them except for long-term planning. The authors suggest that teachers and administrative staff need greater input into the planning of curriculum so that it reflects their own views of an appropriate instructional program. They recommend that curriculum developers provide only skeletal outcome frameworks and then engage teachers in defining the content appropriate to their situations. But Werner (1988), who interviewed twenty teachers regarding their implementation of a mandated reading program, found time to be an important variable in this regard. According to Werner, if curriculum innovation is to be successful, program developers must take into account the element of time and how it affects teachers' attitudes toward implementation. Also principal leadership was found to be an important factor in influencing both teacher development and program implementation (Pravica and McLean, 1983; Wideen, 1988).

Focus on Classrooms. Studies in this cluster dealt with individual teachers' professional development through various forms of classroom-focused interaction and intervention. These studies offer a miscellaneous collection, since they vary greatly in both topics and methodologies. They range from studies which ask how and from whom teachers seek advice regarding classroom instruction (Holdaway and Millikan, 1980) to action research (Chorny, 1988; Hart, Ripley, Poulin and Maguire, 1989). Responses revealed that teachers most frequently seek advice and assistance from other staff members in their own schools, but that they do so infrequently due to lack of time.

Two studies focused on action research as a form of in-service. Chorny (1988) followed several teachers involved in self-directed studies focusing on their own language arts instruction. Participating teachers reported a variety of different learnings from their action research activities. For example, 'Through the study I learned how to listen to my students carefully and to try to structure their learning according to what I heard...I believe I am a better teacher.' Hart, Ripley, Poulin and Maguire (1989) describe an action research project involving teachers in self-evaluation. Their school-based research group looked at customized evaluation procedures by experimenting with different models in their school. They make the point that the project was worthwhile as an in-service activity because it arose from a need, it was specific to their school, and it focused on the improvement of instruction.

Emerging Themes in In-service Research. These studies of in-service education suggest a wide range of strategies by which teachers engage in personally meaningful professional development. The need for and the value of ownership by teachers in determining their in-service activities emerged as a theme in this research, both in the recommendations arising from many of the studies but also in the overall directions taken by this body of research. Notably absent are studies focusing on more traditional forms of in-service education such as workshops, conferences, seminars and traditional coursework. Instead, the research focuses on teachers' individual and collaborative efforts to improve instruction through personal involvement in meaningful activities. Similarly, the research methodologies suggest a personal attitude toward investigation, with an emphasis on the close-up look provided by qualitative approaches and participant observation strategies.

However, we think that this research does not adequately reflect the state of affairs in Canadian in-service education. From personal experience we know that much in-service still consists of one-day workshops, conferences and other traditional forms of professional development involving little commitment or ownership on the part of participating teachers. Similarly, many teachers participate in university coursework, yet only three studies deal with this type of activity, and all are reporting on innovative strategies for course delivery. We also know of innumerable studies of teacher professional development not located in this review. Nevertheless, the studies reported here do suggest a measure of agreement about some factors which might contribute to more effective in-service education, and this provides a starting point for future work. The possibilities are endless.

Extending Research in Teacher Education: Some Perspectives

Recent research in Canadian teacher education represents only a beginning in developing our understanding of the continuum of teacher development from pre-service through induction and in-service education. The complexities of teacher education are not about to yield to the type of scattered efforts that we have reviewed. Concerted, focused efforts are required in those areas on which we reported and also in areas which until now have been virtually ignored. For example, in pre-service teacher education we need to look more closely at the organization of faculties of education as well as the background, training and expertise of those in faculties who train teachers. In the area of induction we know little about the lived experiences of beginning teachers, yet we find ourselves embarking on large-scale induction projects. These will need careful study in order to learn what we can about program effectiveness. In the area of in-service education, research is so scattered that it gives only a glimpse of what may or may not be true about the professional development of practising teachers. Perhaps what is needed most of all are focused attempts to push the limits in certain areas with sufficient duplication and variety in approach to produce substantive bodies of knowledge that can provide a basis for program development.

Conclusion

Most Canadian scholars in teacher education, like those elsewhere, would argue that teacher education should be viewed as a continuum. However laudable this aim, its achievement at this time eludes our efforts, both in practice and in research. From the research perspective — our focus in this paper — efforts to understand teacher education as a process of continuous development are impeded by several factors. First, the groups of players in research remain almost totally unfocused and separated. The university provides the primary domain for research in pre-service education, with limited attention to induction and in-service. Teachers' federations, both provincial and local, do much of the work in induction, mostly in the form of needs assessment. School districts support research into teacher education. Individual graduate students associated with various groups tend to span all three. These groups, for the most part, fail to communicate in ways that would focus their efforts. Second, in different jurisdictions the research performs different functions, often the least of which is the improvement of practice. For example, university professors do their research to gain scholarly recognition. Consequently, their published work, which may bear on teacher education, circulates in groups far removed from those directly involved in teacher education. Such works are rarely seen by those in the field because the reward structure in universities does not encourage the sharing of such work with practitioners. Third, the means by which research is disseminated is problematic. For example, much of the research in in-service education involves action research among teachers, most of which does not find publication. Fourth, teacher development in itself remains a mystery. Even if these different players could come together, the conceptual desert of teacher development would limit their dialogue.

Despite this realism, we end this chapter on a positive note. Some very encouraging signs have appeared. Universities show signs of focusing some of their research efforts on teacher education and appear to be reaching out to districts in collaborative ways. These changes have been helped by the general liberalization of research methodology in the past five years. Teachers have begun to speak out and to write about their classroom research in local publications such as the *Research Forum* in British Columbia.[2] The past five years have seen a more collaborative developmental perspective on education in general; for example, a recent conference focused on teacher development.[3] Some in the country see a quiet revolution occurring in education. We hope that research into all aspects of teacher education informs that revolution.

Notes

1 French immersion is a program for English-speaking students where French is the only instructional language.
2 The district of Surrey currently publishes the *Research Forum* which is supported by the Ministry of Education in the province. It is circulated widely throughout the province and in other parts of Canada.
3 This conference was sponsored jointly by the Ontario Institute for Studies in Education and the University of Toronto.

References

ANDREWS, I.H. (1986) Five paradigms of induction programmes in teacher education. Unpublished doctoral dissertation, Simon Fraser University.
ANDREWS, J. (1984) Alternative futures for Faculties of Education. *Canadian Journal of Education*, 9, 3, 261–275.
BEAUCHEMIN, C. (1985) L'impact négatif de l'arrivée des élèves en immersion.

Actes de colloque national sur l'enseignement post-secondaire en langue francise à l'extérieur du Québec, Ottawa, mai 1985. pp. 63–65.

BESSAI, F. and EDMONDS, E. (1977) *Student Opinions of Student Teaching.* Toronto: Canadian Education Association.

CAMPBELL, C.E. (1985) Variables which influence student teacher behavior: Implications for teacher education. *Alberta Journal of Educational Research*, 31, 4, 258–269.

CHORNY, M. (Ed.) (1988) *Teacher as Researcher.* Calgary: Language in the Classroom Project. University of Calgary, Faculty of Education.

CLANDININ, D.J. (1985) Personal practical knowledge: A study of teachers' classroom images. *Curriculum Inquiry*, 15, 4, 361–385.

CLARKE, S.C.T. and COUTTS, H.T. (1975) Toward teacher education in the year 2000. *The Alberta Journal of Education Research*, 21, 4, 221–240.

CLIFTON, R.A. and COVERT, J. (1980) Two experimental programs and the professional dispositions of student teachers. *The Morning Watch*, 7, 3–4, 35–42.

COLE, A.L. and McNAY, M. (1988) 'Induction programs in Ontario schools: Issues and possibilities.' Paper presented at the Annual Meeting of the Canadian Society for the Study of Education, Windsor, Ontario, February.

COVERT, J.R. (1984) *The Extended Practicum: More of the Same.* Technical report; ERIC document #ED 273 605. Newfoundland: Memorial University.

EMERSON, G.J. (1977) Factors related to enlarged perspectives among the students of an Ontario Teacher's College. *Canadian Journal of Education*, 2, 2, 45–63.

FAIR, J.W. (1973) Teachers as learners: The learning projects of beginning elementary school teachers. Unpublished doctoral thesis, University of Toronto.

FLANDERS, T. (1980) *The professional Development of Teachers.* Vancouver: The British Columbia Teachers Federation.

FRIESEN, D. and COOPER, L. (1985) 'Implementing the cooperative learning model of teaching: Helping to make it a reality.' Paper presented to the third International Conference for the Study of Cooperation in Education, Regina, Saskatchewan.

GREENE, M.L. (1980) 'Follow-up studies on the success of education graduates.' Paper presented at the Annual Meeting of the American Educational Research Association, Boston.

GRIMMETT, P.P. and RATZLAFF, H.C. (1986) Expectations for the cooperating teacher. *Teacher Education*, 37, 6, 41–50.

HARPER, F.B.W. (1977) Practice teaching performance and resultant achievement motivation. *Alberta Journal of Educational Research*, 23, 2, 104–108.

HART, C. and RIPLEY, D., with POULIN, L. and MAGUIRE, N. (1989) Involving teachers in their evaluation. *Alberta Teachers' Magazine*, 69, 2, 4–7.

HOLBORN, P. (1983) 'Integrating theory and practice from the student teacher's perspective.' Paper presented at the Annual Meeting of the American Educational Research Association, Los Angeles.

HOLBORN, P. and OLLIVER, S. (1988) 'Supervision of student teachers.' Paper presented at the Annual Meeting of the American Association of Colleges for Teacher Education, New Orleans.

HOLDAWAY, E. and MILLIKAN, R. (1980) Educational consultation: A summary of four Alberta studies. *Alberta Journal of Educational Research*, 26, 3, 194–210.

HOPKINS, D. (1980) Survey feedback and the problem of change in teacher education. Unpublished doctoral dissertation, Simon Fraser University.

HOUSEGO, B.E. and BOLDT, W.B. (1980) Critical incidents in the supervision of student teaching. *The Alberta Journal of Educational Research*, 31, 2, 113–124.

HUTCHEON, D. (1972) Follow-up study of Regina B.Ed. graduates. *Saskatchewan Journal of Educational Research and Development*, 3, 3–10.

ILAVSKY, J. (1978) *Issues and Themes in Teacher Induction: Prior to First Day of School*. Winnipeg: Manitoba Teachers' Society.

JACKNICKE, K.G. and ROWELL, P.P. (1987) Alternative orientations for educational research. *Alberta Journal of Educational Research*, 33, 2, 62–72.

McINTOSH, J. (1978) The barrier between beginning and experienced teacher. *Journal of Educational Administration*, 16, 1, 46–56.

McMURRAY, J.G., HARDY, M. and POSLUMS, R. (1986) 'Successful life experiences, teaching styles and stress in beginning teachers.' Paper presented at the annual meeting of the American Educational Research Association, Washington, DC.

McRADU, K.A., ALLISON, D.E. and GRAY, R.F. (1985) Implementing a centrally developed curriculum guide. *The Alberta Journal of Educational Research*, 31, 3, 191–200.

MANLEY-CASIMIR, M.E. and WASSERMANN, S. (1988) The teacher as decision-maker: Connecting self with the practice of teaching. Unpublished manuscript.

MARTIN, Y.M., ISHERWOOD, G.B. and RAPAGNA, S. (1978) Supervisory effectiveness. *Administrative Quarterly*, 14, 3, 74–88.

MICKELSON, N.T. and PEARCE, R. (1976) 'The internship programme for secondary students.' Paper presented at an international symposium sponsored by IMTEC Gaustablick, Norway.

MUNDEL-ATHERSTONE, B. (1980) 'A personality profile of students who are successful in student teaching and in teaching,' Paper presented at annual meeting of the Canadian Society for Study in Education, Montreal.

MONTABELLO, S. (1989) 'Theory/practice up close.' Paper presented at the Annual Meeting of the American Educational Research Association, San Francisco.

NEUFELD, J.S. (1974) Why choose the teaching procession? *Saskatchewan Journal of Educational Research and Development*, 5, 1, 21–26.

NIXON, M.T. and BUMBARGER, C.S. (1984) Prospective teachers: Views of programs and needs. *Alberta Journal of Educational Research*, 30, 3, 226–237.

OBADIA, A. (1986) Statistiques sur les inscriptions dans les programmes pédagogiques en français de base, immersion française et français langué maternelle en milieu minoritaire. 2e Congres de l'ACᵖFM, Vancouver, mai 1986.

OVERING, L.R. (1973) Toward a redefinition of teacher education. *Interchange*, 4, 2–3, 19–27.

PANSEGRAU, M. (1984) Teachers' perspectives on inservice education. *Alberta Journal of Educational Research*, 30, 4, 239–258.

PRAVICA, S. and McLEAN, L.D. (1983) The effects of principal participation in curriculum implementation: Support from an evaluation of a new mathematics curriculum. *Alberta Journal of Educational Research*, 29, 1, 46–53.

RANDHAWA, B.S. and KIRKPATRICK, J.B. (1975) Teacher employment and job assignment. *Saskatchewan Journal of Educational Research and Development*, 5, 2, 53–63.

RATSOY, E.W., BABCOCK, G.R. and CALDWELL, J.C. (1978) *Evaluation of the Education Practicum Program 1977–1978. Program Evaluation Report No. 1.* Edmonton: University of Alberta, Faculty of Education.

RATSOY, E., FRIESEN, D. and HOLDAWAY, E. (1987) *Evaluation of the Initiation to Teaching Project.* Edmonton: Alberta Education, May.

REIMER, E.P. (1978) *The Manitoba Teacher Induction Project: A Final Evaluation Report.* Winnipeg: Manitoba Department of Education.

SANDERS, J.T., ANDRESINO, H.S., ISAACS, L.M., and IRVINE, S.M. (undated). Teacher education: Expectations and experience. Unpublished manuscript, available from University of Western Ontario.

SEDGWICK, K.H., HILL, R. and RUSSELL, T.L. (1981) 'Training teachers in observational skills to improve their judgements of student achievement: a pilot study.' Paper presented at the annual meeting of the American Educational Research Association, Boston.

SLOAN, L.V. (1981) *Final Report on the Development of the Extended Practicum at the University of Alberta.* Edmonton: University of Alberta, Faculty of Education.

TARDIF, C. (1985) On becoming a teacher: A student teacher's perspective. *The Alberta Journal of Educational Research*, 31, 2, 139–148.

TATTERSALL, W.R. (1979) Patterns of change in teaching anxiety, professional self-concept and self-concept during an extended practicum: A study of student teachers in Simon Fraser University's Education 405 practicum. Unpublished master's thesis, Simon Fraser University.

THOM, D.J. and KLASSEN, D. (1986) One more time — what makes a good teacher? Unpublished manuscript, Thunder Bay, Ontario: Lakehead University.

TURNER, L.E. (1985) Towards understanding the lived world of three beginning teachers of young children. *Alberta Journal of Educational Research*, 31, 4, 306–320.

UNRAH, W. (1981) *Evaluation of the Faculty of Education.* Evaluation Report 1978–1981. Calgary: University of Calgary, Faculty of Education.

WEBER, S.J. (1986) Teacher education: A search for meaning. *Elements*, 18, 1, 22–23.

WERNER, W. (1988) Program implementation and experienced time. *Alberta Journal of Educational Research*, 34, 2, 90–108.

WIDEEN, M.F. (1988) School improvement in Canada. *Qualitative Studies in Education*, 1, 1, 21–38.

WIDEEN, M.F., and HOLBORN, P. (1986) Change and survival in faculties of education. *Interchange*, 17, 1, 33–47.

WIDEEN, M.F. and HOPKINS, D. (1984) Supervising student teachers: A means of professional renewal? *Alberta Journal of Educational Research*, 39, 1, 26–37.

Chapter 3

Research on Teacher Education in Japan

Akira Sato and Jun Ushiwata

Introduction

The past ten years have seen many problems in the elementary and secondary schools of Japan. Because many of these problems were attributed to lack of competence among teachers, national advisory groups made the improvement of the teacher force the main theme for educational reform in Japan. This reform has made teacher education a national concern. As a result, research on teacher education has become one of the most noteworthy fields in education, as academic societies have come together to hold a symposium on the reform of teacher education, and featured this theme in their journals. This chapter reviews the past ten years of research on teacher education in Japan reported in some 400 books, articles and reviews. Although some reviews have simply reported research in a fragmented way, others have intensively analyzed the studies they reported. The chapter describes the distinguishing features of the research, identifies trends and issues, describes the research methods used, and presents the findings obtained. We restricted ourselves to investigative papers, except for the historical studies and those on teacher education in foreign countries. The paper begins with a brief sketch of the context in which teacher education occurs in Japan and of the system of teacher education.

Context and Teacher Education System

School System

Kindergartens, elementary schools, lower secondary schools, upper secondary schools, technical colleges and universities including junior colleges and graduate schools make up the formal school system in Japan. More than twenty million pupils are enrolled in both elementary and secondary schools. Public schools are established by units of local government within forty-seven prefectures. These units may include municipalities, cities, towns and villages which administer the schools. Public schools amount to 99 per cent of elementary schools (24,901), 94 per cent of lower secondary schools (11,265), and 76 per cent of upper secondary schools (5512).

Compulsory schooling lasts nine years between the ages of 6 and 15, six years of elementary school (grades 1 through 6) and three years of lower secondary school (grades 7 through 9). Ninety-four per cent of the graduates from lower secondary schools enter upper secondary school (grades 10 through 12) after taking an entrance examination. About 40 per cent of graduates from upper secondary schools advance to university after passing another entrance examination. Japan's prospective teachers are drawn primarily from this pool of university students.

Statutes specify that the elementary and lower secondary school curriculum should consist of academic subjects, moral education and special activities. The Ministry of Education, the principal educational administration agency at the national level, prescribes the Course of Study and curriculum standards not only for compulsory schools but also for non-compulsory kindergarten and upper secondary school. The Course of Study establishes national standards for the content of what is to be taught and other minimum standards required of all pupils, whether they are in private, national or public elementary and secondary schools.

Pre-service Teacher Education

In the pre-war era normal schools held a position equivalent to secondary schools and had little articulation with the institutions of higher education. They provided initial teacher education. Normal schools invited criticism because of their perceived weak emphasis in the liberal arts and their non-academic technical approach. This resulted in the training of students called the 'normal school type' characterized by an unquestioning attitude and narrow view.

Immediately after the war the normal school was abolished and responsibility for pre-service teacher education could be assumed by any university that developed a curriculum required for teaching certification. This pre-service education system, called the open system, has aroused discussion concerning its merits and demerits. Many now believe that pre-service education for prospective teachers of compulsory schools should be provided exclusively at colleges of education which concentrate on teacher education, and would then accommodate the number of students required by schools.

At present 84 per cent of junior colleges (543) and universities (460) have teacher education courses leading to certification that has been approved by the Minister of Education. These universities include sixty-five colleges of education of which fifty-eight are affiliated with national universities and seven with private institutions.

Requirements for Teaching Certificates

To become a teacher of an elementary or secondary school, one requires a teaching certificate granted by the prefectural board of education. Teaching certificates remain valid for life in all prefectures, regardless of differences in the class of certificate. For teachers of pre-school, elementary school and lower secondary school the bachelor's degree provides the basic qualification for a first class certificate; a second class certificate requires two years of study in college or other post-secondary institution. Upper secondary school teachers require a master's degree for a first class certificate, and a bachelor's degree for a second class certificate.

In addition to the basic qualifications, the teaching certificate requires a prescribed number of credits both in professional educational subjects such as principles of education, pedagogical psychology, teaching methods and teaching practice, and in the subject to be taught. The latter means the subject in which the prospective teacher specializes. The certificate for elementary school teachers, which requires six subject areas, qualifies a teacher to teach all subject areas from grades 1 through 6, whereas secondary school teaching certificates authorize teachers to teach only specified subject fields. Student teaching occurs mostly in the final year of a student's course. The minimum requirements are four weeks for elementary school candidates, and two weeks for secondary school teacher candidates.

Selection and Appointment of Teachers

Teachers of elementary and secondary schools who hold a relevant teaching certificate are recruited by the competent authorities. Candidates for private schools are selected and appointed by the corporations establishing the schools. To obtain a post in a public elementary or secondary school, a candidate must take a recruitment examination which includes a written test in general education, professional educational subjects and subjects to be taught, as well as interviews and practical tests.

About one million full-time teachers staff elementary and secondary school schools. Elementary school teachers comprise 45 per cent, lower secondary school teachers 28 per cent, and upper secondary school teachers 27 per cent. In 1986, 28 per cent of university graduates gained teaching certificates, and of these 21 per cent found teaching posts. Recently the decline in pupil enrolments makes employment as teachers more difficult.

In-service Teacher Education

The law governing educational public service personnel requires teachers to exert effort in continuing study and the cultivation of the spirit. This law also prescribes that educational administration agencies should provide such teachers with opportunities for continuing education. In-service education has been vitalized since the 1970s under the national government subsidy. But there has been criticism because internship has never been institutionalized, though induction has been discussed repeatedly.

Formal in-service education is provided partly by the Ministry of Education for a selected number of teachers, and extensively by the local educational administration agencies. Among administrative agencies, the prefectural education centre plays the most important role in in-service education conducted outside the school. In-service education activities are provided generally for beginning teachers, experienced teachers (in fifth, tenth, twentieth year of employment), headteachers, vice-principals and principals. Besides these, formal and informal in-service education is conducted in each school by teachers themselves in various groups. Participation in or completion of any in-service education program is not followed by salary increments.

Since 1989 twenty days of in-service education for beginning teachers, both at education centres and under supervising teachers within school, have been institutionalized as required by law. Few universities offer advanced study courses for practising teachers.

Teacher educators at universities are responsible for fundamental and theoretical education, which includes education in subject matter and which forms the whole of pre-service education for prospective teachers. The educational administration agencies are responsible for almost all in-service education for practising teachers, especially for training in technical or practical knowledge and skills needed for educational activities at schools.

The Trend in Research on Teacher Education[1]

Pre-service Education

Research in pre-service education has focused on the role of pre-service education, curriculum, student teaching, students' aspiration for teaching and so on.

We discuss the role of pre-service education for two reasons. First, the improvement of teachers' competency became a national concern; pre-service education was criticized as too theoretical, and the teacher certification law was revised to stress the professional aspect of pre-service education. Second, as a result of the decline of enrolments in primary and secondary schools, recruitment into the teaching profession has been decreasing drastically. The purpose of the schools of education and teachers' colleges had been limited to teacher education. It was now proposed to change these one-purpose schools or colleges into a new type that would be open to students other than those wanting to become teachers.

Yamada (1987), tracing the history of pre-service education after the Second World War, criticized the national policy stressing practical competencies of teachers in the universities and colleges. He argued that in-service education should play that role, not universities and colleges. Yaosaka and Ushiwata (1988) found, from a questionnaire administered to 499 college teachers who teach foundation courses, that many college teachers wanted to stress fundamental and theoretical aspects rather than practical ones in pre-service education. On the other hand, Matsudaira (1982) evaluated pre-service education through questionnaires sent to beginning teachers, and found that many considered pre-service education to be weak in practical knowledge and technique. A big gap exists between school teachers and college teachers regarding the role of pre-service education, and these two perspectives need further examination. Hirahara (1987) reported the reorganization of some national teachers' colleges and schools of education in the light of these concerns. Ebata (1987) compared professional education in the department of medicine, whose purpose is limited to prepare doctors, with that in the department of law, whose purpose is not limited to prepare lawyers but to include students who do not plan to become lawyers. He proposed to change the pre-service education of teachers, which resembled the medical model, to one which resembles the legal model. This theme came mainly from researchers from the national teachers' colleges and schools of education.

As for the curriculum of pre-service education, we have the research conducted by Maki and others (1980) on the foundations of education as a professional subject. They examined the content and methods used through a survey of the staff which asked about such things as the titles and credits of courses, and the conditions for study; they also examined textbook content. Their findings indicated vagueness in the character of the foundations of education as a professional subject. Takagi and Shimizu (1984) did a similar study involving educational psychology. Apart from these, we have few studies which evaluate the curriculum or teaching methods in pre-service education.

Student teaching has attracted a great deal of attention. Fujieda *et al.* (1980, 1981) conducted the most comprehensive set of studies, including three different surveys. First, they surveyed forty-one national and private universities and colleges through a questionnaire. They also followed up with case studies of six universities and colleges by interview. Second, they surveyed primary and secondary schools attached to national universities and colleges through questionnaires. Third, they surveyed college students (teacher candidates) through questionnaires. These investigators found that a huge gap existed between universities and colleges and between primary and secondary schools about the significance and role of student teaching in pre-service education. Other researchers have directed their attention to the attitudes held by student teachers toward the teaching profession. Akiyama (1981), for example, surveyed student teachers' aspirations for teaching, using a questionnaire given before and after student teaching. He found that 27 per cent of those surveyed strengthened their aspiration for teaching as a result of their student teaching. On the other hand, 20 per cent weakened their aspiration for teaching because they became aware that they were inadequate for teaching. Suzuki and others (1983) also completed a similar survey with comparable results. Using the psychological approach, Sato (1979) found a positive relationship between the grades given to student teachers and their education, empathy and experience, and Inoue (1979) found a high correlation between student teachers' self-esteem and their student teaching practice experiences.

We have other researchers who focused on the college students' aspirations for the teaching profession. Matsuo (1982) surveyed freshmen of Fukuoka Teachers' College five times during a ten-year period. College students' aspirations for teaching grew during that period. In their vocational preference they ranked teaching, especially primary teaching, first among eighteen different jobs. On the other hand, only half of them thought that they were adequate to be teachers. He concluded that a big gap existed between their high aspirations and their feelings of inadequacy to become teachers. Further, he thought that this gap should be considered in pre-service education.

Ito (1980) examined the development of students' orientation to teaching. He found that those who had a high aspiration for teaching when they applied for admission had decided to become teachers when they were young. This aspiration remained and developed through pre-service education, as 91.9 per cent of them wanted to become teachers when they graduated from the college. On the other hand, only 67.5 per cent of those having no aspiration for teaching when they applied for admission wanted to become teachers. Hayashi (1986) also focused on the relation of the development of a professional orientation eligibility for teaching among college students. He found a relationship between their aspirations for teaching, eligibility for teaching, leadership and emotional stability. He concluded that pre-service education should be planned to enhance not only the students' teaching abilities, but also to make them aware of the teaching profession. Programs should also offer the students abundant opportunities for self-insight and self-acceptance in order to understand their character and their teaching aptitude so that they can be aware of what they should improve.

As to the research on pre-service education, Mukoyama (1985) has examined the teacher certification law and Wakai (1979) the accreditation of teacher education programs and institutions. It is interesting to note that we have few researchers examining the quality of teacher educators (college teachers).

Teacher Selection

There was little research on the selection of teachers after the Second World War, but during the past ten years there have been more studies. These have focused on three problems. First, the standards and procedures of teacher selection have not been clear and open to the public; as a result, selection is suspected to be arbitrary and non-democratic. Tsuchiya (1987), quoting the results of the investigation done by the Japan Senior High School Teachers' Union, pointed out that the freedom of thought and religion of the applicants were trespassed on through interviews during teacher selection. Maejima (1981) quoted the same study and showed that 21.6 per cent of the teachers surveyed heard of or experienced unfair selection influenced by personal considerations or through a relative. However, it is impossible to obtain clear evidence for these unfair selections, and no comprehensive research has been done on the real conditions of teacher selection so far. On the other hand, Tsuchiya (1981) examined the qualifications for taking the examinations for teacher selection, and found discrimination against age and nationality. Suzuki (1986) compared the number of examination applicants to the number hired, and found that the proportion of women was higher than men. As a result, he suggested that priority was being given to male applicants in the selection and appointment of teachers.

Second, the decreasing demand for teachers means increased competition in the examinations for teacher selection. This trend has appeared especially since the late 1970s, and researchers have focused on this problem during the past ten years. For example, Maejima (1981), through a case study of one university, found that in some lectures a collection of questions from past examinations became the textbook where students memorized a lot of words to pass the teacher selection examination instead of trying to understand and think deeply on the subject. Horiuchi and Mizumoto (1986), through a questionnaire administered to college students, found that 80 per cent of the students began to prepare for examination a half-year in advance, and one-third prepared for three months. Almost all the students surveyed crammed for the teacher selection examination using collections of questionnaires on the market; they found their college education unhelpful in preparing them for the examination. The researcher criticized the selection system which lessened the importance of preparation in the universities.

Third, the national policy to appoint as teachers those having practical teaching competencies and a natural disposition for teaching brought diversity into teacher selection which consisted of a primary and secondary component (Tsuchiya, 1981). The primary one contained an exercise and a written examination, and the secondary one an exercise, aptitude test, interview and essay. Supervisors and principals, according to a survey by Ueda and others (1987), wanted diversified but accurate selection methods, and new teachers with natural dispositions for teaching, plenty of knowledge and techniques who could, immediately after entry to teaching, work as well as experienced teachers. Many researchers criticized these efforts by administrative agencies and administrators, because they were not connected with teacher preparation in the universities and colleges (Maejima, 1987; Ueda and others, 1987).

Fourth, we have a heated controversy on 'the Inservice Education System for the Beginning Teachers' (IESBT) starting formally in 1989. It is a teacher selection problem. IESBT, first planned as an internship, included both the functions of in-service education during one year and teacher selection (exclusion of unqualified teachers) after completing one probational year. The latter function was criticized by researchers, and later it was changed. But it is still suspected to be a function of IESBT (Tsuchiya, 1987; Maejima, 1987). Researchers criticized the plan as they thought this teacher selection system was unfair and violated political neutrality; in other words, they distrusted it (Yamada, 1981).

A great gap exists between administrative agencies and researchers on the teacher selection issue; thus it is important to study the selection system collaboratively.

In-service Education of Teachers

Studies of in-service education have increased dramatically in number and become diversified in content during the past ten years. The foci of researchers are divided into the systematization of the in-service education of teachers, in-service education by the administrative agencies, in-service education in the schools, and in-service education for beginning teachers.

In the 1970s the national advisory committee on education proposed that teacher education should be lifelong education. For this they proposed the 'systematization' of in-service education so that teachers could receive the appropriate in-service according to their ages and experiences, and to adjust the plans of the Ministry of Education, prefectural and local agencies accordingly. Kishimnoto, Okatoo, Hayashi and Koyama (1981) tried to identify the actual conditions related to the professional development of teachers in order to establish a professional growth and development model as the foundation of the 'systematization'. They surveyed 1040 teachers using a questionnaire designed to obtain a score on a set of competency items, the degree of importance attributed to those items, and identify the competency items that teachers felt they needed to learn. In thirty-six out of forty-eight teacher competency items, teachers' age and length of experience played a central role in explaining the score patterns, showing that it was appropriate to consider the teachers' need for competencies according to their age and experience. Prefectural education authorities eventually developed a model of teacher development and began to provide in-service education according to teachers' age. Ojima (1982) administered a questionnaire to teachers in their 20s and 30s and over 40s, chiefs of the research and instruction departments, assistant principals and principals, asking about the content of in-service education provided. He showed that the routes of teacher development and the needs of in-service education were many and varied. He concluded that the systematization of the content of in-service education should not be fixed and forced on teachers. Haitani (1981), who has been engaged in establishing the systematization of in-service education in Hiroshima prefecture, analyzed the systematization in many prefectures and found that some administrative agencies enforced systematized in-service education on teachers without considering their needs or voluntarism. He criticized these plans which were based on professional development models made by administrative agencies; he proposed changes so that the in-service system for teachers would reflect their own professional development model and in-service plan.

Thus the role of the administrative agencies in the in-service education of teachers has been a controversial one. Many researchers, using questionnaires administered to teachers, have evaluated the in-service education programs provided by these groups outside the school. Hori (1982) drew three conclusions from his survey. First, he found school personnel in managerial positions rated in-service education by administrative agencies higher than teachers did. Second, teachers rated in-service education in the schools higher than that given by the administrative agencies. Third, the teachers rated in-service education by the prefectural school boards and education centres higher than that given by the Ministry of Education, cities, towns, school boards and higher institutions. Ueda and others (1987) surveyed administrative agencies and found that 71.6 per cent of the school supervisors who prepared and provided in-service education to teachers thought it met with good results, whereas only 28.6 per cent of the teachers agreed with it. These studies suggest that teachers wanted to move in-service education into the schools rather than having it conducted by administrative agencies or higher institutions. But Izuno, Yoshida, Enomoto and Ueno (1981) found that teachers differed among themselves regarding the type of school in-service they wanted. Those in their 20s and 30s liked informal, spontaneous and individual in-service education in the schools, whereas the teachers in their 40s and 50s liked formal, planned and collaborative in-service education in the schools. Whether formal or informal, in-service education in the school was considered the most effective by teachers. But why? Izuno and others explained the reason as follows: teaching competencies cannot be developed through theory but rather develop through teaching experience. In-service education conducted in the school is the most effective way to integrate theory and practice. Furthermore, Amagasa (1981) concluded that the group-oriented way of life, a characteristic of Japanese behaviour, explained why teachers liked in-service education conducted in the school. He analyzed the elements of organizational climate which promoted this group-oriented behaviour pattern, and found a combination of 'professional', 'competitive' and 'stable' elements in the school and teaching profession.

Although universities and colleges have played only a small role in in-service education for teachers since the new type of in-service education was established in the 1970s, researchers have begun to direct their attention to the role the new universities might have in in-service education (Nishi, 1987; Satake, 1983).

During the past ten years researchers have paid much attention to in-service education for young teachers, because of their different needs compared to experienced teachers. Also in 1978 the National Advisory Committee on Education to the Minister of Education proposed an in-service education system that required beginning teachers to get in-service training for one year. Ojima (1980) and Ojima, Nagai and Amagasa (1981) tried to clarify young teachers' awareness of their teaching ability, identify the factors making them mature teachers, and assess their morale to participate in several kinds of in-service training. They found that one of the main factors helping young teachers grow on the job was on-the-job training by their elder colleagues during daily school life. They concluded, therefore, that in-service education for beginning teachers should be school-based. Ojima (1983) also showed why young teachers liked the support from colleagues. First, young teachers were extremely unprepared for teaching; thus they needed advice and support in the school. Second, he pointed to the poor independence of youth as another reason. Minamimoto (1986) also found that in-service education in schools had an effect on the young teachers as they model themselves after experienced teachers. But Minamimoto found big differences in the conditions in each school that influenced the upgrading of the qualifications of young teachers. After all, it is necessary to study the proper conditions of schools (including personnel administration) that could improve in-service education for young teachers.

As for the new Inservice Education System for Beginning Teachers which is to start in 1989, it will be necessary to study the actual conditions of the program and examine this with regard to the in-service needs and characteristics of future young teachers.

A Brief Epilogue

We have three concluding observations. First, there is a great deal of distrust in Japan among university personnel, administrators and teachers but, we believe, there should be more collaborative research on such issues as selection and in-service education. Second, the small amount of research on the effects of teacher education implies that more evaluations of these should be undertaken. Third, this review must be regarded as a beginning. Periodical regular reviews are essential from now on for our understanding to grow.

Note

1 More than 95 per cent of the reported research involves university personnel.

References

AKIYAMA, M. (1981) A study on the changes of student-teachers' attitudes (2): Changes in their attitudes toward teaching profession and the analysis of their factors. *Journal of the Faculty of Education, Saga University*, 29, 1, 53–71.

AMAGASA, S. (1981) The fundamental study on the organizational climate in the in-service education of teachers. *Bulletin of Japan Educational Administration Society*, 7, 115–128.

EBATA, H. (1987) Theoretical problems in faculties of education: The dilemma of those only in teacher education. *Japanese Journal of Educational Research*, 54, 3, 279–288.

FUJIEDA, S. and SHIRAI, M. (1981) Study on the improvement of student teaching (the third interim report), Japanese Society for the Study of Education, Study Committee on Teacher Education, *A study on the Practical Strategies for the Improvement of Teacher Education*, 3, 28–58.

FUJIEDA, S., MAEJIMA, Y. and SHIRAI, M. (1980) Study on the improvement of student teaching (the second interim report), Japanese Society for the Study of Education, Study Committee on Teacher Education, *A Study on the Practical Strategies for the Improvement of Teacher Education*, 2, 34–103.

HAITANI, J. (1981) A study of the systematization of in-service education for teachers. *Bulletin of the Japan Educational Administration Society*, 7, 37–50.

HAYASHI, T. (1986) Students' aspiration for the teaching profession: An analytical study of students' self-evaluation of their teaching aptitude. *Technical Bulletin of Tokushima Bunri University*, 31, 21–41.

HIRAHARA, H. (1987) A study of teacher education in national teachers' colleges and national schools of education. *Japanese Journal of Educational Research*, 54, 3, 268–278.

HORI, K. (1982) The organization of supervision. Japan Educational Administration Society, Special Committee on Supervision, *A Comprehensive Study on the Improvement of the Quality of Teaching Profession and Supervision*, Tsukuba City, 303–319.

HORIUCHI, T. and MIZUMOTO, N. (1986) Students' attitudes toward and interests in teacher selection. *Bulletin of Kyoto University of Education*, 69, 11–35.

INOUE, S. (1979) Effects of self-esteem level in student teaching. *Bulletin of School of Education, Okayama University*, 52, 185–198.

ITO, K. (1980) Developmental process of professional orientation of students of the faculty of education. *Bulletin of the Faculty of Education, Shizuoka University, Liberal Arts and Social Sciences*, Series No. 31, 115–128.

IZUNO, T., YOUSHIDA, H., ENOMOTO, K. and UENO, K. (1981) A study on the elements making for leadership in teachers. *Bulletin of the Japan Educational Administration Society*, 7, 129–143.

KISHIMOTO, K., OKATOO, T., HAYASHI, T. and KOYAMA, E. (1981) A study of the teachers professional development model (II): A factor analysis of teaching competencies. *Bulletin of Faculty of Education, University of Hiroshima*, 30, 119–129.

MAEJIMA, Y. (1981) A study on the teacher selection and appointment system. *Bulletin of the Educational Administration, Tokyo University*, 2, 104–116.

MAEJIMA, Y. (1987) The problem of selection of teachers and formation of teacher competencies. *Bulletin of the Japanese Society of Education Law*, 16, 48–61.

MAKI, M. *et al.* (1980) A developmental study on 'foundation of education' as a required subject for teacher certification. *Bulletin of the National Institute for Educational Research*, 97.

MATSUDAIRA, N. (1982) Education in the universities and colleges perceived by beginning teachers: The evaluation of teacher education in universities and colleges. Japanese Society for the Study of Education, Study Committee on Teacher Education, *A Study of the Practical Strategies on the Improvement of Teacher Education*, 4, 130–144.

MATSUO, Y. (1982) A study on teachers: College students' consciousness about becoming a teacher. *Bulletin of Fukuoka University of Education*, 32, 169–175.

MINAMIMOTO, O. (1986) A study on the young primary school teacher's competence perceived by school leaders. *Journal of the Japanese Association for the Study of Educational Administration*, 23, 79–94.

MUKOYAMA, H. (1985) The problems of the current teacher certification system. *Bulletin of the Japanese Society of Education Law*, 14, 45–63.

NISHI, J. (1987) Actual conditions of in-service education of teachers in the university. Joetsu University of Education, *A Study on the Relationship between Education in the University and In-service Education.*

OJIMA, H. (1980) The 'self-analysis' of teachers under five years' experience of teaching. *Journal of the Japanese Association of Educational Administration*, 22, 1–13.

OJIMA, H. (1982) Improvement of the quality of the teaching profession and the systematization of content of in-service education. Japan Educational Administration Society, Special Committee on Supervision, *A Comprehensive Study on the Improvement of the Quality of Teaching Profession and Supervision*, Tsukuba City, 266–279.

OJIMA, H. (1983) A study on the characteristics of competence improvement in 'junior teachers' through an opinion survey of INSET. *Bulletin of Institute of Education, the University of Tsukuba*, 7, 17–47.

OJIMA, H., NAGAI, S. and AMAGASA, S. (1981) An empirical study of young teachers' teaching ability and their demand for in-service training. *Bulletin of Institute of Education, the University of Tsukuba*, 5, 71–110.

SATAKE, K. (1983) A study on in-service education in the graduate course of Naruto University of Education. *Bulletin of Research Center of School Education, Naruto University of Education*, [entire issue]

SATO, S. (1979) A psychological study of student teaching (III): Grades received and education experience. *Memoirs of the Faculty of Education, Kumamoto University*, 28, 219–229.

SUZUKI, M. *et al.* (1983) Effect of student teaching practice on personal desire to be a teacher (II) *Bulletin of the Faculty of Education, Kobe University*, 71, 245–277.

SUZUKI, S. (1986) Selection and appointment of teachers, in SHINBORI, M. (Ed.) *Re-Examination of Preservice Education*, Tokyo: Kyoiku Kaihatsu Kenkyusho.

TAKAGI, H. and SHIMIZU, T. (1984) The present conditions and problems of psychology of education and psychology for youth as professional subjects. *Bulletin of Faculty of Education, Yokohama National University*, 24, [entire issue].

TSUCHIYA, M. (1981) Some problems concerning teacher selection and appointment. Japanese Society for the Study of Education, Study Committee on Teacher Education, *A Study on the Practical Strategies for the Improvement of Teacher Education*, 3, 194–206.

TSUCHIYA, M. (1987) What will change with the establishment of the system of in-service education for beginning teachers?: In relation to the selection of teachers, in Yamada and Tsuchiya (Eds) *What Will Change with the Establishment of the System of In-service Education for Beginning Teachers*. Tokyo: Kyoiku Shiryo Shuppankai.

UEDA, M. *et al.* (1987) The actual figures and problems of teacher-selection procedure and in-service training. *Bulletin of the Japan Educational Administration Society*, 13, 159–184.

YAMADA, N. (1981) A study of the history of the probational system for teachers. Japanese Society for the Study of Education, Study Committee on Teacher Education. *A Study of the Practical Strategies on the Improvement of Teacher Education*, 3, 152–168.

YAMADA, N. (1987) Teacher education in the university. *Japanese Journal of Educational Research*, 54, 3, 247–257.

YAOSAKA, O. and USHIWATA, J. (1988) The consciousness of the college teacher on the improvement of teacher education concerning student guidance. *Research Bulletin of the National Institute for Educational Research*, 17, 13–34.

WAKAI, Y. (1979) A study of the accreditation of teacher education programs and institutions. *Bulletin of Japan Educational Administration Society*, 5, 179–193.

Chapter 4

A Decade of Research on Teacher Education in the Netherlands

Frans K. Kieviet

This chapter provides a brief survey of the Dutch system of teacher education and educational research, and a discussion and evaluation of the development of research and the main topics examined by that research in pre-service education, induction and in-service education.

Teacher Education and Research in the Dutch Educational System

Some facts about the Dutch educational system and the position of teacher education within it help us to understand the position of research on teacher education in the Netherlands (Ministry of Education and Science, 1988; Nijhof and Streumer, 1985). In the Netherlands separate training institutes prepare teachers for *primary* and *secondary* education.

Primary. The institutes providing this education were formed in 1984 by amalgamating the former training institutes for infant schools (pupils aged 4–6) and training institutes for elementary school (pupils aged 6–12). This amalgamation became necessary because of the integration of infant and elementary schools into a quite new type of school for primary education for the whole age range from 4 to 12. The many original training institutes — over 140 — fused and integrated into some sixty, which for a country as small as Holland is still rather a lot. An operation like this produces numerous problems, and related research questions. The teacher training institutes for primary education are regarded as higher vocational education; their one course lasts four years. The students receive instruction in various school subjects and in educational theory and didactics. Practical training takes place through exercises within the institute and through student teaching in primary schools.

Secondary. Many separate types of secondary school exist in the Netherlands. The types of institutions for initial secondary teacher education reflect this. Teacher training for secondary education includes:

> teacher training departments at the universities for teachers for higher levels of general secondary education. Until recently teacher training at university consisted of an approximately four months course at the end of academic study;
>
> new teacher training institutes running a four-year course, preparing for lower levels of general and vocational education, the first of which started in 1970;
>
> institutes running secondary teaching certificate courses which provide training comparable with that mentioned above but on a part-time basis;
>
> initial training courses on a part-time basis especially for teachers for technical vocational education;
>
> specific institutes that train for teaching in a particular subject, e.g. academies for teachers of physical education. There are also institutes that train for teaching in agricultural education.

For tertiary levels of the Dutch education system (higher vocational and university education) teacher training is not compulsory.

Presently all teacher training institutes (with the exception of the university departments) are fusing with other types of higher vocational education institutions into larger institutes.

Initial teacher training institutes carry out in-service education in the Netherlands. However, the Dutch educational support system, with its separate national educational advisory centres and local or regional counselling services, supports school staff and teachers in various ways. These include such things as the introduction of new curricula, the implementation of innovations, and support for school-focused improvement. These many players make it difficult to define at which point in-service education, or more generally staff development, ends and some other form of support starts. Such agencies and the teacher training institutes are obliged to cooperate, but such cooperation and mutual 'tuning' of support are often poor.

Several remarks about the conditions for research on teacher education in the Netherlands are pertinent. First, teacher training institutes have no facilities for research, and university departments have limited facilities. So a major proportion of research on teacher education is executed by specific research institutes having no direct relation with teacher education. This might be an obstacle to the implementation of research findings because they are seen to have a low involvement in teacher education.

Second, the various types of teacher training institutes face different problems which create barriers for an integrated research program. Each institution has the constitutional right to develop its own policies and programs which militates against the constructive policy the government wants to implement in teacher education. A debate continues about whether the government, in view of the recent innovations in primary education, should determine the objectives for primary teacher education, or allow the teacher training institutes leeway to define their own objectives.

The financing of educational research is also relevant to research on teacher education in the Netherlands. Broadly speaking, three possibilities exist. First, university research can be financed directly from the Ministry of Education and Science and, depending on the policy of each university, research on teacher education may form part of the research program. This is termed the first stream of financing. The second stream is through grants for research projects for which research institutes take the initiative. A third possibility is to commission research, and a great deal of educational research is done on the basis of commissions. The Ministry of Education and Science gives the opportunity to educational organizations to propose research topics while the Ministry presents themes which are important to its own policies. A National Institute for Educational Research selects from among these research applications and drafts research programs for various educational areas on the basis of these applications. One example is the program on Post Secondary Education/Teacher Education, where several projects are in progress on the new teacher training for primary education. The fact that the research applications originate from different sources contributes to a lack of coherence in these programs. The National Institute for Educational Research is also responsible for managing the finances for projects and it invites research institutes to tender and negotiates their contracts.

The research financed out of the third stream of financing has a decision-oriented character: the results are meant to facilitate decisions on definite problems. More often than not this research does not contribute much to theory. Only a small part of the funds from the National Institute is available for more fundamental research, but these are spread over a number of themes, and teacher education is unfortunately not designated as a separate theme.

Pre-service Education

Problem Analyses and Innovation-related Studies. A significant amount of research on teacher education in the Netherlands is decision-oriented. We present examples where changes have taken place during the last twenty years in pre-service education and which were the object of research. First there is the foundation of new teacher training institutes preparing for lower levels of general and vocational secondary education.

In connection with the goals of the new teacher training institutes, Olgers and Riesenkamp (1980) did an extensive investigation into the objectives that teacher training institutes should realize with their students to prepare them for their future work, and the demands which follow for the institutes. Twenty-seven different groups of informants were involved in this project, such as teachers and pupils of secondary schools, and teachers of teacher training institutes. A list of ninety-one statements, which contained demands which should be made on teachers and training institutes, formed a questionnaire presented to representative samples from the twenty-seven different groups of informants. Approximately 2900 persons were involved and the response rate was 60 per cent. Each person was asked to indicate the level of importance of the statement on a scale of one to six. Among other things it turned out that teachers in the new training institutes clearly favoured changes in the secondary education system and a sound theoretical and educational basis for the teaching profession, whereas the teachers in secondary education tended more to the practical needs in everyday teaching. The students too proved to have a fairly strong inclination towards theoretical, educational aspects of the teaching profession; in this respect they might be characterized as a progressive party. It appeared, however, that graduates from the institutes adapted their views very quickly (within eighteen months after graduation) to the view of their colleagues within the schools, who were more conservative and directed towards daily practice.

In connection with the ways in which the institutes functioned a large, long-term (1978 to 1981) investigatory study revealed they had to cope with a variety of serious problems (NIVOR/SCO, 1981) including integration between the general educational preparation of students and domain-specific instruction, and the recruitment of competent teachers as supervisors for practice teaching.

Second, the establishment of teacher training institutes for primary education in 1984 was a major innovation in itself. As explained above, these institutes prepare, over four years, future teachers for pupils aged 4 to 12 years. This task supposes that teachers must have a wide range of professional competencies at their disposal. One of the uncertainties is whether the insititutes will be able to teach this wide range in such a way that the new teacher can indeed make a good start. To examine this De Jong, Matthijssen and Van der Wal (1988) collected the judgments of several groups of persons who were involved in teacher training for primary education. The research instrument consisted of fifty-seven item competencies on a questionnaire (Likert-type scale) based partly on the Connecticut's Beginning Teacher Supports Program. Most respondents (N = 639) thought that some specific competencies (e.g. realizing an attractive and orderly learning environment, or diagnosing and remediating learning problems) would not be acquired under present conditions and that more training time should be available.

The problem mentioned above is not the only one facing the new training institutes for primary education. Coonen (1987) surveyed by questionnaire (Likert-type scale) a representative sample of 489 lecturers in these institutes (response rate was 62 per cent). He reported many problems (some of which have also been mentioned in the international literature), for instance: the low entrance level of students; the limited possibilities for selection; the fact that the majority of students are women; the lack of coherence in the program; and the relations with the schools intended for practising. More specific problems proved to be the ageing population of lecturers and the disappearance of specific competence among the staff with regard to the younger age groups in the primary school. The rather negative image of the training institutes was further supported by the results of some investigations into the academic level of competence of the students of these institutes in arithmetic and language, which proved to be insufficient.

More generally a rather extensive inventory and analysis were carried out concerning problems in the various types of pre-service and in-service teacher education (Tillema and Veenman, 1985; Tillema, 1986a). This study made it possible for the National Institute for Educational Research to draft a research program for this area, taking into account the demands for research from professional organizations and the government. A survey was completed by interviewing many persons and organizations involved, such as experts in teacher education, trade unions and administrators. The named problems that emerged included: relations between teacher training institutes and the external environment; the input and output of teacher training; the quality of teacher education; student practice teaching; realization and organization of teacher education; in-service education; plus some special topics like student guidance and inequality policy.

In the Netherlands much decision-oriented research occurs in teacher education with respect to definite problems, however, the investigations of these problems and possible solutions are usually not carried out early enough. There is a lack of research programs which investigate aspects well before decisions are taken or which accompany implementation of innovations.

Instructional Methods of Pre-service Education. One of the central domains of research on teacher education remains the didactics of teacher education, which includes the instructional theory and technology used. In the 1970s research on microteaching (Kieviet, 1972), minicourses (Van der Plas and Veenman, 1975) and interaction analysis (Veenman, 1981) were important. Topics which received much attention in the past decade are: the theory-practice relation, reflective teaching and student (practice) teaching.

Before discussion of the more important studies in this area, it should be repeated that most teacher training institutes have no research facilities of their own. Thus outsiders do research into instructional methods, which is an unfavourable situation. Though much interest exists in this area (see Tillema and Veenman, 1987a, 1987b), the limited research capacity results in a small number of studies.

The gap between theory and practice remains an important area in research on teacher education. Out (1986) developed a strategy for teacher training based on the problem–oriented paradigm which integrates theory and practical training. The practical problems included the teachers' tasks in individualized education in primary schools. The strategy has three parts:

1 six categories of student activities, for instance, the student plans learning activities;
2 teaching activities that must be carried out in order to perform teaching functions that start and stimulate the student activities; and
3 conditions for the above-mentioned teaching activities, for instance, the cooperative activities between college teachers.

The strategy has been elaborated in a number of modules and working schemes, and practised and evaluated in three training institutes during three years. The strategy was evaluated in eight different groups of students at three teacher training institutes using nine modules. A variety of observation instruments was used in the research. Generally speaking, the strategy proved to be feasible in strengthening the relation between the achievement of the objectives by the student and the execution of the student activities, as well as execution of the student activities and the execution of teaching activities.

Verloop's study (1984, 1989) provides a second example of an attempt to connect theory to practice. He tried to influence student-teachers' interactive cognitions and teaching behaviour by means of specially designed video materials (compare the protocol materials movement), which contained detailed illustrations of educational theories (e.g., Ausubel's advance organizer model and Shaftel's role playing model). He used three randomly composed experimental groups, each consisting of ten student-teachers from primary and secondary teacher training institutes. One group studied the educational theory and worked through the treatment videotape, one group only studied the educational theory verbally and one group received no specific treatment and followed the normal program.

The interactive cognitions were registered by means of stimulated recall with reference to two lessons videotaped in the classrooms in which the student teachers practised. The interactive behaviour was analyzed by means of specially developed observation instruments. The superior value of the video treatment with regard to the number of interactive cognitions as well as the number of interactive behaviours was confirmed. Considering the relations between the interactive cognitions and the interactive behaviour, it appeared that the group with the video materials treatment also had a higher degree of theory-related cognitions for the majority of theory elements. So one might say that with this group not only was the theory more fully employed but this employment was also relatively steered more by relevant cognitions.

Reflective teaching also received attention as part of the theory-practice relationship. Korthagen (1982, 1985), in a case study, described how a teacher training institute taught secondary maths education student-teachers to use reflective teaching to direct their own development using Skemp's (1979) training model. Over a four-year period the students learned to choose their own goals of development, and to go through the various phases of the process needed to improve their own internal steering (director) systems. The phases included: action, looking back on the action, awareness of essential aspects, creating alternative methods of action. Korthagen also reports that more than half the forty-nine former students surveyed through questionnaire and interview spontaneously mentioned learning about reflective thinking and directing one's own development. However, some respondents simply wanted external steering. It was assumed that this difference between students is related to their conceptions of learning.

In a longitudinal study, in progress, Korthagen (1988) investigated the development of these conceptions and the influence of the training institute on them. He developed the IEO test, which measured whether a person is directed by an *internal* or *external* orientation (Korthagen and Verkuyl, 1987). This test consists of a questionnaire containing six scales, each with about ten items rated on a five-point scale. The instrument was used in a study in which thirty-seven first and second year students from a maths department using reflective teaching were compared with fifty-five students in the maths departments of two other training institutes. No differences in the preference for learning by means of reflection could be found (Korthagen, 1987). A remaining question is: do differences occur when fourth year students are included?

A second and more extensive comparative study was executed by Korthagen and Wubbels (1988). They compared a group of thirty-seven former students from the above-mentioned maths department using reflective teaching with thirty-six former students from a maths department in another institute. They used the IEO test, the QTI (Questionnaire on Teacher Interaction, see below on beginning teachers) and a questionnaire to determine readiness for innovation and job satisfaction. No differences were found in the disposition to reflect. However, according to their pupils, teachers from the experimental group who had left the training institute three or more years ago demonstrated more behaviours with a positive effect on learning outcomes. Moreover, these teachers seemed to have a more adequate self-image, and demonstrated a higher job satisfaction. So there are some cues for a positive effect of training in reflective teaching.

An important part of teacher education in the Netherlands is student teaching, or 'school practicum'. During the past decade this has received research attention. We give two examples. A relevant question is in what way can the school practicum be structured? Vedder (1984) and Vedder and Bannink (1988) evaluated 'one-to-one' lessons, in which the student teaches only one pupil. These lessons occurred at the beginning of the school practicum since it was thought that this approach would reduce the complexity of the situation. Vedder followed fifteen student maths teachers for secondary education, who gave one lesson per week during seven or eight weeks to the same pupil. These seven or eight lessons were the object of extensive reflection by the student and discussion with fellow students and a tutor (the lessons were audiotaped and the student had to keep a diary). Vedder used these diaries and the data derived from interviews and a questionnaire to reconstruct the learning experiences of the student teachers and the learning effects as perceived by the student teachers. He estimated that the one-to-one method was promising: it contributed especially to contacts the teacher-to-be made with the pupil and subject matter to be taught.

De Jong's (1988) project in which a new organization model of student teaching in the primary school was developed and evaluated provides a second example of research into the school practicum. The leading principle held that teacher education programs should develop action-relevant cognitions and that these could be enhanced by inquiry into teaching (compare the inquiry-oriented paradigm of Zeichner, 1983). For this purpose a 'study of teaching model' was developed. Its main characteristics are: first, the student teacher reflects on his own learning needs, and next, he explores some educational issue in depth by collecting data, trying to answer the learning questions he formulated. Using outcome measures no difference was found between a treatment and a control group on that measure. However, a relation existed within the experimental group between the outcome measures and the quality of realization of the model.

I have discussed the three lines of research on pre-service education in the Netherlands, namely the theory-practice relation, reflective teaching, and student (practice) teaching, and some findings holding promise of more effective teacher training have emerged. However, I hold little optimism about the implementation of these insights. In the epilogue I shall comment on this point.

A new line of research came into existence from the teacher thinking movement. In the Netherlands there appears to be a great deal of interest in this area, as is evidenced by researchers' participation in the International Study Association on Teacher Thinking (ISATT). Several studies, including those by Halkes and Deykers (1984), Halkes and Olson (1984), Peters (1984), Corporaal, Van Hunen, Boei and Starren (1986), Ben-Peretz, Bromme and Halkes (1986), Buitink and Kemme (1986), Corporaal (1987), Boei and Van Hunen (1988), Corporaal (1988), have been undertaken. In these the cognitions of student teachers or practising teachers were examined in order to gain more insight into them in order to assimilate this insight into the instructional approaches for pre-service and in-service education making use of information-processing theories or activity theories. Until now research has been restricted to describing these cognitions. We expect that this line of research will be fruitful, but there is still a long way to go.

Beginning Teachers

In line with international interest in beginning teachers Dutch educational research examined some problems of beginning teachers and considered how they could be redressed. Several studies have obtained data about the problems of beginning teachers (Vonk, 1982, 1983, 1984; Vonk and

Schras, 1987; Bergen, Peters and Gerris, 1983; Veenman, Berkelaar and Berkelaar, 1983; and Gerris, Peters and Bergen, 1984). The findings fit in with the international ones given in Veenman's (1984) review, which presents the results of eighty-three empirical studies that appeared between 1960 and 1984 on the perceived problems of beginning teachers in their first year(s) of teaching. Studies from Western Europe, the United States, Australia and Canada were included. The eight most frequently perceived problems were, in rank order: classroom discipline, motivating pupils, dealing with individual differences, assessing pupils' work, relationships with parents, organization of class work, insufficient and/or inadequate teaching materials and supplies, and dealing with problems of individual pupils. There was a high correspondence between the problems experienced by elementary and secondary beginning teachers, and classroom discipline was definitely the most highly ranked problem.

The challenge for teacher education is to find methods by which beginning teachers can be helped to overcome these problems. Créton and Wubbels (1984) undertook a very extensive empirical study into ways in which beginning teachers could be helped. In their book (see also Wubbels, Créton and Hooymayers, 1985) they describe the activities and results of clinical supervision of beginning teachers in their first professional year in secondary education. In the supervision, attention was directed to the interrelational aspects of behaviour in classrooms, since discipline was the most important problem for beginning teachers. Of special importance was whether the teachers were able to manipulate their own behaviour. The researchers adopted a systems communication perspective (Wubbels, Créton and Holvast, 1988). Two products from this project are described below.

The first is the Questionnaire on Teacher Interaction (QTI). It is a classroom adaptation of the Interpersonal CheckList associated with Leary's (1957) model, and deals with pupils' and teachers' perceptions. The QTI consists of seventy-seven items allocated to eight scales, and from the data they provide, relatively stable patterns in the teacher-pupil relationship in the classroom can be made visible. The instrument proved to be reliable and reasonably valid (see Wubbels, Brekelmans and Hermans, 1987). It has also been used in research on pre-service teacher education (Holvast, Wubbels and Brekelmans, 1988), where classroom interactions of student teachers and their supervising teachers were compared. Indications were that the classroom atmosphere that supervising teachers build up with their pupils has a considerable influence on the classroom atmosphere student teachers attempt to establish. This indicates there are severe limitations to the school practicum.

Another outcome was a supervision program which was developed, implemented and evaluated using qualitative and quantitative methods (interviews, questionnaires, lesson observations, case studies). The program is conducted by specially trained teachers from the school and incorporates class visits by the supervisor and a supervision conference in which special attention is paid to topics such as 'interacting with pupils' and 'use of classroom organization procedures'. An evaluation demonstrated that beginning teachers were very positive about the supervision which they felt was a great support and a contribution to their self-confidence. The superiority of the supervision program could not be proven unequivocally, due perhaps to several unexpected problems (Wubbels, Créton and Hooymayers, 1987).

In conclusion, we have a rather good idea about the problems of beginning teachers, but research into how to prevent or solve these problems is still insufficient in the Netherlands.

In-service Education

In the past decades interest in in-service education and training has been growing in the Netherlands. Three reasons can be given (see also Tillema, 1986b). First, the growing conviction that pre-service education can only contribute to an initial competence to start a career as a teacher makes continuing education necessary. Second, the idea of the relatively autonomous school which has to work on its own self-renewal makes staff development necessary. The third reason is associated with the constructive policy of the government to start large-scale innovations in the educational system. In-service education and training become necessary to implement those innovations.

As a consequence of this greater interest more research began on in-service education, but it was also deemed to be necessary as it was obvious that a solid empirical basis for the practice of in-service education was lacking. Researchers adopted an international orientation and sought international cooperation. The minicourse research project involving several Western European countries, including the Netherlands, who participated under the auspices of CERI (a division of OECD) (1975) provides one example. Another includes the INSET project, also conducted by CERI, in which several European countries worked together in comparative case studies on important topics of in-service education, such as training the trainers (see Bolam, 1982).

The international literature on effective methods of in-service education and training is scarce. In the Netherlands some projects have been undertaken during the past decade to broaden our knowledge of the design and instruction aspects of in-service education, so-called didactics. We discuss three of them. The study of Van der Sijde (1987) arose from the Classroom Environment Study of the IEA (International Association for the Evaluation of Educational Achievement) in which the Netherlands participated. This project aimed to identify teaching behaviours that correlate with pupils' performance and attitudes. These teaching behaviours could be the basis for teacher training. Van der Sijde developed short (one-day) programs for in-service training of secondary school teachers intended to change the script of teachers according to a proposed lesson script consisting of five scenes (presentation, monitored practice, guided practice, tutoring, homework check). He developed the script using the results from the IEA study and other sources. From experiments, using observation and achievement tests, it appeared that the training did have an effect on students' achievement and on teachers' behaviour. Pupils also showed more favourable perceptions on the Classroom Environment Scale.

A second study on effective methods of in-service education involved the work of De Jong, Matthijssen and Tillema (1988), who investigated the effects of different proportions of time spent on explanation and practice. They examined a part of an in-service course for a group (N = 75) of secondary school teachers to develop thematic learning materials for the subject of technics. Teachers reported learning more if the practice part was relatively greater. Coaching by a tutor after the course appeared to strenghten the knowledge level.

Van Tulder, Veenman and Sieben (1988a) carried out a Delphi study to find out which characteristics of in-service activities for primary school teachers experts would label important. A list of thirty-four statements resulted such as: in-service must lead to concrete changes in everyday practice. After this Delphi study they carried out an evaluation examining a number of in-service courses between 1984 and 1987 on these characteristics (Van Tulder, Veenman and Sieben, 1987, 1988b). The course lecturers (112) were approached by means of questionnaires and interviews. It turned out that the characteristics considered important had been realized in a reasonable measure. It is worth noting that differences appeared to exist between lecturers in team-oriented and individual-oriented in-service training courses. The former more often gave priority to knowledge and comprehension in comparison with skills. Futhermore, a problem appeared to be that lecturers generally had no possibilities for coaching in the classroom, while cooperation with local or regional school counselling services, which did have these possibilities, was superficial and incidental. Likewise peer-teaching hardly occurred.

De Jong, Matthijssen and Tillema (1987) concluded from their research with sixty-three teacher training institutes for primary education that a significant difference exists between what is known about effective training components (according to people like Joyce, Showers and Sparks) and what is offered in in-service courses. It turned out that in the team-oriented courses demonstration and practice occurred much less than in the individual-oriented ones. This finding is comparable to that of Van Tulder *et al.* (1988b). The outcome of in-service courses is often the object of criticism. In several evaluation studies participants thought that problems in the classroom did not receive sufficient attention. A weak point about these studies is that often they only concentrated on the opinion of participants or lecturers, while other criteria for the effectiveness of in-service courses, and the effects in classroom practice in particular, were rarely applied.

When the results of these studies (see also Tillema and Veenman, 1985, and Stokking, 1988) are put together, the following bottlenecks in in-service education and training in the Netherlands emerge.

Little knowledge exists about how to realize in-service education and training in an efficient and effective way.

Not much knowledge and experience exist with regard to the design and organization of large-scale in-service training projects.

The initial teacher training institutes charged with in-service education and training are not sufficiently prepared for this task. This is also true for lecturers.

The correspondence between supply and demand is often insufficient.

The tuning between the teacher training institutes and the various institutions in the support structure is problematic. This applies especially to the teacher training institutes for primary education and the school counselling services.

School teams and individual teachers are not always sufficiently motivated.

The acknowledgment of in-service education as an intrinsic part of professional development is still in progress.

Conditions corresponding to this insight are not sufficiently adequate.

Epilogue

In this review of a decade of research on teacher education in the Netherlands, several points emerge for further consideration.

It becomes apparent that a great part of the research on teacher education in the Netherlands has a decision-oriented character, designed to help make decisions with regard to definite problems. This research contributes little to theory. Nevertheless, decision-oriented research is important for further development of the national educational system. Unfortunately, much of this research begins too late; thus possible solutions to problems are not implemented in time. Morever, the research program for teacher education funded from the third stream demonstrates little coherence.

In comparison with decision-oriented research, research of a more fundamental nature takes a modest place. This holds for the first stream of financing (university finances) as well as for the other streams of financing. As we saw, this more fundamental research is restricted to a small number of themes. Partly because of scanty finances, much of the research has the character of a survey. Relatively little research is directed at the actual processes which take place in learning situations. Yet we require this if the didactics are to develop. Socialization aspects are neglected too (with the exception of De Frankrijker, 1988).

Considering this situation, a better tuning of the research financed out of different streams seems important. This should make it possible to use fundamental as well as decision-oriented research to maximum benefit at the same time as achieving maximum coherence. Furthermore, it would be useful to reach national agreement about which topics should have the highest priority (for instance, variables of effective in-service training) in order to prevent a dispersion of research potential and attention. What is more, one should guard against segmentation: all too often types of teacher education are considered in isolation, while many of the problems are common ones.

Given the scarce means for fundamental research, an international orientation is necessary. In this respect the Dutch situation can be assessed positively. A strong international orientation offers the possibility of linking up with the mainstream of scientific research in order to contribute to the development of the body of knowledge. International contacts are also important for decision-oriented research. International cooperation offers the possibility of looking for solutions for problems that countries have in common.

With regard to implementation, we see a number of restrictive conditions: autonomous teacher training institutions; weak professional ties; and inattention to research findings. Because institutes have little or no research capacity, much of the research comes from outside. This lowers their involvement. The relative autonomy of the institutes augurs against a national agreement on priorities.

All in all, with regard to preconditions as well as to pragmatic matters, room for improvement exists. Research in teacher education must be developed, become more coordinated, if the quality of teacher education and schooling is to be improved.

References

BEN-PERETZ, M., BROMME, R. and HALKES, R. (Eds) (1986) *Advances of Research on Teacher Thinking*. Lisse: Swets and Zeitlinger.

BERGEN, V.A.M., PETERS, TH.C.M. and GERRIS, J.R.M. (1983) Een exploratieve studie naar de probleemsituaties van ervaren en beginnende docenten tijdens hun beroepsuitoefening [An exploration study into the problem situations of experienced and beginning teachers], in S.A.M. VEENMAN and H.W.A.M. COONEN (Eds) *Onderwijs en Opleiding* [*Education and Teacher Training*]. Lisse: Swets and Zeitlinger.

BOEI, F. and VAN HUNEN, W. (1988) Experts and novices: Differences measured with the RepGrid. In *Teaching and Action, Evolution of Perspective. Proceedings of the Fourth ISATT Conference*. Nottingham: University of Nottingham.

BOLAM, R. (1982) *Inservice Education and Training of Teachers*. Paris: OECD.

BUITINK, J. and KEMME, S. (1986) Changes in student-teacher thinking. *European Journal of Teacher Education*, 9, 1, 75–84.

CERI (Centre for Educational Research and Innovation) (1975) *The International Transfer of Microteaching Programmes for Teacher Education*. Parijs: OECD.

COONEN, H.W.A.M. (1987) De opleiding van leraren basisonderwijs [Teacher education for primary schools]. Doctoral dissertation, with English summary. 's-Hertogenbosch: Katholiek Pedagogisch Centrum.

CORPORAAL, A.H. (1987) Six shared dimensions concerning good teaching. *European Journal of Teacher Education*, 10, 57–67.

CORPORAAL, A.H. (1988) Bouwstenen voor een opleidingsdidactiek: Theorie en onderzoek met betrekking tot cognities van aanstaande onderwijsgevenden [Buildingblocks for the didactics of teacher training: Theory and research concerning cognitions of prospective teachers]. Doctoral dissertation, with English summary. De Lier: Academisch Boekencentrum.

CORPORAAL, A.H., VAN HUNEN, W.H., BOEI, F. and STARREN, S. (1986) Thinking about good teaching: Some central dimensions used by (student) teachers, in J.H.C. VONK and E. DE VREEDE (Eds) *Inservice Edcuation and Training of Teachers*. Brussels/Amsterdam: ATEE (Association for Teacher Education in Europe).

CRÉTON, H. and WUBBELS, T. (1984) Ordeproblemen bij beginnende leerkrachten [Problems of classroom discipline with beginning teachers]. Doctoral dissertation, with English summary. Utrecht: W.C.C.

DE FRANKRIJKER, J.J.G.B. (1988) De Katholieke onderwijzersopleiding: Organisatie en ideologie, 1889–1984. [Catholic teacher training: Organization and ideology, 1889–1984]. Doctoral dissertation, with English summary. Nijkerk: Intro.

DE JONG, J.A. (1988) 'Je wordt aan het denken gezet', ontwikkeling en evaluatie van een model voor de schoolstage van de PABO [Inquiry-based student teaching, development and evaluation of a student teaching model for the Dutch Teachers' College for Primary Education]. Doctoral dissertation, with English summary. Utrecht: ISOP/State University.

DE JONG, R., MATTHIJSSEN, C. and TILLEMA, H.H. (1987) Kenmerken van nascholingscursussen [Characteristics of in-service training course], in J.J. PETERS and H.H. TILLEMA (Eds) *Scholing in onderwijs en bedrijf [Schooling in Education and Industry]*. Lisse: Swets and Zeitlinger.

DE JONG, R., MATTHIJSSEN, C. and TILLEMA, H.H. (1988) 'Effecten van training en coaching van leraren' [The effects of training and coaching of teachers]. Paper presented at the annual convention of the Dutch Association for Educational Research (ORD), Leuven.

DE JONG, R., MATTHIJSSEN, C. and VAN DER WAL, G. (1988) 'De brede bekwaamheid toegepast? [The broad competence, now applied?]. Paper presented at the annual convention of the Dutch Association of Educational Research (ORD), Leuven.

GERRIS, J.R.M., PETERS, V.A.M. and BERGEN, TH.C.M. (1984) Teachers and their educational situations they are concerned about: Preliminary research findings, in R. HALKES and J.K. OLSON (Eds) *Teacher Thinking: A New Perspective on Persisting Problems in Education*. Lisse: Swets and Zeitlinger.

HALKES, R. and DEYKERS, R. (1984) Teachers' teaching criteria, in R. HALKES and J.K. OLSON (Eds) *Teacher Thinking: A New Perspective on Persisting Problems in Education*. Lisse: Swets and Zeitlinger, pp. 149–162.

HALKES, R. and OLSON, J.K. (Eds) (1984) *Teacher Thinking: A New Perspective on Persisting Problems in Education*. Lisse: Swets and Zeitlinger.

HOLVAST, A.J.C.D., WUBBELS, TH. and BREKELMANS, M. (1988) Supervising teachers and the teacher behavior and teaching ideals of student teachers, in J.T. VOORBACH and L.G.M. PRICK (Eds) *Teacher Education 4: Research and Developments on Teacher Education in the Netherlands*. Den Haag: SVO/ATEE.

KIEVIET, F.K. (1972) Microteaching als methode in de opleiding van leerkrachten [Microteaching as a method in the training of teachers]. Doctoral dissertation, with English summary. Vaassen: Van Walraven.

KORTHAGEN, F. (1982) Leren reflecteren als basis van de lerarenopleiding [Learning to reflect as a basis for teacher training]. Doctoral dissertation, with English summary. SVO-reeks 67. 's-Gravenhage: SVO.

KORTHAGEN, F.A.J. (1985) Reflective teaching and preservice teacher education in the Netherlands. *Journal of Teacher Education*, 36, 5, 11–15.

KORTHAGEN, F.A.J. (1987) Intern en extern gestuurd leren in de opleiding van onderwijsgevenden [Internally and externally steered teaching in the training of teachers], in J.J. PETERS and H.H. TILLEMA (Eds) *Scholing in onderwijs en bedrijf* [Schooling in Education and Industry]. Lisse: Swets and Zeitlinger.

KORTHAGEN, F.A.J. (1988) The influence of learning orientations on the development of reflective teaching, in J. CALDERHEAD (Ed.) *Teachers' Professional Learning*. Lewes: Falmer Press.

KORTHAGEN, F.A.J. and VERKUYL, H.S. (1987) 'Supply and demand: Learning conceptions and their importance for teacher education programs'. Paper presented at the AERA annual meeting, Washington.

KORTHAGEN, F.A.J. and WUBBELS, TH. (1988) 'De effecten van een opleiding die tot doel heeft a.s. leraren te leren reflecteren ['The effects of a training that aims at teaching prospective teachers to reflect']. Paper presented at the annual convention of the Dutch Association for Educational Research (ORD), Leuven.

LEARY, T. (1957) *An Interpersonal Diagnosis of Personality.* New York: Ronald Press Company.

Ministry of Education and Science (1988) *The Dutch Education System.* Docinform. no. 332E. Zoetermeer: Ministerie van Onderwijs en Wetenschappen.

NIJHOF, W.J. and STREUMER, J.N. (1985) Netherlands: System of education, in T. HUSEN and T.N. POSTLEWHAITE (Eds) *The International Encyclopedia of Education.* Oxford: Pergamon.

NIVOR/SCO (1981) *Overzichtsrapport zes jaar NLO-onderzoek* [Review of Six Years of Research into the NLO.] Nijmegen: Amsterdam.

OLGERS, A. and RIESENKAMP, J. (1980). De onderwijskundige voorbereiding van aanstaande leraren [The educational preparation of prospective teachers]. Doctoral dissertation, with English summary. Den Haag: Staatsuitgeverij.

OUT, T.J. (1986) Probleemgericht opleiden [Problem oriented teacher training]. Doctoral dissertation, with English summary. Selectareeks. Den Haag: SVO.

PETERS, J. (1984) Teaching: Intentionality, reflection and routines, in R. HALKES and J.K. OLSON (Eds) *Teacher Thinking: A New Perspective on Persisting Problems in Education.* Lisse: Swets and Zeitlinger, pp. 19–34.

SKEMP, R.R. (1979) *Intelligence, Learning and Action: A Foundation for Theory and Practice in Education.* Chichester: Wiley.

STOKKING, K.M. (1988) Nascholing basisonderwijs: Onderzoek 1980–1987 [Inservice education for primary education: Research 1980–1987]. *Pedagogische Studien,* 65, 363–367.

TILLEMA, H.H. (1986a) *De universitaire lerarenopleiding: Een aanvullende probleemverkenning ten behoeve van de SVO programmalijn opleiding onderwijsgevenden* [*Teacher Training at University: A Supplementary Survey of Problems on Behalf of the SVO Program on Teacher Training*]. 's-Gravenhage: SVO.

TILLEMA, H.H. (1986b) In-service education in the Nederlands, in W. HOEBEN (Ed.) *In-service Education of Educational Personnel in Comparative Perspective: Report of a Unesco Joint Study in the Field of Education.* Den Haag: SVO/Unesco.

TILLEMA, H.H. and VEENMAN, S.A.M. (1985) *Probleemverkenning opleiding onderwijsgevenden* [Problem Survey of Teacher Training]. 's-Gravenhage: SVO.

TILLEMA, H.H. and VEENMAN, S.A.M. (Eds) (1987a) Developments in training methods for teacher education. *International Journal of Educational Research,* 11, 5, [entire issue].

TILLEMA, H.H. and VEENMAN, S.A.M. (1987b) Conceptualizing training methods in teacher education, in H.H. TILLEMA and S.A.M. VEENMAN (Eds) Developments in training methods for teacher education. *International Journal of Educational Research,* 11, 519–529.

VAN DER PLAS, P.L. and VEENMAN, S.A.M. (1975) De Minikursus (The minicourse]. *Pedagogische Studiën,* 52, 285–295.

VAN DER SIJDE, P.C. (1987) Training the teaching script. Doctoral dissertation. Almere: Versluys.

VAN TULDER, M., VEENMAN, S. and SIEBEN, J. (1987) Nascholing leraren basisonderwijs: vormageving van de cursussen 1984–1986 [In-service training for primary teachers: design of the courses 1984–1986], in J.J. PETERS and H.H. TILLEMA (Eds) *Scholing in Onderwijs en Bedrijf* [Schooling in Education and Industry]. Lisse: Swets and Zeitlinger.

VAN TULDER, M., VEENMAN, S. and SIEBEN, J. (1988a) Features of effective in-service activities: Results of a Delphi-study. *Educational Studies,* 14, 209–223.

VAN TULDER, M., VEENMAN, S. and SIEBEN, J. (1988b) 'Nascholing leraren basisonderwijs: Opzet en vormgeving in de cursusjaren 1984 t/m 1987' ['In-service training for primary teachers: Plan and design in course years 1984–1987]. Paper presented at the annual convention of the Dutch Association for Educational Research (ORD), Leuven.

VEDDER, J. (1984) Oriëntatie op het beroep van leraar: Praktische vorming en reflecteren aan het begin van de lerarenopleiding [Teaching profession, an orientation: Practical training and reflecting at the start of teacher training]. Doctoral dissertation, with English summary. Lisse: Swets and Zeitlinger.

VEDDER, J. and BANNINK, P. (1988) The development of practical skills and reflexion at the beginning teacher training, in J.T. VOORBACH and L.G.M. PRICK (Eds) *Teacher Education 4, Research and Developments on Teacher Education in the Netherlands.* Den Haag: SVO/ATEE.

VEENMAN, S.A.M. (1981) Evaluation of a teaching-learning programme based on interaction analysis and microteaching, in A. SALMON (Ed.) *The Evaluation of In-service Education and Training of Teachers.* (Council of Europe). Lisse: Swets and Zeitlinger.

VEENMAN, S.A.M. (1984) Perceived problems of beginning teachers. *Review of Educational Research,* 54, 143–178.

VEENMAN, S.A.M., BERKELAAR, A. and BERKELAAR, J. (1983) Problemen van beginnende leraren in het basisonderwijs [Problems of beginning teachers in elementary education]. *Pedagogische Studiën,* 60, 28–37.

VERLOOP, N. (1984) 'The effects of video materials on student-teachers' cognitions during their interactive teaching.' Paper presented at the annual meeting of the AERA, New Orleans.

VERLOOP, N. (1989) Interactive cognitions of student teachers: An intervention study. Doctoral dissertation. Arnhern: CITO.

VONK, J.H.C. (1982) Opleiding en praktijk [Training and practice]. Doctoral dissertation, with English summary. Amsterdam: VU Boekhandel/ Uitgeverij.

VONK, J.H.C. (1983) Problems of the beginning teacher. *European Journal of Teacher Education,* 6, 133–150.

VONK, J.H.C. (1984) *Teacher Education and Teacher Practice.* Amsterdam: Free University Press.

VONK, J.H.C. and SCHRAS, G.A. (1987) From beginning to experienced teacher. *European Journal of Teacher Education,* 10, 95–110.

WUBBELS, TH., BREKELMANS, M. and HERMANS, J.J. (1987) Teacher behavior, an important aspect of the learning environment? In B.J. FRASER (Ed.) *The Study of Learning Environments 3.* Perth: Curtin University.

WUBBELS, TH., CRÉTON, H.A. and HOLVAST, A.J.C.D. (1988) Undesirable class-room situations: A systems communication perspective. *Interchange,* 19, 2, 25–40.

WUBBELS, TH., CRÉTON, H.A. and HOOYMAYERS, H.P. (1985) 'Discipline problems of beginning teachers, interaction teacher behavior mapped out.' Paper presented at the AERA annual meeting, Chicago. ERIC document 260040.

WUBBELS, TH., CRÉTON, H.A. and HOOYMAYERS, H.P. (1987) A school-based teacher induction programme. *European Journal of Teacher Education,* 10, 81–94.

ZEICHNER, K.M. (1983) Alternative paradigms of teacher education. *Journal of Teacher Education,* 34, 3, 3–9.

Chapter 5

One and a Half Decades of Research on Teacher Education in Australia

Richard P. Tisher

The Educational Context

Australian tertiary education approaches the 1990s in a state of turmoil, uncertainty and impending restructuring.[1] Our federal government, through its Green Paper on Higher Education (Dawkins, 1987), shows a determination to change the face of university and college education. As might be expected, the federal moves have also been challenged by students and academics who have raised their voices in protest. Our federal government, however, controls the purse strings, and is clearly determined to bring about changes in the ways higher education institutions are administered, receive funds and go about their business. Consequently tertiary education is in a state of flux as universities and colleges review working conditions for staff, become more entrepreneurial, accept more full fee paying students, generate a greater proportion of their own income, establish stronger links with industry and business, amalgamate to form larger multi-campus institutions, review course offerings, and try to be more accountable to the community at large.

As part of the tertiary shake-up national reviews are being undertaken. Reports have already been completed on training in engineering and law. A national review of the training of mathematics and science teachers will look at the quality of the specialist subject matter and education components in pre-service programs, scrutinizing many aspects of mathematics, science and education faculties. It remains to be seen what impact the review will have on the pre-service education of maths and science teachers, and on teacher education generally.

At present pre-service education is offered in Colleges of Advanced Education (CAEs) and universities, and may be of either three or four years' duration. The three-year Diploma of Teaching program is designed for pre-school, kindergarten or primary teachers who may, after one or more years in employment, complete another year of equivalent full-time study to receive a Bachelor of Education degree. The majority of the four-year programs are designed for secondary teachers who follow either a concurrent subject specialist plus education program, or a three-year specialist bachelor's course followed by a one-year Diploma in Education course.

Qualified teachers are employed in either state government or non-government schools. The latter, comprising Catholic, other denominations and private schools, provide education for 25 per cent of Australia's school children. While pre-service education is provided in the federally funded colleges and universities, the government and non-government school sectors are responsible for the induction and in-service education of their employees. The universities and colleges, however, offer graduate diploma and master's programs which may be deemed as in-service activities, and at the same time provide formal qualifications. No doubt these formal courses will remain, but there is increasing pressure upon the colleges and universities to grant credit for short in-service courses done elsewhere. We are likely to see many changes in the near future in the number, variety and length of in-service courses offered by universities, colleges and employing agencies, and in the ways these may be put together for credit for formal awards.

At present educational researchers must apply to bodies that distribute funds for scientific, sociological and psychological research in competition with scholars from all of these fields. No special educational research funding agency exists, although one did exist for a time during the 1970s. However, educational researchers, who are drawn predominantly from the schools of education in the colleges and the universities, win a reasonable proportion of the competitive funds, though not as much as in the 1970s. My own perspective is that educational research is funded poorly in relation to research in other disciplines, especially research in the sciences. This may be due to the fact that there is no national policy on educational research, and research on teacher education in particular, or to the fact that educational researchers have not been as aggressive as their scientific colleagues in submitting applications for research funds.

The preceding provides a somewhat roughly painted background to the ensuing discussion — a condensed review of the nature of the research on teacher education undertaken in Australia during the last one and a half decades. More detailed reviews are available elsewhere.[2] This chapter simply highlights essential features of the research, presenting a series of snapshots of the research methods used, the kinds of issues studied, the findings obtained and changes in the research. As well, I present my own views about the strengths and limitations of these research endeavours.

Methods Used by Investigators

During the period spanned by this review numerous debates appeared in the educational literature about the merits and de-merits of quantitative and qualitative approaches to research in education. Australian researchers followed, and entered into, the debate, but at the same time chose to use a variety of approaches to study teacher education.

Although there is variety, about 40 per cent of the Australian investigations belong to the empirical–analytical tradition. They consist of: (1) cross-sectional surveys of trainees' characteristics, e.g., reasoning patterns (Garnett and Tobin, 1984) and value systems (Boyce, 1977); and (2) pre/post-test designs, with or without a manipulation or intervention. Naturalistic studies include those dealing with trainees' preferences for various strategies for teaching primary science (Appleton, 1984), the self-perceived needs of trainees (Gunstone and Mackay, 1975), beginning teachers' problems and concerns (Tisher, Fyfield and Taylor, 1979), and the associations between trainees' self-reported teaching patterns and their personal and situational stresses (Taylor, 1980). Studies involving experimentation include attitudinal changes to teaching science (Dooley and Lucas, 1981), changes in trainees' constructs of self, teacher and pupils (Diamond, 1985), changes in trainees' verbal behaviours (Tierney, 1984) and increases in the correspondence between trainees' teaching style and that shown in a particular model (Tobin, Pike and Lacey, 1984). The majority of these pre/post-test projects used only one group to be compared with itself and, as a consequence, extraneous variance could have occurred due to history, maturation or the measurement procedure. One of the more sophisticated manipulative studies used multivariate procedures to evaluate six experimental treatments in a competency-based teacher education program (Thompson and Levis, 1980), but this kind of study is rare.

The sociological or ethnographic styles, including case studies and action research, have been favoured ways to study in-service education and professional development. They do not figure often in pre-service projects, although a modest proportion of studies on the practicum and the supervisory process use case studies and action research.

In in-service education, case studies have centred on the teacher as a 'reflexive' classroom researcher (Beasley, 1981), the role of clinical supervision in enhancing skills and confidence (Smyth and Henry, 1983) and teachers' desires to play a significant role in their own in-service education (Ingvarson, 1982). Action research projects have included school controlled in-service teacher education in Victoria (Fenton, 1983) and the fostering of school-focused development programs in New South Wales (Eltis, Braithwaite, Deer and Kensall, 1981). This New South Wales project, involving three Sydney high schools and a university School of Education, incorporated illuminative evaluation throughout its operation. Reports of these projects appear to be very well received by practitioners since they show 'what works'.

Some Characteristics of the Research

Before I turn to the foci of, and findings from, this research, I will describe and reflect on some of its characteristics.

First, the investigatory sample in the majority of studies has been a 'captive group' usually in the researcher's institution. In the case of studies on science teacher education, the captive sample has generally been primary trainees in a College of Advanced Education.

Second, the time interval between testings in projects involving pre- and post-tests has been short, somewhere between two weeks and six months on average. For a few studies where interventions occurred, the time intervals were a fraction longer, ranging from five weeks to a little over one year. But even this longer time span is often too short for changes to be noted in some outcomes. Why are the time intervals so short? Why are there few projects tracing teachers' professional development through pre-service, induction and in-service? I can only speculate on these questions. There may be an unwillingness by Australian researchers to take on lengthy, labour-intensive, longitudinal studies, or there may be an insufficient number of research teams, resulting in a number of longitudinal studies foundering due either to a lack of resources or determination on the part of the researchers. It is to be hoped that the future will see more reports of completed longitudinal studies, especially ones which trace teachers' professional development through various phases of their education. There is an intriguing, burgeoning beginning. As part of a three-year project on the teaching and learning of science in schools, a research team (Baird, Fensham, Gunstone and White, 1987) asked fourteen science graduates in a one-year Diploma in Education program to keep diaries in which they recorded thoughts and impressions about their teacher education and their own development. The program is predicated on the propositions that transition from learner to teacher is facilitated greatly when intending teachers work closely with their colleagues; a student teacher is actively constructing views of teaching based on personal experiences; and reflecting on one's practice helps trainees construct their views of teaching. The findings (Gunstone, Slattery and Baird, 1989) indicate that learning to become a teacher is facilitated through personal reflection and a pre-service program that takes account of, and builds upon, a trainee's competencies.

Third, published evaluations of teacher education programs are rare. Only a few have been reported. One, a 'post-hoc evaluation' of a primary pre-service program in a Victorian country college (Reed, 1986), asked graduates through a mail questionnaire to express their opinions about their pre-service program. The respondents believed it had definitely helped them with their organization of lesson content, schemes of work and pupil motivation and evaluation. A more detailed evaluation carried out in Victoria about six years ago (Owen, Wyn and Senyard, 1983) considered the four modes for conducting the Diploma in Education program at the Melbourne College of Advanced Education and documented what ex-students considered were discrepancies between what was important to them in their current teaching positions and the emphases in the course. The largest discrepancies occurred with respect to classroom management, catering for individual differences, self-evaluation and translating curriculum plans into action. The results also indicated that the school-based mode for conducting the program yielded greater benefits for trainees than the other three: drawing up contracts, selecting from a wide choice of options, and following a set core of studies with a few options.

Fourth, very few studies are repeated or replicated. Some repetitions have occurred with studies on the effects of training practice supervisors (Preston and Baker, 1985), and on the perceived problems of beginning teachers (e.g., McCahon and Carpenter, 1987; Otto, Gasson and Jordan, 1979; Tisher, Fyfield and Taylor, 1979), but the investigatory samples and survey instruments have differed, so findings tend to complement each other rather than reaffirm a previous result for a comparable sample.

Given the complexities of teacher education, the research on it, and the changes occurring in the higher education milieu in this country, Australian researchers must now consider the benefits to be derived from repetitions or replications of existing studies. Elsewhere (Tisher, 1987) I have argued that positive pay-offs occur with replications. For example, more teacher educators will most likely regard findings as relevant since some projects will have been conducted in contexts approximating their own; moreover, our understanding of the nature of the teacher education process will grow in an iterative manner.

Issues and Findings

Australian researchers have, as implied already, pursued a wide range of often unrelated issues. The research appears to be driven more by individual curiosity than by an overarching plan or framework. Consequently the studies are difficult to categorize but they may be clustered into four broad groups, namely, those dealing with:

1   the characteristics of trainees at various stages in their training;
2   the nature and impact of pre-service training, with special attention given to skills development and to the practicum;
3   induction; and
4   in-service education.

Characteristics of Trainees

What issues have been studied and what does the research tell us about those who enter and complete pre-service education? Answering this question proves difficult because some findings apply to primary trainees, others to Diploma in Education students, and some to students in units of these kinds of programs. Nevertheless, there are implications for teacher selection and the conduct of pre-service programs. Many trainees enter teaching by default (Carpenter and Foster, 1979), with no clear commitment, while less than half enter because they are interested in it, desire security and recognition or are influenced by their teachers. If a Western Australian study (Ryan and Reynolds, 1982) is indicative of what Australia's Year 12 students think, then at least one-third of graduating high school students believe teaching is poor employment with poor promotion prospects, limited prestige, limited income and excessive after-hours work. For more qualified students to be attracted to teaching, education authorities, as well as teacher educators, will have to publicize the better features of teaching, more so than is done now. Also training programs will have to take better account of the proportion of entrants with low commitment.

It may be considered fortunate that by the conclusion of pre-service at least 40 per cent of trainees have a strong commitment to teaching (Elsworth and Coulter, 1978). But that has to be set against the facts that male trainees have become more custodial than the females, science trainees more custodial than their humanities colleagues (McArthur, 1975), survival is now regarded as an important aspect of a teacher's role, and a proportion of trainees have developed unfavourable attitudes to teaching and pessimistic views about pupils and school administrators

(Dymond, 1976; Hogben and Petty, 1979; Hogben and Lawson, 1984). These findings imply that pre-service programs, including the times spent practising in schools, have deleterious effects on future teachers and require major overhaul. The results cannot be dismissed simply by stating that these kinds of outcomes occur because the trainees are, for the first time, experiencing teaching from a new perspective: that of teacher rather than pupil. Fortunately, the story does not end here. Further experience with pupils results in a proportion of teachers perceiving them as patient, kind and willing to help, and believing teachers should be interested in, patient with and helpful towards them (Diamond, 1983).

The Nature and Impact of Pre-service Training

During the last decade a small proportion of Australian studies, some commissioned, has looked at the nature of pre-service programs (Campbell, Evans, Philp and Levis, 1979; Deschamp and Tripp, 1980), the benefits students derive from them (Beasley, 1981; Symington, 1982; Appleton, 1983, 1984; Tierney, 1984) and ex-students' reactions to them (Tisher, Fyfield and Taylor, 1979; Young, 1979; Hewitson, 1981; Telfer, 1982; Reed, 1986). From these reports a collage can be constructed of some aspects of the nature of pre-service education and its impact.

By and large the programs aim to foster personal development, along with general education, specialist knowledge and professional skills, but appear to place a lower emphasis on personal development. Trainees are taught to plan, but it seems improvements are required in the examples used and the instructions given. School-based programs provide more peer support and opportunities for discussion than other courses.

Positive outcomes from pre-service programs are that trainees' teaching competencies improve; they develop realistic views about their own curriculum knowledge and teaching prowess; their professional attitudes are enhanced; their general level of anxiety about teaching decreases; their teaching confidence increases in direct relation to the increase in their content knowledge; and, as noted earlier, about 40 per cent finish their training with a strong commitment to teaching. In passing it should be noted that for most new teachers there is a strengthening in commitment during the first five years of teaching (McArthur, 1981).

Skill Development and Micro-teaching. The early 1970s saw a strong interest in skill development, and micro-teaching courses in particular. Training institutions tried out various courses that had originated in the USA or

Australia, and a few studies relating to their benefits were undertaken (Hewitson, 1979). These indicated that trainees liked this mode of training and that a number of their questioning and probing skills could be enhanced. There was not, however, a large-scale adoption of micro-teaching, although most training institutions appear to have retained elements in their pre-service offerings. The cost, the labour-intensive nature of the courses, and in some instances a concern about 'principles' on which the courses were based seem to have deterred Australian teacher educators from a large-scale commitment to this mode of skill development.

In the 1970s competency-based teacher education was also being debated, and, as noted earlier, at least one experimental study attempted to evaluate aspects such as explicit objectives, criterion-referenced assessment, controlled school experience and mastery criteria (Thompson and Levis, 1980). The investigators reported that when these aspects were included the competency-based program was more effective than a conventional teacher education course in helping trainees acquire explanatory skills, especially verbal fluency and terminal review.

Since 1980 studies on micro-teaching or skill development have been rare. Exceptions include an experimental investigation of the effectiveness of a value claim strategy in teacher education (Butcher, 1981), a study of the effect of practicum on the acquisition of teaching skills (Pegg, 1985), a thirteen-week time series design involving classroom analyses to produce changes in trainees' verbal behaviours (Tierney, 1984), and an experimental study involving strategy analysis to improve teaching skills (Tobin, Pike and Lacey, 1984). This last project involved 112 college students enrolled in science education courses. The pre-service teachers learnt about models appropriate for activity-oriented science and engaged in peer-teaching (i.e., behaviour modelling). These activities were followed by (1) an analysis of their teaching, to note whether it corresponded to the proposed models, and (2) feedback about their teaching. The investigators concluded that the various activities were effective in improving the quality of the trainees' activity-oriented science teaching skills.

As mentioned earlier, Australian teacher educators appear to favour only moderate doses of skill development, or micro-teaching courses, in their pre-service programs. This may account for the fact that in recent years few studies have been conducted on these aspects.

The Practicum and the Supervisory Process. Unlike skill development the practicum and its supervision have, in recent years, received increased attention. Twelve years ago a small group of teacher educators convened our first national, special interest conference, and every five years since about 100 persons have met to share information about research and development on the practicum and supervision. At the first conference only one research paper was read. At the second there were five, and in January 1986, fifteen.

So, what issues have been deemed important? Research workers have studied trainees' anxiety during practice (Sinclair and Nicholl, 1981), the impact of the practicum on trainees' socialization into teaching (Matthews, 1980), changes in self-assessments of knowledge of curriculum content, teaching competencies and attitude to teaching (Young, 1979), alterations in professional self-image (Coulter, 1974), perceptions about the quality of the practicum (Hewitson, 1981; Love and Swain, 1980; Thursby, 1980), its effect on the concerns of pre-service teachers (Sellars, 1988), and whether trainees learnt a lot during their school experience (Poole and Gaudry, 1974). Studies also exist which ascertain the ways in which student teachers are implicitly guided in their thinking about, and analysis of, teaching by their supervising teachers (Grundy, 1986), and gather information about trainees' perceptions of inquiry teaching and the extent to which they implement lessons with inquiry characteristics (Skamp and Power, 1981).

These projects confirm school experience to be an extremely important, practical, satisfying component of pre-service education. The trainees say they gain a lot from it; that it is the most realistic aspect of their courses, helps reduce their anxiety about teaching, fosters their practical teaching skills, helps them develop realistic perspectives about pupils and their own curriculum knowledge, highlights their inability adequately to implement inquiry teaching, and allows them to explore their own capabilities. Finally, they feel it should be increased. It has the potential to affect management and other classroom skills, and for some supervising teachers it may well be a form of in-service education. These last two 'potentials' have not, however, been the foci for research in Australia. We must await studies on these issues.

As indicated earlier, some action research projects also deal with the practicum. I mention three of these: a working model for reflective teaching practice (Evans, 1980); the utilization of a clinical observation system (Preston and Baker, 1985); and a collaborative planning review exercise (Fawns, 1984). In each project trainees had to reflect on their own and their supervising teachers' classroom behaviours. In the exercise on clinical observation, for example, the trainees examined their supervising teachers' skills after they had been briefed about recording data, setting objectives and post-observation conferences with the teachers. All investigators reported some successes such as commitment to the program, valuing the experience, and developing positive perspectives about pupils. In this clinical observation study trainees saw a great deal of value in the system, but very few used it during practice teaching. Reasons for this may be that too much time and effort were required to gather the data and discuss them with the teachers. Alternatively, the mode of briefing students in the study, through a compulsory seminar and printed handout, may not have been highly effective. This feature highlights the importance of clear communication among trainees, teacher educators and supervising teachers.

The matter of supervision is one that has received a great deal of attention during the past eight years. More and more teacher educators have emphasized that it is the most important, yet least adequately resourced and developed, component of practice teaching. The need for top quality supervisors has also been stressed and, consequently, an increasing amount of research has dealt with their characteristics and ways in which their supervisory skills may be enhanced. The matters of quality supervision, characteristics of supervisors, who should supervise, and the training needed are not of easy resolution in Australia. They are complicated by the facts that we must pay supervisors, some experienced teachers are reluctant to take on the responsibility, and school principals maintain they should control the choice of supervisors.

The studies about characteristics have looked generally at the qualities of supervising teachers (Yarrow *et al.*, 1984); or have dealt with the characteristics of excellent supervisors as perceived by trainees assigned to them (Price and Sellars, 1985). Issues such as supervisors' effectiveness (Eltis and Cairns, 1982), responsibilities (Briggs, 1984; Danaher, Elliot and Marland, 1982), and clear communication with trainees (Osborne and Henderson, 1986) have also received attention, as has the quality of supervision (Duck and Cunningham, 1985). The researchers found that teachers, school administrators and trainees believed the highly desirable qualities of a practice teaching supervisor are fairness, approachability, consistency, friendliness and the ability to be considerate and tactful. It was also found that problems with respect to practice supervision were generally related to failures in communication between trainee and supervisor. Furthermore, both trainees and supervisors believed that the ideal practice supervision could not be achieved. There would always be discrepancies between actuality and the ideal, especially with respect to discussion and development of curriculum plans, feedback about these plans and review of trainees' lessons.

But steps are being taken to enhance the quality of supervision. A most important and significant feature of teacher education in Australia during the last few years is the effort directed towards the research and development of programs to enhance supervisory skills (Edmonds, 1980; Eltis and Turney, 1984; Meggit, 1980; Preston, 1986; Sellars, 1981; Swinburne, 1983). A majority of the programs, which have been formulated through action research projects, incorporate concepts derived from the literature on 'clinical supervision', or 'partnership supervision'. The researchers and developers have varied the length of time for 'training' in supervisory skills from two hours in a seminar to ten hours in a one-day workshop, and have found that several short (three by two-hour) seminars can develop supervisors' awareness of and understanding about the role of feedback to trainees. The longer sessions, on the other hand, which have more time for the presentation of models of supervision, opportunities for role-play and practice of supervisory skills, appear to be more beneficial in helping supervisors in their role. Supervisors state that they like these programs but, unfortunately, no information has been published about the extent to which their supervisory practices have changed as a result of the programs, or whether their supervision is now of better quality. We must await reports on these matters.

Induction of Beginning Teachers

The early and mid-1970s saw great interest in beginning teachers' mode of entry to teaching (Tisher, Fyfield and Taylor, 1979), how they were socialized into the profession (McArthur, 1981), their attitudinal changes (Marsh, 1976; Rentoul and Fraser, 1981), job satisfaction (Tisher and Taylor, 1982) and their problems and concerns (Otto, Gasson and Jordan, 1979; Tisher, Fyfield and Taylor, 1979). This was a period when large numbers of new teachers were being recruited, employing authorities were concerned about how they were coping with their job, and information about induction schemes and related studies in the United Kingdom was being disseminated. It was also the period when our only national educational research funding committee existed. This commonwealth committee supported many individual studies on beginning teachers and commissioned the only large-scale national study on induction (Tisher, Fyfield and Taylor, 1979), funded the dissemination of the findings to all state education departments, and sponsored a national follow-up conference two years after the national survey was completed. But even then the research had little impact on practice since the state departments had put their own induction schemes into operation in the interim and were not prepared, for financial and political reasons, to adjust them according to the implications from the national findings. The Catholic education system in Victoria, however, appears to have made use of our research knowledge about induction. It began reshaping its induction programs after the national follow-up conference.

Induction, the period during which beginning teachers enter the profession, receive some planned support and become professionally competent at a basic level and at ease in their job, is generally considered by Australian researchers to span the first year of teaching. One exception to this focus on the first year was a project (McArthur, 1981) that traced teachers through their first five years in schools, noting that most adjustment in occupational socialization occurred during the first year. The 'reality shock' phase was, however, considerably modified over time, and a more stable period of internalization of subcultural values ensued over the following few years. The study noted that most new teachers strengthened their commitment, or career-orientation, during the first five years of teaching, and showed an increase in guardianship or custodialism in the first year, followed by a plateau period over the next four.

The findings from the various studies on induction are generally congruent with those of the commissioned national project; they include the following:

> the majority of beginning teachers are satisfied with their teaching appointments, consider they manage most teaching tasks adequately, and believe they are fully accepted within their school. About one in five, however, expected greater opportunities to participate in curriculum planning, to influence school philosophy, and for intellectual stimulation, than actually was the case;

> beginning teachers are concerned about their abilities to evaluate their own teaching, to motivate pupils, to control classes, and to teach pupils with wide ability ranges; and

> beginning teachers are generally satisfied with the variety of existing induction provisions such as visits to schools prior to appointment, meetings with colleagues in the schools after appointment, conferences away from their school, and personal tutoring within the school.

Education employing authorities are now not recruiting the same number of new teachers as they were twelve years ago, even though teacher shortfalls exist in some areas. Consequently, induction has not received the same amount of publicity or research attention, although it is still regarded as an important phase in a teacher's professional development and socialization. Three recent reports, however, have taken another look at beginning teachers' perceived problems, concerns and confidence (Reed, 1986; McCahon and Carpenter, 1987), and commitment to teaching (Carpenter and Byde, 1986). The findings are comparable to those of earlier projects. In the study on commitment to teaching, for example, the researchers reported that for some beginning teachers commitment was related to the extrinsic rewards associated with teaching, while for others it was interwoven with what they saw as the intrinsic rewards, variety, contact with young people and the satisfaction of assisting pupils to achieve.

In-service Education

Australian teachers and teacher educators believe in-service education plays an important role in professional development and fosters positive attitudes about education, pupils, the content of curricula and classroom processes. Consequently, they have a strong commitment to it, and there is richness and diversity in its activities and the research on them.

The richness and diversity create problems for a reviewer in tracing and synthesizing projects scattered through many broadsheets, 'in-house' reports, newsletters, published reports, conference proceedings and journal articles. We once had a national broadsheet, *In-Service Education and Training* (INSET), that informed us about numerous initiatives and investigations relating to them, but it is no longer published, and it is now very difficult to obtain a quick overview of all that is happening in the country.

Naming a few projects will illustrate the diversity and richness of research on in-service education. We have, for instance, surveys of the in-service needs of teachers (Reynolds and Clark, 1984), teachers' attitudes towards professional development (Archdall, 1983), and the nature of our in-service provisions (Coulter and Ingvarson, 1985), including school-focused programs for principals (O'Callaghan and Johnson, 1981), the Schools' Commission Development Program (Batten, 1979), educational computing courses (Ingvarson and MacKenzie, 1987), and the role of education centres (Bowd and Boylan, 1982). Case studies deal with our own responsibilities for in-service (Ingvarson, 1982), being a reflexive classroom researcher (Beasley, 1981), and the role of clinical supervision in enhancing teaching skills (Smyth and Henry, 1983). Action research projects, mentioned earlier, include school-controlled in-service education (Fenton, 1983) and fostering school-focused development programs (Eltis *et al.*, 1981). These were greatly appreciated by those involved, as the projects showed 'what it was that worked'. The Eltis *et al.* study showed, for example, that the individual designated to coordinate the activities within the school became the key teacher in the development of school-focused in-service education. Moreover, the project gave teachers a greater appreciation of the complexities accompanying the initiation and execution of school focused programs.

Some in-service researchers (Robson, 1984; Diamond, 1985) have attempted to alter teaching styles by first making teachers more aware of their own views about teaching, pupils and teaching methods, before presenting alternatives. For example, in one project (Diamond, 1985) the participating teachers were asked to model for a period of ten days a teacher whose role characteristics were slightly different from their own self-portraits that had been obtained using the Kelly Repertory Grid (Kelly, 1955). That is, they were to teach in a slightly, but not dramatically, different way from their 'usual' pattern. A subsequent administration of the Repertory Grid showed that there had been some changes, for example, with respect to helping pupils and with classroom routines. These applications of the Grid look very promising, but I doubt that they will be emulated by many, since the associated work requires a great deal of time and is labour-intensive.

What has the research told us about in-service education in Australia? First, teachers have a range of needs for in-service education which vary considerably depending on experience and school location. Their most highly rated needs are for skills in curriculum development, interpersonal relations, general teaching methods and helping the less able and the gifted. Unfortunately, present offerings do not seem to cater adequately for these. About half of our in-service activities focus on matters associated with organizational development, while only a third deal with curriculum development, and less than one-fifth with staff development. It is no wonder that a decline has occurred in the number of in-service activities being attended by teachers. But curiously, over the years the average length of in-service programs has increased. The attrition in attendance can be accounted for, in part, by the failure to meet teachers' needs, to reduced funding and resources for in-service education, and the unhelpful stance of employers about their responsibilities for professional development. They produce disappointingly vague statements about these and the purposes of in-service education.

On a positive note, it has been shown that in-service education fosters professional development; clinical supervision in particular provides a powerful way of converting ideas into action; teachers can be helped to become reflexive classroom researchers; and human achievement skills training courses can affect principals' behaviours. Such positive outcomes should encourage more teacher educators to offer in-service education. Unfortunately, the very diversity of Australian research and development has both positive and negative features. On the one hand, the diversity seems to reduce the powerfulness and compelling nature of the findings. On the other hand, as there is no one best way to achieve professional development, the diversity of in-service education is a strength. There is, however, no discernible, coherent pattern to our in-service education, and no one model has emerged to demonstrate the best way to achieve professional development in this country.

Reflections

In the preceding discussion I have referred to the changing milieu for tertiary education in Australia, the foci for research on teacher education, the methods researchers have used, the research findings, changes in the research, who does it, its limitations and the compelling nature of some projects which show what works in practice. I conclude from this review that research on teacher education in Australia is alive and moderately well. The studies are diverse, essentially descriptive but with implications for practice, and guided by the researcher's interests rather than an overall national policy. Rarely are they replicated, and no attempt is made to integrate the efforts in pre-service with those in induction and in-service.

Some studies, such as those on the training of practice supervisors in Western Australia (Preston and Baker, 1985), have had an impact on local practice; but the research does not appear to have had much effect at a state or national level. This is not due entirely to its diversity, its ad hoc nature or lack of integration. It could be due to the fact that many major policy issues, at state and national levels, tend to be resolved on the basis of political, economic and social considerations rather than on the basis of research evidence which identifies successful and unsuccessful practice.

What else can be said about the Australian research? Does it have a conceptual base, and have the canons of good research been adhered to? With respect to the latter issue, I have already referred to limitations of the Australian studies such as 'captive' non-representative samples, use of only one group to be compared with itself, short time intervals between pre/post-testing, and lack of replication. I have also commented on the strengths of several studies, but overall a great variation exists across projects. Some researchers have been very thoughtful and careful about the conduct of their studies, others not so.

With respect to the issue of whether the research has a conceptual base, my quick response is, 'not clearly so', although a proportion of the researchers refer to some theory that has guided parts of their investigation. For instance, there are references to Fuller's theory of concerns, the bases underlying clinical supervision, and the role played by personal constructs. However, no guiding, overarching or second-order theory about how one becomes a teacher has been used by the investigators. Whether such a theory is possible is a moot point, although it is suggested elsewhere in this book that it is.

The Australian research has given us insights into the nature and impact of the various phases of teacher education, but unfortunately too few teacher educators appear to have been compelled to act on its findings. One reason may be that the areas they deem important have received very little or no research attention. Certainly, a number of areas have received limited attention. For example, it has been argued elsewhere (McIntyre, 1980) that it is important to study the associations between practices in teacher education and the ideologies of teacher educators, since these features can filter the effects of a program. If that point of view is accepted, then it is salutory to note that studies of teacher educators are rare in this country. There was one national survey (Beswick *et al.*, 1980) on the views and characteristics of teacher educators but none on ideologies and their association with practice.

Given the major changes we are likely to see in the structure and funding of tertiary education, including teacher education, it does seem essential for some research effort to be directed to the impacts that teacher education contexts, administrative structures, government policies and fiscal arrangements have on the delivery of effective teacher education programs. To date we have seen few studies on these issues in Australia, but we can expect that to change in the future.

The matters of new research foci, conceptual bases and methodology constitute many challenging tasks for the Australian researcher; tasks which require individuals and teams with ingenuity, fortitude, persistence and longevity, but which, when complete, will provide challenging knowledge to teacher educators, and governments, to compel them to act.

Notes

1 This is post-secondary education provided in universities, Colleges of Advanced Education and Technical and Further Education (TAFE) institutions.
2 The other reviews are reported in R.P. Tisher (1986), New directions for Australian research on science teacher education, *Research in Science Education*, 16, 125–134; R.P. Tisher (1987), A decade of research on teacher education in Australia. Paper presented at the Annual Meeting of the American Educational Research Association, Washington, April, ERIC reference No. SP 028 935; R.P. Tisher (1987), Research on teacher education in Australia, in K. Eltis,

(Ed.) *Australian Teacher Education in Review*, Inaugural Yearbook of the South Pacific Association for Teacher Education, Bedford Park, South Australia. About 260 articles and reports were consulted in compiling the reviews, about 160 were summarized and catalogued and more than half of these appear in the review reference lists.

References

APPLETON, K. (1983) Beginning student teachers' opinions about teaching primary science. *Research in Science Education*, 13, 111–119.

APPLETON, K. (1984) Student teachers opinions: A follow-up. *Research in Science Education*, 14, 157–166.

ARCHDALL, T. (1983) Preferences and attitudes of Victorian teachers towards professional development activities. Master of Education Studies project, Faculty of Education, Monash University.

BAIRD, J., FENSHAM, P., GUNSTONE, R. and WHITE, R. (1987) Individual development during teacher training. *Research in Science Education*, 17, 182–191.

BATTEN, M. (1979) *Report of a National Evaluation of the Development Program.* Schools Commission Evaluation Studies, Canberra: Schools Commission.

BEASLEY, B. (1981) The reflexive spectator in classroom research. *In-Service Education and Training*, 1, 2, 8–10.

BESWICK, D., HARMAN, G., ELSWORTH, G., FALLON, B. and WOOCK, R. (1980) *Australian Teacher Educators and Education Policy*, Report of a National Study, Melbourne: University of Melbourne, Center for the Study of Higher Education.

BOWD, A. and BOYLAN, C. (1982) A report on the effectiveness of the Wagga Wagga Education Centre. Mimeo report, Wagga Wagga Education Centre, June.

BOYCE, M.W. (1977) Value systems of prospective teachers. *The Australian Journal of Teacher Education*, 2, 1, 1–8.

BRIGGS, F. (1984) The organisation of practicum, the responsibilities of the teacher and the college supervisor: A pilot study. *The Australian Journal of Teaching Practice*, 4, 2, 15–25.

BUTCHER, P.M. (1981) An experimental investigation of the effectiveness of a value claim strategy unit for use in teacher education. Unpublished MA (Hons) thesis, Macquarie University, Sydney.

CAMPBELL, W.J., EVANS, G.T., PHILP, H. and LEVIS, D. (1979) A study of the pre-service and initial in-service development of primary school teachers, in M. HEWITSON (Ed.) *Research into Teacher Education.* ERDC Report No. 19. Canberra: Australian Government Publishing Service.

CARPENTER, P. and BYDE, P. (1986) The meaning of commitment to teaching: The views of beginning teachers. *The South Pacific Journal of Teacher Education*, 14, 1, 13–25.

CARPENTER, P. and FOSTER, W. (1979) Deciding to teach. *Australian Journal of Education*, 23, 121–131.

COULTER, F. (1974) The effects of practice teaching on professional self-image. *Australian Journal of Education*, 18, 149–159.

COULTER, F. and INGVARSON, L. (1985) *Professional Development and the Improvement of Schooling: Roles and Responsibilities.* A report to the Commonwealth Schools Commission, Canberra.

DAWKINS, J.S. (1987) *Higher Education: A policy discussion paper.* Canberra: Australian Government Publishing Service, December.

DANAHER, P., ELLIOTT, D. and MARLAND, P. (1982) Trial and occasional trauma: The student teacher perspective on teaching practice supervision. *The Australian Journal of Teaching Practice*, 3, 1, 27–40.

DESCHAMP, P. and TRIPP, D. (1980) Training teachers to plan. *The Australian Journal of Teacher Education*, 5, 1, 1–19.

DIAMOND, C.T.P. (1983) Theoretical positions: A comparison of intending and experienced teachers constructs. *The South Pacific Journal of Teacher Education*, 11, 1, 43–53.

DIAMOND, C.T.P. (1985) Becoming a teacher: An altering eye, in D. BANNISTER (Ed.) *Issues and Approaches in Personal Construct Theory.* London: Academic Press.

DOOLEY, H. and LUCAS, K. (1981) Attitudes of student primary teachers towards science and science teaching. *The Australian Science Teachers' Journal*, 27, 1, 77–80.

DYMOND, W.F. (1976) Change in student teachers' perceptions of the teacher's role: An empirical study. MEd thesis, University of Western Australia.

DUCK, G. and CUNNINGHAM, D. (1985) Roles of supervisors in school experience. *The South Pacific Journal of Teacher Education*, 13, 2, 19–29.

EDMONDS, J.M. (1980) Rationale, development and evaluation of a course to train school supervisors in supervision skills, in W. NEWMAN and B. ARKINS (Eds) *The Role of School Experience in Teacher Education: Recent Trends and Future Developments.* Collected papers of a national conference on the practicum, Armidale College of Advanced Education.

ELSWORTH, G. and COULTER, G. (1978) Relationships between professional self-perception and commitment to teaching. *Australian Journal of Education*, 22, 25–37.

ELTIS, K. and CAIRNS, L. (1982) Perceived effectiveness of supervisors of the practicum. *The Australian Journal of Teaching Practice*, 2, 2, 101–109.

ELTIS, K. and TURNEY, C. (1984) Supervisor development programme: Field test one — the feedback role. *The South Pacific Journal of Teacher Education*, 12, 1, 19–30.

ELTIS, K., BRAITHWAITE, R., DEER, C. and KENSALL, H. (1981) Fostering school-focussed development programs. Mimeo report of a project supported by the Schools Commission, School of Education, Macquarie University.

EVANS, B. (1980) A working model for reflective teaching practice, in W. NEWMAN and B. ARKINS, (Eds) *The Role of School Experience in Teacher Education: Recent Trends and Future Developments.* Collected papers of a national conference on the practicum, Armidale College of Advanced Education.

FAWNS, R. (1984) The sources of theoretical principles for science method programs: A new setting explored. *Research in Science Education*, 7, 203–211.

FENTON, J. (1983) *School-controlled In-service Teacher Education.* Report of a joint project sponsored by Horsham Regional Office and Deakin Institute for Studies in Education.

GARNETT, P. and TOBIN, K. (1984) Reasoning patterns of pre-service elementary and middle school science teachers. *Science Education*, 68, 5, 621–631.

GRUNDY, S. (1986) The image of the teacher in the post-lesson conference. *The Journal of Teaching Practice*, 6, 1, 60–73.

GUNSTONE, R. and MACKAY, L. (1975) The self-perceived needs of student teachers. *The South Pacific Journal of Teacher Education*, 3, 1, 44–51.

GUNSTONE, R., SLATTERY, M. and BAIRD, J. (1989) Learning about learning to teach: A case study of pre-service teacher education. Paper presented at the annual meeting of the American Educational Research Association, San Francisco, March.

HEWITSON, M. (Ed.) (1979) *Research into Teacher Education: The Practical Teaching Skills.* ERDC Report No. 19. Canberra: Australian Government Publishing Service.

HEWITSON, M. (1981) A survey of student opinion and its implications for school and institutional roles in teaching practice. *The South Pacific Journal of Teacher Education*, 9, 2, 29–37.

HOGBEN, D. and LAWSON, M. (1984) Attitude stability and change during teacher training. *The South Pacific Journal of Teacher Education*, 12, 2, 34–44.

HOGBEN, D. and PETTY, M. (1979) From student to primary school teacher: Attitude stability and change. *The South Pacific Journal of Teacher Education*, 7, 92–98.

INGVARSON, L. (1982) Some effects of the teacher development program in Victoria. *Australian Journal of Education*, 26, 86–98.

INGVARSON, L. and MACKENZIE, D. (1987) *Factors Influencing the Impact of In-service Courses for Teachers in Educational Computing: Implications for Policy.* Report to the State Coordinating Committee of the Commonwealth Schools' Commission's Computer Education Program in Victoria.

KELLY, G.A. (1955) *The Psychology of Personal Constructs.* Vols 1–2. New York: Norton.

LOVE, J. and SWAIN, M. (1980) Success in practicum programs: Student teacher perceptions, in W. NEWMAN and B. ARKINS (Eds) *The Role of School Experience in Teacher Education: Recent Trends and Future Developments.* Collected papers of a national conference on the practicum, Armidale College of Advanced Education.

McARTHUR, J.T. (1975) Teacher socialization: The influence of initial teaching experience on the pupil control ideology of beginning teachers, PhD thesis, Monash University.

McARTHUR, J.T. (1981) *The First Five Years of Teaching.* ERDC Report No. 30. Canberra: Australian Government Publishing Service.

McCAHON, K. and CARPENTER, P. (1987) The induction of beginning secondary teachers. *The South Pacific Journal of Teacher Education*, 15, 2, 27–35.

McINTYRE, D. (1980) The contribution of research to quality in teacher education. *The South Pacific Journal of Teacher Education*, 8, 14, 4–19.

MARSH, C.J. (1976) A study of the maintenance of some pedagogical attitudes held by social studies teachers after their first year of teaching in a school. *Australian Journal of Education*, 20, 316–324.

MATTHEWS, R.J. (1980) Stages in the socialization of trainee teachers, in W. NEWMAN and B. ARKINS (Eds) *The Role of School Experience in Teacher*

Education: Recent Trends and Future Developments. Collected papers of a national conference on the practicum, Armidale College of Advanced Education.

MEGGITT, P.H. (1980) Training supervisors in secondary schools, in W. NEWMAN and B. ARKINS (Eds) *The Role of School Experience in Teacher Education: Recent Trends and Future Developments.* Collected papers of a national conference on the practicum, Armidale College of Advanced Education.

O'CALLAGHAN, G. and JOHNSON, B. (1981) *An Evaluation of the South Australian Principals Professional Development Programme.* Adelaide: Education Department of South Australia, Research and Planning Directorate.

Osborne, B. and HENDERSON, L. (1986) A case study of communication breakdown during cross-cultural teaching practice, Paper presented at the Third National Conference: The Practicum in Teacher Education, Geelong, January.

OTTO, E., GASSON, I. and JORDAN, E. (1979) Perceived problems of beginning teachers. *The South Pacific Journal of Teacher Education,* 7, 1, 28–33.

OWEN, J., WYN, J. and SENYARD, J. (1983) The use of a discrepancy approach in the evaluation of a teacher education program, in *Collected Papers* of Annual Conference of Australian Association for Research in Education, Canberra.

PEGG, J.E. (1985) The effect of practice on the acquisition of teaching skills: A micro-teaching study. Unpublished PhD thesis, University of New England, Armidale.

POOLE, C. and GAUDREY, E. (1974) Some effects of teaching practice. *Australian Journal of Education,* 18, 255–263.

PRESTON, R. (1986) Student teachers: A role in in-service for supervisors, in the collection of papers for the Third National Conference: The Practicum in Teacher Education, Geelong, January.

PRESTON, R. and BAKER, R. (1985) An exploratory study of the clinical observation system: A systematic approach to student teacher observations during field experience. *The South Pacific Journal of Teacher Education,* 13, 1, 29–43.

PRICE, D. and SELLARS, N. (1985) A synthesis of effective supervising teacher behaviours in the final year of the primary practicum. *The South Pacific Journal of Teacher Education,* 13, 2, 9–18.

REED, K. (1986) Teaching tasks and beginning teachers. *The South Pacific Journal of Teacher Education,* 14, 1, 1–12.

RENTOUL, A.J. and FRASER, B.J. (1981) Changes in beginning teachers attitudes towards individualised teaching approaches during the first year of teaching. *The Australian Journal of Teacher Education,* 6, 1, 1–13.

REYNOLDS, P. and CLARK, M. (1984) *In-service Needs of Teachers and Administrators in Western Australian Schools 1983.* A report of the WA In-Service Teacher Education Project, Western Australian College of Advanced Education.

ROBSON, M. (1984) Teacher perceptions and classroom behaviours: An intervention. Unpublished PhD thesis, Monash University.

RYAN, A.S. and REYNOLDS, P. and collaborators (1982) *Perceptions of Teaching as a Career: Report No. 1. Survey of Year 12 Students.* Report of a joint project by Western Australian College of Advanced Education and the Western Australian Institute of Technology, December.

SELLARS, N. (1981) A training course for supervisory teachers: An exercise in nettle-grasping. *The Australian Journal of Teaching Practice,* 2, 1, 29–45.

SELLARS, N. (1988) The effects of practice teaching on the concerns of pre-service primary teachers. *The South Pacific Journal of Teacher Education*, 16, 3, 21–32.

SINCLAIR, K. and NICHOLL, V. (1981) Sources and experiences of anxiety in practice teaching. *The South Pacific Journal of Teacher Education*, 9, 1, 10–18.

SKAMP, K. and POWER, C. (1981) Primary science, inquiry and classroom demands: Pre-service teachers' responses and perceptions. *Research in Science Education*, 11, 34–43.

SMYTH, J. and HENRY, C. (1983) Case study experience of collaborative and responsive form of professional development for teachers, in *Collected Papers* of Annual Conference, of Australian Association for Research in Education, Canberra.

SWINBURNE, D. (1983) *Report on the Teaching Practice Improvement Project*. Melbourne: Monash University, Faculty of Education.

SYMINGTON, D. (1982) Lack of background in science: Is it likely to always adversely affect the classroom performance of primary teachers in science lessons, *Research in Science Education*, 12, 64–72.

TAYLOR, J.C. (1980) Path analysis applied to a study of the effectiveness of teacher education, in W. NEWMAN and B. ARKINS (Eds) *The Role of School Experience in Teacher Education: Recent Trends and Future Developments*. Collected papers of a national conference on the practicum, Armidale College of Advanced Education.

TELFER, R. (1982) Differences and perceived differences in teacher education programmes at a CAE and a university. *The South Pacific Journal of Teacher Education*, 10, 2, 9–21.

THOMPSON, H. and LEVIS, D. (1980) An experimental evaluation of competency-based teacher education. *The South Pacific Journal of Teacher Education*, 8, 1, 38–48.

THURSBY, P.M. (1980) An extended practice teaching program: Preparing art teachers, in W. NEWMAN and B. ARKINS (Eds) *The Role of School Experience in Teacher Education: Recent Trends and Future Developments*. Collected papers of a national conference on the practicum, Armidale College of Advanced Education.

TIERNEY, J. (1984) Incident analysis: The integration of micro-teaching and interaction analysis. *The South Pacific Journal of Teacher Education*, 12, 1, 2–11.

TISHER, R.P. (1987) A decade of research on teacher education in Australia. Paper presented in a symposium at the Annual Meeting of the American Educational Research Association, Washington, April.

TISHER, R.P. and TAYLOR, S. (1982) New teachers' job satisfactions. *The South Pacific Journal of Teacher Education*, 10, 1, 9–16.

TISHER, R.P., FYFIELD, J. and TAYLOR, S. (1979) *Beginning to Teach. Vol. 2.* ERDC Report No. 20. Canberra: Australian Government Publishing Service.

TOBIN, K., PIKE, G. and LACEY, T. (1984) Strategy analysis procedures for improving the quality of activity-oriented science teaching. *European Journal of Science Education*, 6, 1, 78–89.

YARROW, A. *et al.* (1984) The characteristics of college personnel involved in field studies. *The South Pacific Journal of Teacher Education*, 12, 1, 39–51.

YOUNG, W. (1979) Teaching practice: Effects on knowledge, skills and attitudes in initial training. *The South Pacific Journal of Teacher Education*, 7, 1, 23–27.

Chapter 6

Research on Teacher Education in West Germany

*Hans Gerhard Klinzing**

This chapter provides a synopsis of the empirical-analytical research on teacher education in West Germany in the last two decades. As this research involves similar methodological problems to those discusssed in other chapters in this volume, this paper focuses merely on its main findings. Research on demographic variables, sex differences and teacher training personnel is not included because of space limitations.

In West Germany research on teacher education is conducted primarily by individuals from universities and teacher training institutions, and consists mainly of short-term projects. The long-term project at the University of Konstanz on teacher attitudes and the projects on laboratory training at the University of Tübingen provide exceptions. The institutions produce about 100–120 publications on teacher education each year, mainly of a 'theoretical' nature. Empirical-analytical research is relatively rare. Educational research in Germany, including research on teacher education, remains predominantly a matter of hermeneutics. Fruitful approaches in the area of empirical research developed in the 1920s and early 1930s were stopped by the Hitler regime. The 'geisteswissenschaftlich'-oriented educationists continued their domination after the Second World War and maintain their resistance to empirical research. Thus in the last two decades less than 10 per cent of all publications concerning teacher education and training involved empirical-analytical studies.

* With the assistance of Günter L. Huber and Gisela Klinzing-Eurich, University of Tübingen.

Schooling and Teacher Education in West Germany

In the Federal Republic of Germany (FRG) the ten states and West Berlin control primary, secondary and tertiary education. This creates a great diversity among schooling systems in the states and in teacher education programs. Schooling consists of primary school, secondary school and tertiary education. A 'Kindergarten' (ages 3 to 6) may precede the four compulsory years of primary school; three kinds of secondary schools follow: Hauptschule (grades 5 to 9/10), Mittelschule/Realschule (grades 5 to 10), and the Oberschule/Gymnasium (grades 5 to 13). A number of schools establish (in grades 5 and 6) special classes for orientation to help pupils decide on which type of secondary school to attend.

The Hauptschule and Mittelschule generally lead to a two- to three-year vocational education (vocational school and training in business or works). The Gymnasium (attended by about 30 per cent of the respective age group) leads to university or college. Because of unemployment among students graduating from colleges and universities, nowadays about 30 per cent of graduating Gymnasium students enter vocational training. In all states regular or experimental comprehensive schools also exist, and disabled pupils attend a variety of special schools.

Teacher education caters to the different state school systems and different school types. Elementary and Hauptschul teachers used to attend teacher training colleges for three years (six semesters) but now these are integrated into universities in most of the states. These pre-service teachers follow a curriculum which consists of four components: subject matter studies, subject matter didactics, educational studies, and induction into professional practice through periods of practice teaching.

Realschul and vocational school teachers study two or three subjects at university for three to four years. Gymnasium teachers do this for four to six years. The Realschul, vocational school and Gymnasium teachers also study some education, ranging from four to twenty credit hours. Teachers of the disabled study at Padagogische Hochschulen, universities or special institutions for four to five years.

After graduation all teachers must complete an additional one and a half to two years induction in special state teacher training institutions (Studienseminare). This stage of teacher education consists of courses in education, subject matter didactics, classroom observation, and supervised practice for about 68 per cent of the total. This stage leads to teacher certification.

Research on Teacher Education

Drawing on over 200 empirical-analytical studies published in the last twenty years, this review provides a comprehensive and representative picture of the state of the art of German research on teacher education in the last two decades, but the reference list does not contain all the reports which were consulted.[1] The studies have been clustered under three headings according to the major themes addressed:

1 teachers in pre- and in-service education;
2 teacher socialization;
3 components of teacher education programs.

Teachers in Pre- and In-service Education

The first cluster of studies, about seventy, assessed a vast range of variables including personality characteristics and abilities of prospective teachers, their values, interests, attitudes, the expectations of teaching as a profession, their motivation to enrol in studies related to teacher education or to become a teacher, their opinions about their teacher education, their perceived problems, and interests in in-service teacher education. These studies often involved comparisons with students studying for other professions, or students studying education for other professions, or comparisons between subgroups of teachers. The investigators used interviews, a variety of questionnaires, semantic differentials and attitude and personality inventories, in all cases administered to non-randomized samples. Sample sizes ranged from 80 to 6198. The data were analyzed by descriptive statistics, for example factor analyses and cluster analyses. Where comparisons were made (mainly in the more recent studies), common inferential statistics were used. Broad sketches of the findings follow.

Personality Characteristics, Attitudes, Values and Interests of Prospective Teachers. The personality of the teacher remains a predominant subject of many studies as the teaching profession is perceived to have a key position in influencing the next generation, and thus the development of society. Generally, the speculative literature paints a rather negative picture of the teacher's personality; teachers are seen to be neurotic, possessed of lower intelligence, having broad but unspecific interests, and being ignorant of the real world. However, many of these speculations are not confirmed by research (see, e.g., Müller-Fohrbrodt, 1973: Müller-Fohrbrodt, Cloetta and Dann, 1978).

The research literature finds few differences between the personality characteristics of those enrolled in teacher education courses and those studying for other professions (see Müller-Fohrbrodt, 1973; Müller-Fohrbrodt *et al.*, 1978).[2] Some findings imply prospective elementary and Hauptschul teachers may be more neurotic, anxious and conservative than those studying as Gymnasium teachers and for other professions, and have slightly lower school grades, but they nevertheless appear to be more idealistic and regard teaching as a definite 'calling'.

Evaluations of Teacher Education by Prospective and Experienced Teachers. In a number of studies prospective and experienced teachers' judgments of their teacher education, and the quantity and quality of its components, were assessed. In general, the findings from about forty-five surveys (Müller-Fohrbrodt, Cloetta and Dann, 1978) about the quality of teacher education and perceived problems point to massive deficiencies at every stage of teacher education.[3] More than 50 per cent of Elementary, Hauptschul and Gymnasium teachers felt that their preparation for their profession was insufficient.

For the first stage of teacher education most student teachers criticized the lack of balance between theoretical studies and studies oriented to teaching practice. Most elementary — and Hauptschul — teachers preferred less subject matter and educational theory and more practice-oriented studies (especially practice-oriented courses in educational psychology, instructional psychology, school education, instructional methods). They also wanted more practice (but in more effective forms than their current practicum). Gymnasium teachers were satisfied with the quality and quantity of their subject matter studies, but considered the compulsory educational studies of no value.

As we have already mentioned, the second stage of teacher education in West Germany consists predominantly of practical training in schools (classroom observation and supervised praxis), supplemented with theoretical courses in a special state institution (Studienseminar). Considering their rating of the first stage, their rating of the second stage becomes important. They considered the quality and quantity of the coursework (especially psychology and general education) to be insufficient, poorly integrated with studies at the university or college, inadequately related to school problems and of little practical help. The final compulsory examination reinforced their perception of being under pressure in the program.

Prospective teachers' perceptions of the quality of supervision, help and guidance received in the training schools were also discouragingly negative. They felt inadequately prepared to cope with school situations, for example, large classes and pupils with learning and behavioral problems, and felt they received little help at the school with their lesson preparation and presentation, and advice about pupil assessment. They also believed their supervising teachers spent an inadequate amount of time with them in post-observation conferences and were inadequately trained to act as supervisors or mentors. Consequently they felt anxious, stressed and overworked during their second stage of training. They also tended to jettison some progressive teaching procedures to which they had been introduced in the first phase of their education as unrealistic.

Interests and Needs for In-Service Education. Another group of seventeen interview and questionnaire studies dealt with needs and interests for in-service education.[4] The high interest in in-service, particularly among young teachers, reflects in part the deficiencies of pre-service teacher education. Many of the in-service activities seem to be carried out by individuals using professional publications and exchanges of experiences with colleagues. Teachers, by the way, read fewer professional texts than members of other professions, and few teachers attend in-service activities offered by universities, teacher training colleges, school administrators or teachers' unions. Participation in in-service activities would be higher if they were of higher quality and more practice-oriented, if more time were available to attend, if more incentives (like higher income) were offered, and if in-service activities were accorded higher reputation and status.

Teachers express high interest in subject matter offerings and in activities oriented to teaching. Elementary school, Hauptschul, comprehensive school and special education teachers are more interested in practical topics related to classroom teaching, while Gymnasium, vocational school and science teachers prefer to study their subject matter and methods of teaching subject matter.

Teacher Socialization

This section reviews thirteen studies which compare prospective teachers in different stages of their studies, or prospective teachers with experienced teachers (cross-sectional studies) — often interpreted as changes — and seven longitudinal studies on the effects of teacher education. Sample sizes ranged from 85 to 2400.

Experiences in schools, universities, training institutions and practice teaching situations and induction had an effect upon individuals' attitudes and values. A socializing effect occurred. Researchers in West Germany have attempted to understand this effect by surveying prospective teachers at different stages of their professional development, and by observing trainee teachers over longer time periods. Several clear trends emerge from these cross-sectional and longitudinal studies.

The cross-sectional studies (e.g., Koch, 1972; Müller-Fohrbrodt, 1973; Walter and Rohr, 1976) indicate that a liberalizing socialization effect occurs for trainees studying in teachers' colleges and universities. They are less conforming, conservative and dominating and more in favour of change and reform in education than final year Gymnasium pupils who aspired to be teachers. However, the studies also show that during intense periods of praxis in the second stage of teacher education and during induction, trainee and beginning teachers become more conservative, dominant and concerned about academic progress and classroom control than was the case earlier in their teacher education (e.g., Deffner, 1977; Neubauer, 1983; Koch, 1972).

Furthermore, the cross-sectional studies imply that teacher education does not have the positive effects we believe it should have. As trainees progress through their course work and praxis they appear to become more sceptical about educational theory and their practical studies, less optimistic about teaching as a profession, and less idealistic (e.g., Deffner, 1977; Niessen, 1974; Merz and Madjaric, 1976).

By and large the findings from the longitudinal studies, which include ones spanning six months (Roth, 1981) and up to six years (Bartmann, Bischoff and Ebel, 1978; Dann *et al.*, 1978), are similar to those derived from the cross-sectional research. Trainees tend to become more conservative, conforming, dominating and concerned about classroom control as they progress through their second stage of teacher education and enter the profession. Some longitudinal studies (Dann *et al.*, 1981; Liebhart, 1970) suggest that elementary and Hauptschul teachers continue to become more conservative and authoritarian during their final stages of teacher education and first three years of teaching.

Finally, it appears appropriate to comment on some other features that emerge from these 'socialization effect' studies. There is little change in trainees' attitudes towards teaching during the first phase of their teacher education in university or college. A greater shift occurs in the second stage when they are more involved in educational studies and praxis. The pressures from supervisors, teachers and school administrators during practice teaching to conform are paramount in producing shifts from progressive to traditional educational attitudes. Also the greater the discrepancy between what they learned about teacher and pupil behaviour at college and what they experienced at praxis, the greater was the increase in their conservative attitudes and irritability, and the greater the decrease in their professional self-respect and positive conceptions of themselves as teachers. The liberalizing influence experienced during university or college studies is not sufficient, due to a separation of theory from practice, to sustain progressive attitudes under the difficult conditions pertaining during practice teaching.

Components of Teacher Education

Academic Courses. Although subject matter is emphasized and valued highly in teacher education in West Germany, its role and effect are rarely studied. Three evaluations of content-oriented courses on mastery teaching (Zachmann-Hintermeier and Treiber, 1986) and psychology (Koch, 1975) and of courses for correspondence studies developed at the Deutsches Institut für Fernstudien, Tübingen (Heller and Wichterlich, 1982) indicate that student teachers gained basic knowledge, valued the content and form of the program, and became positive in their attitudes towards education.

The Teacher Practicum. Practica supposedly enlighten theoretical studies, induct trainees into the profession, and ascertain whether they can 'stand the test'. The West German literature finds the teacher practicum both a necessary and valuable component and also a doubtful one. Few empirical studies exist to confirm or to reject these opinions about the practicum and document its effects. Only nine studies were located. They used questionnaires to teachers, supervisors and student teachers, interviews, analysis of written evaluations by mentor teachers and attitude scales. Results indicate that in general the practicum has an important place in the perception of the student teachers and they valued it very much for their professional development (Baege, 1973; Roth, 1974; Fitzner, 1978). On the other hand, these and other studies (e.g., Lindemann, 1984) indicate that student teachers felt they were insufficiently prepared. They desired more praxis-relevant courses before the practicum and criticized the insufficient supervision by college supervisors and mentors. According to Fitzner (1978), a barrier exists between the world of school, especially the world of the practicum in the school and the college, which hinders the development of a skilful and reflective professional.

The effects of spending the first six months of college in schools as an introductory practicum have been compared to those from traditional courses supplemented by protocol materials (Roth, 1981). There were no significant differences between groups, although the prospective elementary and Hauptschul teachers became more permissive, liberal, pupil-oriented and non-directive. At the same time, however, they accepted to a greater degree the dominant role of the teacher and to a lesser degree his role to diagnose and cope with pupils' learning difficulties. The explanation for these findings does not reside entirely in the praxis experience, since other factors may have produced these changes.

Unfortunately, the practicum as it is usually conducted in West Germany does not appear to fulfil the expectations outlined earlier.

Protocol Materials. Protocol materials in the form of videotransmissions, video or films plus lectures and printed materials are used in a number of universities and colleges. Video was first recommended as a feasible instructional tool for teacher education in the 1960s and by the early 1980s about fifteen universities and colleges were using video or film demonstrations (Brunner, 1985). Only seven studies deal with video and films in teacher education, and the research has produced mixed results about the attitudes of trainees to video demonstrations, the perceived benefits and the impact on trainees (Brunner, 1976; Roth, 1981). Video is also used in teaching laboratories, where a larger research literature exists on its role in teacher education.

Teaching Laboratories Training Teachers. Dissatisfaction with traditional teacher education programs, especially with the separation of educational and subject matter studies from practical experience, doubts about the effectiveness of induction into professional practice, and the movements for a democratic structure and more practice-oriented teacher education in West German universities and colleges led to the development of teaching laboratories in West Germany in the 1960s. Since then we have seen a strong and increasing interest in laboratory training for teachers. During the 1970s and 1980s about 10 per cent of publications in the field of teacher education dealt with teaching laboratories, and in the 1980s about 50 per cent of teacher training colleges and universities in West Germany were using them (Brunner, 1985).

West German teaching laboratories use either 'indirect' or 'direct' training programs. The indirect programs attempt to improve teaching skill by focusing on changes in trainees' personality characteristics, including attitudes, perceptions, cognitive constructs and various affective variables. The approaches followed by these centres are often derived from group dynamics and the work of Tausch (1963). The direct programs have been influenced by the work of Zifreund (1966) and Allen and

Ryan (1969). Direct training is used by the majority of the institutions with teaching laboratories (Brunner, 1985).

Research on teaching laboratories began in the 1960s and it constitutes about 50 per cent of all empirical studies on teacher education in West Germany.

The effects of indirect training programs. About one-quarter (i.e., twenty-seven studies) of the teaching laboratory research (as reviewed by Klinzing and Klinzing-Eurich, 1988) deals with indirect programs which attempt to change personality characteristics, promote learner-supportive attitudes, improve abilities to improvise, and foster assertiveness through case studies, play, simulations, group encounters and exercises in reacting to and interpreting educational situations. Using a variety of criterion measures including attribute tests, personality inventories, self-concept and attitude scales and tests of performance, the investigators were able to show that generally the programs were favourably received, trainees stated they learned a great deal (see, e.g., Signer, 1979) and were able to write satisfactory solutions to 'hypothetical' critical incidents in the classroom (e.g., Tausch, 1963; Nickel, Schwalenberg and Ungelenk, 1974). However, the research is not without difficulties and has no clear findings regarding changes in variables like attitudes, personality characteristics and performance (e.g., Royl and Minsel, 1973).

Effects of programs using direct training programs. More success has been achieved in studies of direct programs of training. About three-quarters of the training laboratory research (i.e., seventy-seven studies) focus on the direct training programs designed to enhance such classroom skills as teacher indirectness, higher cognitive questioning and probing, management, lecturing, non-verbal communication and counselling.

The programs consisted of the following elements: theory presentation, self-analysis, conceptual interventions (model demonstrations, discrimination training), and controlled practice with feedback, or various combinations of these components. Sometimes the training was integrated into the practicum. The duration of programs varied from fifteen to forty hours, conducted as traditional courses in weekly sessions, or as whole-day courses over a number of days.

The research was predominantly experimental with pre-experimental or quasi-experimental designs or case studies. Success was assessed using various procedures, such as questionnaires (e.g., assessing trainees' attitudes), performance tests, high- and low-inference observation instruments, teacher and student ratings, and tests for discrimination, attribution, reactions and divergent thinking.

By and large, the research indicates that this kind of training was rated very favourably, knowledge was acquired successfully (e.g., Langthaler, Schultz and Elsinghorst, 1986), verbal and non-verbal perceptiveness was enhanced (e.g., Klinzing, 1982; Klinzing, Leuteritz, Schiefer and Steiger, 1986), reactions of trainees to hypothetical discipline problems were improved (Tennstädt, 1987), and the quantity and quality of teacher classroom behaviours were improved in the skill areas mentioned before. Findings from measures which go beyond the judgment of training effectiveness in terms of merely their enhancement of the frequency of target skills indicate that the trainees learned not only the use of skills but also *when* and *how* to use them *appropriately* (e.g., Klinzing, Klinzing-Eurich and Floden, 1989).

The acquired behaviours seemed to be integrated into the repertoire of the trainees as they were still observed some months after training. Comparisons across pre- and in-service studies indicate that training seemed to be equally effective for pre-service and in-service teachers.

Most studies point to the benefits to be derived from direct training programs. Research on components of programs yielding minimal success indicates that this can be attributed to insufficient duration of the program, little opportunity for trainees to practise the necessary skills (Thiele, 1978), and the inclusion of a complex set of behaviours to be mastered (Schmitz, 1974). In addition to adequate opportunity for practice, other messages are the need for feedback and group discussion, and clear understanding about and retention of concepts related to the training research; for instance, the indirect research is not clear regarding the change of attitudes and personality characteristics.

Concluding Remarks

Although 'geisteswissenschaftlich'-oriented educationists have dominated the field and had a large influence on the funding and conduct of research and of research, development and education projects in West Germany during the last twenty years, empirical research on teacher education in some domains has reached international standards. Though the studies are diverse, they give some insight into the nature and impact of the different stages of teacher education in West Germany (e.g., the liberalization effect of university and college studies), and uncover severe deficiencies which have implications for reform. These deficiencies (e.g., an insufficient integration of theory and practice, insufficient quantity and quality in preparation for practice, insufficient conditions in the second stage of teacher education) have undesired effects, as the research also indicates. If we accept that teachers should be, for example, emancipated, innovation-oriented, idealistic, 'progressive' personalities, then the findings regarding the reported patterns of change in teachers throughout their teacher education (e.g., 'reality shock', experience of discrepancies in their teaching practice that leads to a revision of attitudes and personality characteristics towards more conformism and conservatism and lower idealism) are alarming and cry for reform. The research also offers some promising innovative instructional strategies, e.g., teaching laboratories, which could be used for a reform of teacher education.

There is still much more unknown territory on the teacher education map than known ground. Most often only narrow, single, isolated aspects of the complex process of teacher education and socialization have been studied. For example, for the general effects of teacher socialization most often only a limited number of attitude and personality characteristics were studied. For the development of other important qualities, like cognitive abilities (e.g., reflective and critical thinking, creativity) which represent another dimension of professional–interpersonal teaching skills, we have only some indications from evaluations of their influences in the complex process of teacher education. More research is necessary, especially research which, in addition to the data sources used in previous studies, uses other research methods, like qualitative ones, in order to broaden the scope of research on teacher socialization processes, to broaden the scope of research methods, and to overcome the limitations and fallacies (especially self-reports) in many instruments.

The low level of funding for research on teacher education compared to the funding for research in computer sciences or natural sciences, and the resistance to empirical research in West Germany, however, provide little hope for an improvement of knowledge from research in the near future. What we probably need in West Germany is a teacher shortage to increase readiness and to stimulate financial support for research in teacher education.

Unfortunately, the knowledge obtained from research has very little impact on the organization and content of teacher education. Other forces than research evidence, like governmental policy, administrative decisions and economic factors, lead to retaining prevailing structures or to changes in teacher education in an undesired direction. Factors such as the frequent lack of innovation or reform orientation of the governments and administrations in West Germany of today, economic difficulties, the expected lowering of the birth rate, unemployment of academics, especially teachers (at present more than 80,000), prevent the necessary expansion of the universities, especially in subjects related to teacher education and in educational sciences, and block reforms, like attempts to integrate the first and second stages of teacher education. Governmental efforts to cut down expenditure, and the tremendous increase in numbers of students studying at universities, lead to the shortening and greater regulation of academic studies, to increased examination pressure, and block the expansion of educational studies related to practice, all of which is likely to bring about undesired effects, like more rigid, less liberal attitudes in student teachers and retention of the prevailing, insufficient preparation for practice with its detrimental consequences.

Even in areas where opportunities exist for internal reforms in both stages of teacher education, educationists do not often use available research knowledge for improving teacher education. Perhaps teacher educators tend to find teaching theoretical knowledge more important and more prestigious; perhaps educational research and research in teacher education have lost credibility because they are seen as too dependent on prevailing research trends and fads; or perhaps it simply requires too much effort by teacher educators to examine the consequences of knowledge obtained by research for designing instruction and training.

Notes

1 This research review is based on studies listed in the German bibliographic indices *Bibliographischer Index Bildungswissenschaften* from 1974 to 1987, the *Auswahl-Dienst: Informationen für Erziehung und Unterricht (ADIEU)* from 1976 to 1986, four journals publishing empirical-analytical studies (*Die deutsche Schule, Psychologie in Erziehung und Unterricht, Unterrichtwissenschaft, Zeitschrift für erziehungswissenschaftliche Forschung*) and references found in the studies located in these journals and indices.

2 A number of studies are reviewed by Müller-Fohrbrodt, 1973, and Müller-Fohrbrodt *et al.*, 1978. Other studies on personality characteristics include those by Dann, Cloetta, Müller-Fohrbrodt and Helmreich, 1978; Merz, 1982; Merz and Madjaric, 1976; Pfeiffer and Stiksrud, 1981; Stahr, 1975.

3 In addition to studies reviewed by Müller-Fohrbrodt *et al.*, 1978, others include those by Bayer, 1976; Breunig and Müller, 1977; Durchholz, Seisenberger and Schmidt, 1979; Eckinger, 1979; Gnad, Klisa and Prasse, 1980; Hampe, 1978; Kürten and Wegner, 1984; Lademann and Lietzke, 1977; Liepe, 1982; Pfeiffer and Stiksrud, 1981; Raufuss, 1982; Roth, 1972; Steltmann, 1986; Walter, 1980; Warnken, 1977.

4 A number have been reviewed by Schönig, 1989. Others include those by Born and Euler, 1977; Kuntz, 1973; Susteck, 1975.

References

ALLEN, W.D. and RYAN, K. (1969) *Microteaching*. Reading, Mass.: Addison-Wesley.

Auswahl-Dienst: Informationen für Erziehung und Unterricht (1976–1986). Duisburg: Verlag für Pädagogische Dokumentation.

BAEGE, K. (1973) *Probleme schulpraktischer Ausbildung: Eine Befragung von Studenten an den Pädagogischen Hochschulen des Landes Baden-Württemberg.* Zulassungsarbeit zur ersten Dienstprüfung für das Lehramt an Grund- und Hauptschulen des Landes Baden-Württemberg. Weingarten: Pädagogische Hochschule.

BARTMANN, T., BISCHOFF, A. and EBEL, H. (1978) Einfluss der Schulpraxis auf die Berufsmotivation von Lehrerstudenten. *Zeitschrift für Entwicklungspsychologie und Pädagogische Psychologie,* 10, 2, 179–188.

BAYER, M. (1976) Reformplanung und Realität in der Lehrerausbildung. *Bildung und Erziehung* 29, 400–412.

Bibliographischer Index Bildungswissenschaften (1974–1987). Duisburg: Verlag für Pädagogische Dokumentation.

BORN, G. and EULER, M. (1977) *Der Physiklehrer in der Bundesrepublik Deutschland: Eine empirische Untersuchung.* Bonn Deutsche Physikalische Gesellschaft.

BREUNIG, W. and MÜLLER, K. (1977) Lehrer zwischen Studium und Berufspraxis: Eine empirische Untersuchung, in *Informationsschrift zur Lehrerbildung und -fortbildung,* 13. Heidelberg: Pädagogische Hochschule, Studiengruppe Lehrer-Dozenten, pp. 49–66.

BRUNNER, R. (1976) *Lehrertraining: Grundlagen — Verfahren — Ergebnisse.* München: Reinhardt.

BRUNNER, R. (1985) Der Einsatz praxisorientierter Verfahren in der Lehrerausbildung an den Hochschulen der Bundesrepublik Deutschland. *Unterrichtswissenschaft,* 13, 2, 169–181.

DANN, H.-D., CLOETTA, B., MÜLLER-FOHRBRODT, G. and HELMREICH, R. (1978) *Umweltbedingungen innovativer Kompetenz: Eine Längsschnittuntersuchung zur Sozialisation von Lehrern in Ausbildung und Beruf.* Stuttgart: Klett-Cotta.

DANN, H.-D. MÜLLER-FOHRBRODT, B. and CLOETTA, B. (1981) Sozialisation junger Lehrer im Berufi: 'Praxisschock' drei Jahre später. *Zeitschrift für Entwicklungspsychologie und Pädagogische Psychologie,* 13, 3, 251–262.

DEFFNER, W. (1977) Berufsrelevante Einstellungen und Ausbildungsbeurteilungen. *Pädagogische Rundschau,* 31, 302–313.

DURCHHOLZ, E., SEISENBERGER, G. and SCHMIDT, H-L. (1979) Studienerwartungen bei Studierenden pädagogischer Studienrichtungen. *Psychologie in Erziehung und Unterricht,* 26, 44–48.

ECKINGER, L. (1979) Zur Situation des Junglehrers: Versuch einer Bestandsaufnahme des Vorbereitungsdienstes in Bayern und Überlegungen zum Referendariat. Dissertation, Universität Regensburg.

FITZNER, K.D. (1978) *Das Schulpracticum als soziales System.* Weinheim: Beltz.

GNAD, G., KLISA, B. and PRASSE, W. (1980) Lehrerausbildung als Erfahrung, in K. Gründer (Hrsq.) *Unterrichten lernen.* Paderborn: Schöningh, pp 63–188

HAMPE, H. (1978) Probleme der Lehrerausbildung. *Westermanns Pädagogische Beiträge,* 30, 22–26.

HELLER, K.A. and WICHTERLICH, H. (1982) Evaluation des DIFF-Fernstudienlehrgangs 'Ausbildung zum Beratungslehrer'. *Psychologie in Erziehung und Unterricht,* 29 19–29.

HINSCH, R. (1979) *Einstellungswandel und Praxisschock bei jungen Lehrern.* Weinheim: Beltz.

KLINZING, H.G. (1982) *Training kommunikativer Fertigkeiten zur Gesprächsführung und für Unterricht.* Weil der Stadt Lexika.

KLINZING, H.G. and KLINZING-EURICH, G. (1988) Lehrerausbildung im Labor: Ein Überblick über die Forschung in der Bundesrepublik Deutschland, in A. Leuteritz, C. Weisbach and T. Helle (Eds) *Konkrete Pädogogik: Festschrift für Walther Zifreund zum 60, Geburtstag.* Tübingen: Attempto, pp. 121–140.

KLINZING, H.G., KLINZING-EURICH, G. and FLODEN, R.E. (1989) 'Integrating the functions of laboratory practice: Skill acquisition and reflection-based decision making in improving expository teaching.' Paper presented at the annual meeting of the American Educational Research Association, San Francisco.

KLINZING, H.G., LEUTERITZ, A., SCHIEFER, H.J. and STEIGER, S. (1986) Auswirkungen von 'direktem' und 'indirektem' Training auf nichtverbale Sensitivität und nichtverbale Ausdruskraft, in W. Langhthaler and H. Schneider (Eds) *Video-rückmeldung und Verhaltenstraining.* Münster: Maks Publ., pp. 145–194.

KOCH, J.-J. (1972) *Lehrerstudium und Beruf: Einstellungswandel in den beiden Phasen der Ausbildung.* Ulm: Süddeutsche Verlagsgesellschaft.

KOCH, J.-J. (1975) Auswirkungen von Hochschulunterricht auf berufsrelevante Einstellungen von Lehramtskandidaten. *Zeitschrift für Erziehungswissenschaftliche Forschung,* 9, 4, 239–250.

KÜRTEN, C. and WEGNER, K. (1984) Lehrerausbildung und das Problem der lerngestörten Grundschüler. *Psychologie in Erziehung und Unterricht,* 31, 263–273.

KUNTZ, K.M. (1973) *Zur Soziologie der Akademiker.* Stuttgart: Enke.

LADEMANN, H.-R. and LIETZKE, H. (1977) Zur Berufssituation des jungen Lehrers. *Zeitschrift für Erziehungswissenschaftliche Forschung,* 11, 155–161.

LANGTHALER, W., SCHULTZ, R. and Elsinghorst, J. (1986) Effekte eines Lehr-Labor-Training 'Lob und Tadel'. *Unterrichtswissenschaft,* 3, 291–302.

LIEBHART, E.H. (1970) Sozialisation im Beruf: Ergebnisse einer Panelbefragung von Studienreferendaren. *Kölner Zeitschrift für Soziologie und Sozialpsychologie,* 22, 715–736.

LIEPE, J. (1982) Lehreranwärter im Unterricht: Was stört denn nun wirklich? *Schulpraxis,* 2–4, 39–43.

LINDEMANN, H. (1984) Schulpraxis in der Lehrerausbildung: Eine Untersuchung bei Lehramsstudenten des Faches Chemie. *Naturwissenschaft im Unterricht — Physik/Chemie,* 32, 318–322.

MERZ, J. (1982) Einstellungsunterschiede zwischen angehenden Grund- und Hauptschullehrern. *Psychologie in Erziehung und Unterricht,* 29, 140–147.

MERZ, J. and MADJARIC, J. (1976) Unterschiede in der Einstellung zum Lehrerberuf vor und nach Berufseintritt. *Zeitschrift für Entwicklungspsychologie und Pädagogische Psychologie,* 8, 91–98.

MÜLLER-FOHRBRODT, G. (1973) *Wie sind Lehrer wirklich? Ideale-Vorurteile-Fakten.* Stuttgart: Klett.

MÜLLER-FOHRBRODT, G., CLOETTA, B. and DANN, H.-D. (1978) *Der Praxisschock bei jungen Lehrern.* Stuttgart: Klett.

NEUBAUER, W. (1983) Dimensionale Struktur der impliziten Führungstheorie bei Lehrern und Lehrerstudenten. *Psychologie in Erziehung und Unterricht,* 30, 183–191.

NICKEL, H., SCHWALENBERG, R. and UNGELENK, B. (1974). Ein erziehungspsychologisches Verhaltenstraining mit Lehrerstudenten. *Psychologie in Erziehung und Unterricht,* 21, 67–80.

NIESSEN, M. (1974) Berufsbezogene Einstellung von Lehrerstudenten. *Zeitschrift für Pädagogik*, 20, 2, 271–286.

PFEIFFER, H. and STICKSRUD, A. (1981) Berufs- und studienbezogenes selbstkonzept künftiger Diplom pädagogen: Ein Vergleich mit dem Selbstbild zukünftiger Lehrer. *Psychologie in Erziehung und Unterricht*, 28, 257–266.

RAUFUSS, D. (1982) Die fachwissenschaftliche Ausbildung: Vorbild für den Schulunterricht? *Schulpraxis*, 2, 7–13.

ROTH, J.H. (1981) Veränderung berufsrelevanter Einstellungen von Lehrerstudenten. *Psychologie in Erziehung und Unterrichr*, 28, 344–350.

ROTH, W. (1972) Lehrerausbildung und schulische Praxis. *Die Deutsche Schule*, 10, 632–637.

ROTH, W. (1974) Schulpraktikum am Ende? Strukturanalyse aus der Erfahrungsperspektive von Lehrerstudenten. *Die Deutsche Schule*, 66, 3, 200–206.

ROYL, W. and MINSEL, W.-R. (Eds) (1973) *Teacher training*. Hannover: Schroedel.

SCHMITZ, R.A. (1974) Empirische Erprobung eines Lehrertrainings in zwei relevanten Lehrerfertigkeiten durch Micro-Teaching mit Video-Feedback. *AV-Forschung*, 11, 5–33.

SCHÖNIG, W. (1989) Schulinterne Lehrerfortbildung als Beitrag zur Schulentwicklung. Unpublished doctoral dissertation, Universität Tübingen.

SIGNER, R. (1979) *Verhaltenstraining für Lehrer*. Weinheim: Beltz.

STAHR, I. (1975) Die Berufsrolle des Diplom-Pädagogen. *Zeitschrift für Pädagogik*, 21, 4, 587–595.

STELTMANN, V. (1986) Problems der Lehrerausbildung: Ergebnisse einer Lehrerbefragung. *PR (Sankt Angustin)*, 40, 353–366.

SUSTECK, H. (1975) *Lehrer zwischen Tradition und Fortschritt*. Braunschweig: Westermann.

TAUSCH, A. (1963) Ausmass und Änderung des Merkmals Verständnis im Sprachverhalten von Erziehern und Zusammenhänge mit seelischen Vorgängen in Kinder. *Zeitschrift für experimentelle und angewandte Psychologie*, 10, 514–539.

TENNSTÄDT, K.C. (1987) Das Konstanzer Trainingsmodell (KTM): Einführung und ausgewählte Ergebnisse einer ersten Evaluation, in J. Schlee and D. Wahl (Eds) *Veränderungen subjektiver Theorien von Lehrern*. Oldenburg: Universität Oldenburg, 206–235.

THIELE, H.(1978) Steuerung der verbalen Interaktion durch didaktische Intervention: Eine empirische Untersuchung zum Effekt von drei Methoden zum Lehrverhaltenstraining. Unpublished dissertation, Universitat Braunschweig.

WALTER, H. (1980) Junge Lehrer 79: Untersuchung über berufliche und sozialpsychologische Probleme bayerischer Junglehrer. *Der Junglehrer*, 23, 1–27.

WALTER, H. and ROHR, F. (1976) Die Einstellung von Lehrerstudenten zu Erziehungsfragen: Eine Analyse autoritativer Tendenzen mittels der LEKU-Skala. *Psychologie in Erziehung und Unterricht*, 23, 123–128.

WARNKEN, G. (1977) *Das Ausbildungscurriculum in der Zweiten Phase der Lehrerausbildung: Eine empirische Analyse*. Kronberg/TS: Scriptor-Verlag.

ZACHMANN-HINTERMEIER, U. and TREIBER, B. (1986) Zielerreichendes Unterrichten: Erprobung eines Lehrertrainingsprogramms. *Psychologie in Erziehung und Unterricht*, 33, 220–228.

ZIFREUND, W. (1966) *Konzept für ein Training des Lehrverhaltens mit Fernseh-Aufzeichnungen in Kleingruppen-Seminaren*. Berlin, D: Cornelsen.

Chapter 7

Research on Teacher Education in Singapore (1968–1988)

Ho Wah Kam

Except for one general review (Sim, 1983), which touched briefly on more recent teacher education research in Singapore, no extensive review of local research in teacher education has occurred. Teacher education research in Singapore has a longer history than is commonly assumed, although much of the work, lacking close bibliographic documentation, is hardly known outside a very small circle of researchers. The field of teacher education research has become particularly active in the last six years in Singapore. This chapter documents as fully as possible what has been done in the area of teacher education research and explains the new direction that this research has recently taken.

The Context: Teacher Education in Singapore

The Institute of Education (IE) was established in 1973, incorporating the former Teachers Training College (TTC), the School of Education of the then University of Singapore, and the Research Unit of the Ministry of Education. As the only institution in Singapore offering pre-service teacher education and much of the in-service training for teachers, it conducts most of the research in teacher education.

Between 1972 and 1987 several major changes occurred in the training curriculum; some of the research studies conducted during this period reflected those changes. The most comprehensive response to the call for reform in teacher education in Singapore was made in 1972, a year before the setting up of the Institute. In brief, four developmental phases occurred in teacher education in Singapore: (1) the early period (around 1950) right up to 1972, dominated by a traditional model of teacher training; (2) the period from the academic year 1973 to 1980, characterized by institutional change and qualitative improvements in the training curriculum;

(3) the phase from 1981 to 1986, marked by a concerted effort to integrate the programs designed for different languages of instruction; and (4) the introduction in 1986 of the practicum curriculum.[1] The curriculum changes in 1986 took into account the sustained debate about theory-practice linkages and also some of the concerns that former trainees had expressed in the follow-up (induction) studies about their training programs. In addition, the implementation of the new practicum curriculum generated a number of studies carried out as action research. These studies are included in the review.

The Studies in Perspective

This review concentrates on pre-service teacher education because very little research work has been carried out in the field of in-service education. Most of the studies reviewed were quantitative. In the process, forty-five documents were located, of which twenty-seven (or 60 per cent) were empirical, coming from survey questionnaires and from the use of evaluation, personality and attitude instruments interpreted largely from a social-psychological perspective. Many of these studies constituted part of the Institute's program evaluation. Very little experimental or quasi-experimental research occurred. A few of the studies reported here stemmed from dissertation research. Other than those which are MEd or PhD dissertations, most reports do not have elaborate theoretical justification as one of their more prominent features. Based on their content, the studies can be grouped under six main rubrics: reasons for choosing teaching; objectives of the training programs; additional selection criteria; the assessment of coursework; teaching practice; and follow-up studies of former trainees.

Reasons for Choosing Teaching

Two studies (Lau and project team, 1968; Soh, 1983) addressed the question of trainees' motives for choosing teaching as a career. The study by Lau *et al.* (1968), started in 1965, represented the first major project of the Research Unit of the former Teachers' Training College. The sample consisted of 36.5 per cent (N = 2046) of the trainees enrolled in the different regular pre-service programs at the College in December of that year. At that time programs of pre-service training were grouped into the four language streams (English, Chinese, Malay and Tamil) for different trainees being prepared to teach in English-medium, Chinese-medium, Malay-medium or Tamil-medium schools.

Lau *et al.* (1968) reported that 71.9 per cent of the respondents were firm in their decision to teach, while the rest would readily change jobs if they had another option. Reasons for choice of teaching were 'an opportunity to render service to society', 'an opportunity to further [their] education', and 'to help develop and educate the younger generation'. For women, who formed the majority of the trainees in the English-medium program, reasons such as 'fondness for children' and 'teaching is suitable for women' were often given. It would appear that 'idealistic' reasons predominated. In commenting that 'this could be due to genuine idealism in the trainees or to their readiness to profess socially acceptable motives or a combination of both', the researchers drew attention to the basic difficulty in such surveys, which is the degree of frankness that one can attribute to these expressed motives. Another interesting feature of the findings, to which the researchers specially drew attention, was what they called the 'cultural differences' among the trainees with different languages. While acknowledging that it was 'not unusual for the average person to be inclined towards socially desirable statements', the researchers had the impression that the Chinese-educated were more idealistic than the other groups; they explained that either they were genuinely more idealistic or the 'Chinese-educated are more prone to respond to statements which contain certain idealistic sentiments' (p. 101).

In 1981 Soh (1983) repeated the Lau *et al.* (1968) study by adapting the questionnaire used in the earlier project and administering it to 562 trainees at IE. By 1981, when the second study started, the social, economic, political and educational conditions had changed quite dramatically for the better. For example, compared to conditions in 1965, there was a greater variety of jobs available to provide young people with attractive alternative job opportunities. Furthermore, the salaries of teachers in 1981 had increased substantially over those of 1965. So, how different were the 1965 and 1981 samples in terms of reasons given? Soh (1983) noted a few differences. For example, the 1981 trainees were less influenced by motives of self-interest, i.e. they did not have an alternative career in mind, and were less attracted by long school vacations. They therefore seemed less 'utilitarian' in their expressed motives. Instead, the 1981 sample regarded teaching as a way of realizing their potential and ambition through working with children. While the two groups of respondents placed varying emphasis on the different roles of a teacher, fewer respondents in the second sample decided to enter teaching simply because it was a noble profession.

Objectives of the Pre-service Training Programs

In 1981 a survey of teacher education objectives (Mosbergen and project team, 1982) was conducted; it polled the views of students enrolled in the full-time (1980/81) Diploma program on 'the repertoire of knowledge, skills and personal qualities needed by new graduate teachers' (p. 2).[2] The selection of objectives was based on a framework conceptualized in two dimensions: knowledge, skills and attitudes domains, and professional, academic and personal features. These three domains and three features formed a matrix of nine categories, from which twenty-two objectives were generated.

The 229 pre-service trainees surveyed accorded 'high priority' to the knowledge and skills needed directly for effective classroom teaching (collectively the *core* objectives): for example, knowledge of the sylla-buses, assessment procedures and educational policy and goals; skills in subject teaching, motivating pupils, classroom management and communication. However, skills in setting and marking exercises and in the selection of resource materials were of 'medium priority' (collectively named in the report as *supportive* objectives). Objectives accorded 'low priority' (or the *peripheral* objectives) included those set out to develop skills in using and making teaching aids, and in classwork supervision and routine administrative duties. In the area of personal qualities the trainees rated as highly important such qualities as being responsible and confident, having good interpersonal relationships and showing integrity. The report commented that the trainee teachers tended to assign greater importance to qualities closely associated with the conduct of lessons than to other aspects of a teacher's work. This should not be surprising since at the time of the survey the trainees were still undergoing training and had completed only ten weeks of classroom practice.

This study of trainees followed upon a similar survey (Mosbergen and project team, 1980) which gathered and analyzed the views of (1) principals of secondary schools and junior colleges and (2) the academic staff of the Institute, on teacher education objectives. There was considerable agreement between the findings of the two surveys.

The samples of respondents in both studies were agreed on the priority to be accorded to a set of teacher education objectives (the core, the supportive and the peripheral), but the principals and academic staff also believed there were long-term, as well as immediate practical goals for teacher education. The trainees had already developed a pragmatic approach to their expectations from courses and block teaching practice. They would be at what Fuller and Bown (1975) have called the 'survival' stage. Hence the 1982 report concluded as follows: 'An effective teacher education programme in the eyes of the [pre-service] students is therefore one that prepares them to cope with the many and varied day-to-day problems they will encounter within the four walls of the classroom.'

It is appropriate here to note that in 1982 the Institute of Education adopted a framework to guide and coordinate its cooperative research on teacher education. Four teams were formed to investigate different issues, and the first high priority areas were: the development of additional selection criteria for applicants to the Institute's training programs; evaluation of innovative teaching methods in the training of teachers; assessment of the performance of trainees; and follow-up studies of trainees who graduated from the Institute.

Selection Criteria

Selection for teacher training is an important issue here, and people have searched for additional criteria that could be included in the selection process. Several instruments had been examined, in particular the Minnesota Teacher Attitude Inventory or MTAI (Cook *et al.*, 1951), the 16 Personality Factor Questionnaire (Cattell and Eber, 1970), and a locally constructed attitude scale (Tan, 1985). The studies (Yip, 1982; Eng and project team, 1983; Tan, 1985) using these instruments to improve and refine the selection process have had moderate success and predictable outcomes. So far the results indicate that the instruments, as might be expected, contain items that differentiate between effective and less effective trainees on coursework and teaching practice variables. For example, the more intelligent, emotionally stable and less anxious students performed better in the program than other trainees (Tay-Koay, 1985).

Assessment of Coursework

As mentioned earlier, assessment was selected by the Institute as a high priority area, but as only one of the major courses in the foundation studies, Principles and Practice of Education, used multiple-choice and essay tests, the assessment research had to centre on this course. Consequently the discussion of the research will be brief. Studies were completed on the kinds of examination questions used (Lam, Poh and Soh, 1986), the facility and discriminating power of the questions (Lam *et al.*, 1986; Soh, 1987a) and how essay questions were graded (Yip, Lui and Soh, 1986; Soh, 1987b). The findings indicated that although many questions tested a range of students' cognitive abilities, most were relatively easy and did not discriminate well between high and low achievers.

Teaching Practice

Determining the validity and reliability of the measures used to assess trainees during their teaching practice formed an important aspect of the Institute's research. The problem of inter-rater reliability among supervisors was compounded by the fact that they came from different subject specializations. In responding to these issues, Soh, Lam and Poh (1985) administered a questionnaire to eighty-six supervisors of the Diploma and Certificate students to survey their views on teaching practice, their expectations, the process of awarding a grade and the emphasis they gave to the role of teaching practice in the training of teachers.[3] On the whole, the supervisors saw themselves emphasizing their instructor and counsellor roles in their relationship with trainees in both ideal and actual situations. Their evaluator role (i.e. having to make judgments about a trainee's stage of development as a teacher against the objectives as specified for teaching practice) was de-emphasized. At the early stages of supervision they gave top priority to the planning and arrangement of activities to facilitate learning, and the selection of valid, worthwhile and appropriate objectives, while on later visits they saw the use of appropriate instructional strategies and approaches, and the provision of feedback and reinforcement as especially important. Soh, Lam and Poh (1985, p. 14) commented that during the later stages of supervision the emphasis of supervisors shifted 'to the class as a unit as well as a broader perspective rather than focussing almost entirely on the teacher-trainees'. There was fairly substantial agreement among the departments during the early phase of supervision (with correlations ranging from .59 to .79) and modest agreement during the later phase (with correlations ranging from .35 to .76).

Yeap *et al.* (1985) decided to find out whether inter-rater reliability among supervisors could be improved through group interaction after the supervisors had watched videotapes of selected trainees' classroom teaching episodes, and also whether different teaching situations affected the ratings of supervisors. An experimental situation was set up with a control group. The experimental group (of supervisors) had the opportunity to discuss among themselves the lesson and their ratings of it after viewing the lesson together with the control group, whereas the control group did not discuss the lesson or their assessment of it. In the final analysis no consistent treatment effects were observed, and the expectation of reduced variance within the experimental group was only partially borne out. The variance of the scores of the experimental group was reduced after the first treatment but this was not sustained. What emerged as an encouraging sign was that the participating supervisors were at least consistent when rating different aspects of the same lesson a second time.

The Institute's concern about forging a stronger practice-theory linkage led to the adoption of a different practicum curriculum in the Diploma program in 1986. As a consequence it was deemed necessary to find out what impact this practicum curriculum had on the trainees. Sharpe (1986, 1987) surveyed the views and experiences of the first batch of trainees who were introduced to the new arrangements. From the post-teaching practice survey findings it would appear that their major methods course prepared the trainees well for the school-based practicum. While the level of confidence of trainees with regard to their ability to perform the different classroom roles was high over the ten-week period of teaching practice, which reflected creditably on the courses, their confidence in handling their own performance did not improve very much over the same period.

In the attempt to improve the supervision of teaching practice, priority was given to the training of supervisors. Workshops were help at which supervision experiences were shared. Chew-Goh's (1986) study set out to investigate the effects of a training program on selected supervision skills and the evaluative behaviour of some prospective heads of departments who were being trained as supervisors of teachers and trainees. The subjects were thirty-three experienced teachers in a full-time in-service program who were required as part of their training to undergo a supervision practicum aimed at preparing them to supervise teachers and trainees. They were teamed with forty-seven second-year Certificate in Education (pre-service) trainees. The research design consisted of a pre-test, treatment (made up of a series of workshops on supervision skills) and then post-test 1 and post-test 2, without a control group. The pre-test and post-tests were administered to the in-service teachers. On the pre-test the in-service teachers had low scores for the four supervision roles (those of observer, feedback, instructor and evaluator). However, on post-test 1 there was an overall improvement in the scores for supervision, with the largest gain made in the feedback role. The teachers who demonstrated the greatest improvement after the treatment were those with no experience as cooperating teachers and those with more than twenty years of teaching experience. On post-test 2, which took place in the school setting, the results were equally positive, with statistically significant gains made on all supervision roles by the sample of teachers. Although the findings were very encouraging, the researcher, however, did caution against an overoptimistic interpretation of the findings because of the small sample size and the lack of a control group. What this experiment did show was that prospective supervisors would benefit from supervision training workshops that are task-oriented and well organized.

In her exploratory study Ng (1987) investigated the use of a five-phase clinical supervision model (from Goldhammer *et al.*, 1980) for the specific purpose of studying the clinical supervision process within the context of the practicum in the revised training curriculum. Naturalistic inquiry methodology (as developed by Guba, 1978) was used. First, clinical supervision was defined by Ng (1987, p. 34) as a 'systematic approach to supervision which involves the supervisor conferring with the teacher on lesson planning, lesson observation, analysis of observational data and feedback on the teaching.' What makes this model distinctive is its teacher-supervisor relationship, characterized by collegiality, collaboration, skilled service and ethical conduct (p. 34). Second, naturalistic inquiry differs from other modes of inquiry by the degree of manipulation of the conditions prior to the study of the phenomenon and by accepting (or acknowledging) the constraints imposed on the outcomes by those taking part in the study. To the naturalistic inquirer, reality is 'constantly changing in terms of time, people, episodes, settings, and circumstances' (Guba, 1978, p. 15). Ng (1987) used a sample of seven trainees from the 1985/86 cohort of the Diploma program. Though small, the sample reflected variations in student characteristics that were important in the context of the training program. All seven were being trained to teach economics. The natural setting was that of teaching practice. Ng (1987, p. 95) found that clinical supervision worked well with trainees who were mature, able and highly motivated. By contrast, the method worked less well with trainees who felt less secure with a non-judgmental approach. She also found a truly collegial trainee-supervisor relationship difficult to achieve in the local context, where the norms for behaviour are a little different. The traditional respect for superiors requires a hierarchical relationship that must be absent in clinical supervision. Other than this minor problem, the trainees were receptive to this non-directive, collaborative approach to supervision, and there was no serious cultural conflict. In fact, the researcher recommended that a wider use of clinical supervision in the Institute's training programs be considered.

Another arrangement for teaching practice being considered as a possible alternative to the one-supervisor-to-one-trainee set-up is pair teaching. Pair teaching in the practicum was first introduced on an experimental basis both to minimize the adverse effects of a 'cultural unfamiliarity' faced by a group of young teachers from another country doing their teaching practice in Singapore schools, and to maximize experiential learning. According to Skuja (1986), who initiated the use of pair teaching at the Institute of Education, 'the triad nature of the paired arrangement [i.e. two trainees and the supervisor, and occasionally with the school's cooperating teacher in conference] meant that [such] supervision was not as hierarchical as single supervision.' From the interviews with twenty-three pairs of trainees placed in fourteen schools, carried out by Chen and Skuja (1988), it was clear that pair teaching was effective for certain types of trainees and less so for others. Trainees who were more pupil-centred benefited more from the paired arrangement than those who were more concerned with self-development and self-achievement. Chen and Skuja (1988, p. 3) suggested that the most successful candidates for pair teaching are those who are 'other-orientated i.e. open-minded and having concern for others' points of view', and that the least successful candidates are likely to be those who are 'self-orientated...tend to be inhibited and feel threatened by others' perceptions of their performance'. It was inevitable that, given the interactive nature of the paired arrangement, the researchers concluded that based on these preliminary findings the success of the scheme was dependent on the extent to which the trainees were able to relate to each other and work together.

Induction Studies of Beginning Teachers

The early phase of settling into a teaching position (or the period of induction) has been studied quite intensively by researchers in several countries as it is regarded as a crucial stage in the career of a teacher. These studies are broadly of three types: personal accounts of success and failure (e.g. Ryan, 1970, in the US), empirical studies of selected factors (e.g. Tisher *et al.*, 1979, in Australia) and interviews with beginning teachers (Skuja and Lim-Quek, 1984, in Singapore). Such studies kept the teacher education institutions informed of the kinds of problems beginning teachers faced in making the shift from trainee to teacher; in turn, teacher education programs can be modified and more effective support programs designed for beginning teachers.

Such follow-up studies constitute part of the program evaluation scheme at the Institute of Education. Since 1981, three surveys (Ho *et al.*, 1983; Lim-Quek and Tay-Koay, 1987; Mah and Chew, 1988) have been conducted to find out the perceptions that different cohorts of Certificate and Diploma trainees had of their training programs and whether there was any noticeable shift in their views about teaching as a result of full-reponsibility teaching experience. In Ho *et al.*'s (1983) survey of Certificate-trained teachers, for example, which covered seven cohorts of trainees who graduated between July 1980 and July 1982, respondents felt that the preparation at the Institute was 'adequate' for the classes they were teaching. However, for a small number in the sample the basic problem was one of adjustment to the real world of the classroom; they sometimes characterized the training as 'idealistic'. When asked whether they were able to apply in the classroom what they had learnt, the majority of the respondents said that they had applied to some extent different aspects of their training. In particular, the skills learnt in the course on educational technology were found to be most useful. The teachers were also given a number of problem statements to rank in order of seriousness in the light of their classroom experience. Even experienced teachers would find pupils with behaviour problems difficult to handle in a class of some forty pupils, so it was not surprising that many young teachers ranked this experience with difficult children as the most serious problem for them. Despite the differences in working conditions (e.g. see Tisher, 1980), the problems ranked as very worrying were fairly similar across cultural contexts.

A subsequent follow-up study (Skuja and Lim-Quek, 1984), using the interview method, sought more detailed information about the nature of problems encountered by a sample of beginning primary school teachers and the strategies used by them in dealing with their problems. Although this focus on problems and coping strategies might well mask what was productive and exciting in the experience of young teachers, there was much that was positive which came through in the interviews. They said they enjoyed teaching, and that they were able to adapt to the changing demands of a school situation.

Lim-Quek and Tay-Koay (1987) reported on a survey of the 1984 batch of Diploma graduates after they had had one year of full-time teaching experience. Their views were sought on the pre-service training program. In addition, an examination was made of the relationships between the trainees' academic background, performance in course work and teaching practice (observed and self-rated). By and large, these beginning teachers found their training useful. While expressing considerable confidence in their own ability to teach, they rated themselves as being more competent in the social skills area than in the helping skills area. The beginning teachers said that they lacked confidence in such areas as maintaining classroom discipline and helping children with behavioural problems. A relationship existed between their performance in teaching practice and in how they rated themselves as classroom teachers: those who performed well in teaching practice tended to feel more competent in teaching.

Taken together, it seems reasonable to conclude from the results of the induction studies on beginning teachers that they were positive about the training they had undergone, and that whatever concerns they had after a period of full-time teaching in schools were of a practical nature, quite similar to the concerns of experienced teachers, such as feeling less confident about helping pupils with behavioural problems.

Areas Given Little Attention

A number of areas have seen little research attention in Singapore. For instance, although it is generally agreed that the development of classroom skills is a crucial component in any pre-service program, this area has been given limited attention in the research.

Three action research studies examined a related area: the delivery system of pre-service programs. Ho and Wong (1985) and Chin, Teh and Chew (1987) reported on a special arrangement (carried out over four school vacations, 1982–1985) which combined campus-based training with field experience, under the general rubric of 'vacation learning camp'. From the training point of view these field experience arrangements challenged pre-service and in-service teachers to apply what they had learnt in the management of learning/teaching situations for children who experienced learning difficulties. The in-service teachers who took part had to demonstrate how the objectives of the camp could be realized, while the pre-service trainees, acting as teachers, had to develop skills of gaining the pupils' attention and cooperation, to maintain an atmosphere of goodwill that a camp should have and to try out different ways of teaching given topics to classes of different sizes. Pupil progress in terms of cognitive gains and changes in self-concept were closely monitored. At the third (1984) camp, for instance, the trainees tried out, on an experimental basis, three different methods (conventional, task-based and tutoring) of teaching selected topics in mathematics and English. The principal learning experience for the trainees was that they could examine through direct experience the teaching methods being used and their effects on the pupils; they learnt at first hand that there was a great need to help these pupils build up their self-esteem before these same pupils could progress academically.

The shift of interest to the study of cognitive processes involved in training is a useful direction that teacher education research can take. Only one study has explored this question. Seet (1986), noting the limitations of the lecture-demonstration-imitation approach in the training of language teachers and working on the assumption that pre-service trainees having had the practical experience of a method of teaching

English would tend to theorize on their own, developed what he called an 'experiential approach' to the training of teachers of English, by exposing them to 'authentic learning experiences' which they can make use of meaningfully (p. 37). In this way, Seet argued, it was possible to develop trainees' cognitive structure. For the empirical part of the study, using listening comprehension as a teaching topic, Seet (1986) designed a small-scale experiment to test the assumption that those who had had the benefit of the experiential approach would show a better understanding of the underlying principles of teaching listening comprehension than the control group. The results show that after eight weeks of exposure to the special package employing the experiential approach, the experimental group did better than the control group on the overall scores for classroom observation and for the questionnaire administered at the end of the experiment. The mean differences were statistically significant. However, Seet pointed out the limitations of his study and stressed the tentative nature of his findings.

Taking a New Direction

The studies reviewed were characterized by a variety of content and purposes. However, lack of replication and follow-through and the predominant use of questionnaires and survey techniques probably curtailed the scope of the research. While the individual and team efforts were most laudable, what was lacking was an overarching framework to give cohesion and direction to such research.

As part of an overall strategy to develop a research ethos at IE, Sim (1987) developed a conceptual framework for teacher education, designed to generate a number of research questions in four domains, namely, input-throughput-output, theory-practicum linkages, school-teacher effectiveness, and innovative teaching and learning. Briefly, the framework was directed by several propositions, among which were (1) that the traditional issues in teacher education (e.g. theory-practice linkage, the relationship between success in a training program and full-responsibility teaching success, the question of a knowledge base for teacher education) have not been fully resolved either here or in other countries, and they need further research attention; and (2) that much of teacher education research is *predictive* in nature, since we want to know how well the programs prepare trainees for future roles. A predictive concern will require that some consensus concerning teaching effectiveness (i.e. full-responsibility teaching success in the schools) be arrived at and valid measures of teaching success be developed for research purposes. Another proposition was that much more would need to be known about the cognitive development of teachers in service, often expressed broadly as the effect of teaching on teachers.

Initially, twenty-four research questions were generated from the model (Sim, 1987), which form the agenda. However, at this stage of the research program implementation, attention is being paid to only ten of the twenty-four original questions. These ten questions have since formed the basis of seven projects that are now under way. Three of the questions from the agenda are cited below as examples.

> How do additional/alternative selection criteria compare with existing criteria in predicting performance in the pre-service programs and subsequently at school?

> How extensively are theoretical principles and research findings being used in practicum conferencing and practicum experiences being used in theory courses?

> How effective is cooperating teacher training/orientation in helping cooperating teachers use theoretical principles and research findings when they supervise student teachers?

These projects are being undertaken by teams drawn from different departments and schools within IE, coordinated by the Educational Research Unit set up in early 1988. Unlike individual projects, a research program such as this requires a mechanism to mesh the different projects together. In practical terms this has meant, among other possibilities, looking for appropriate points at which to establish linkages between and among the projects.

Concluding Remarks

In this review an attempt was made to provide a broad perspective on teacher education research in Singapore over the last twenty years. The research documents, both published and unpublished, covered studies of the objectives of teacher education, admission criteria, trainees' motives for choosing teaching as a career, the evaluation of training programs, the assessment of coursework and teaching practice, and the experience of beginning teachers. Three staging posts were also identified as having had special significance for the development of teacher education research in Singapore, namely, the establishment of the Institute of Education in 1973, the setting up of a cooperative research strategy in 1982, and the formulation in late 1987 of a research agenda for teacher education.

Although much of the research work completed remains to be systematically disseminated, the findings from some of the studies have had some influence on practice. In particular, the data from the follow-up studies formed the basis of decisions to modify the schedules of the pre-service programs and make changes in the courses. Also, in the project on additional selection criteria, which has since moved into a new phase, the results should be able to build up to some policy decision to select trainees using, in addition to the conventional criteria, empirically verified ones as well.

In the review it was noted that the complexity of teacher education as a process had not been fully addressed in the reported research. Processes in teacher education and teacher development have become the focus of attention as researchers in teacher education seek to understand these processes better and try to find points at which in-depth investigations can be made. Such investigations are necessarily multifaceted and multidisciplinary. It is hoped that with the provision of a unifying conceptual framework and a research agenda, the newly formulated research program, implemented in early 1988, will in due course yield results that directly benefit IE's training programs.

Notes

1 'Practicum' is used in this context as a collective term to cover all those practical experiences that trainees are exposed to either in the lecture hall or in the school and classroom for the purpose of developing and enhancing their teaching competence.
2 The Diploma in Education program (one year, full-time) prepares university graduates for teaching in secondary schools and junior colleges.
3 The Certificate in Education program (two years, full-time) prepares school leavers with the Singapore-Cambridge Certificate of Education (Advanced Level) qualification to teach in primary schools.

References

CATTELL, R.B. and EBER, H.W. (1970) *Handbook for the 16 Personality Factor Questionnaire.* Champaign, Ill.: Institute for Personality and Ability Testing.
CHEN, AI YEN and SKUJA, RITA (1988) The use of pair teaching to improve the practicum experience in pre-service teacher education. Unpublished paper, Institute of Education, Singapore.
CHEW-GOH, GEOK ENG (1986) The influence of training on the performance of teacher supervisors. MEd dissertation, National University of Singapore.
CHIN, LONG FAY, TEH, GEORGE and CHEW, PHYLLIS (1987) *The Effectiveness of*

Different Teaching Approaches in Mathematics and English: Lessons from the Fourth IE Vacation Learning Camp. Singapore: Institute of Education.

COOK, W.W., LEEDS, C.H. and CALLIS, R. (1951) *Minnesota Teacher Attitude Inventory.* New York: Psychological Corporation.

ENG, SOO PECK and project team (1983) Feasibility of the MTAI as a selection instrument for pre-service teacher education: A pilot project. *Singapore Journal of Education,* 5, 2, 20–42.

FULLER, FRANCES and BOWN, O. (1975) Becoming a teacher, in Kevin Ryan (Ed.) *Teacher Education.* Chicago, Ill.: University of Chicago Press.

GOLDHAMMER, R., ANDERSON, R.H. and KRAJEWSKI, R.J. (1980) *Clinical Supervision: Special Methods for the Supervision of Teachers.* New York: Holt, Rinehart and Winston.

GUBA, EGON G. (1978) *Toward a Methodology of Naturalistic Inquiry in Educational Evaluation.* Los Angeles, Calif.: University of California at Los Angeles, Centre for the Study of Evaluation.

HO, WAH KAM and project team (1983) Continuity and discontinuity between training and school experience: Follow-up studies of former students of the Institute of Education. *Singapore Journal of Education,* 5, 2, 49–63.

HO, WAH KAM and WONG YIN MEE (1985) *Continuity in Learning: A Report on the Third IE Vacation Learning Camp.* Occasional Paper 23. Singapore: Institute of Education.

LAM, TIT LOONG, POH, S.H. and SOH, K.C. (1986) *Question Analysis of the 1985 Principles and Practice of Education Examination Paper.* Singapore: Institute of Education.

LAU, WAI HAR and project team (1968) *Why Teach?: A Study of Motives for Choosing Teaching as a Career.* Singapore: Teachers Training College.

LIM-QUEK, MURIEL and TAY-KOAY, SIEW LUAN (1987) The experiences and perceptions of graduate teachers after one year of full-time teaching: A follow-up study. Unpublished report, Institute of Education, Singapore.

MAH, HAZEL and CHEW, PHYLLIS (1988) A follow-up study of Certificate in Education students after one year of full-time teaching. Unpublished report, Institute of Education, Singapore.

MOSBERGEN, RUDY and project team (1982) *Survey on Teacher Education Objectives: The Views of Junior College/Secondary School Principals and IE Lecturers.* Singapore: Institute of Education.

MOSBERGEN, RUDY and project team (1982) *Survey on Teacher Education Objectives: The Views of Full-Time Diploma-in-Education Students in IE.* Singapore: Institute of Education.

NG, MAUREEN (1987) An inquiry into the use of clinical supervision with student teachers. MEd dissertation, National University of Singapore.

RYAN, KEVIN (Ed.) (1970) *Don't Smile Until Christmas.* Chicago, Ill.: University of Chicago Press.

SEET, OLIVER BENG HEAN (1986) An innovative approach to the preparation of English language teachers from an applied linguistics perspective. PhD thesis, National University of Singapore.

SHARPE, LESLIE (1986) An analysis of the student teacher questionnaire. Unpublished paper, Institute of Education, Singapore.

SHARPE, LESLIE (1987) Dipoma in Education Teaching Practice (2 Jan–13 Mar 1987): A report. Unpublished report. Institute of Education, Singapore.

SIM, WONG KOOI (1983) Research and teacher education: A Singapore perspective. *Singapore Journal of Education*, 5, 2, 127–137.

SIM, WONG KOOI (1987) Review, rear-view, real and re-view of RITE. Notes of a talk to IE staff at an in-house workshop. Institute of Education, Singapore.

SKUJA, RITA (1986) Paired teaching: A Singapore alternative, in Verner Bickley (Ed.). *Re-exploring CELT: Continuing Education for Language Teachers*. Hong Kong: Institute of Language in Education.

SKUJA, RITA and LIM-QUEK, MURIEL (1984) The experiences of beginning teachers: A follow-up study report based on interview data. Unpublished report, Institute of Education, Singapore.

SOH, KAY CHENG (1983) *Student Teachers' Backgrounds and Motives for Teaching: A 1968–1981 Comparison*. Occasional Paper 11. Singapore: Institute of Education.

SOH, KAY CHENG (1987a) *Principles and Practice of Education: Question Analyses of 1983 and 1985 Examination Papers*. Singapore: Institute of Education.

SOH, KAY CHENG (1987b) *Analytical and Impressionistic Marking: A Secondary Analysis*. Singapore: Institute of Education.

SOH, KAY CHENG, LAM, T.L. and POH, S.H. (1985) *Teaching Practice Supervision: What Are Supervisors After?* Singapore: Institute of Education.

TAN, ESTHER (1985) The relationship between trainee teachers' attitude and outcome of teacher training. Unpublished paper, Institute of Education, Singapore.

TAY-KOAY, SIEW LUAN (1985) Additional selection criteria research project: Selection and performance of 1983 Diploma in Education students at the Institute of Education. *Singapore Journal of Education*, 7, 2, 65–70.

TISHER, R.P. (1980) The induction of beginning teachers, in Eric Hoyle and Jacquetta Megarry (Eds). *World Yearbook of Education 1980: Professional Development of Teachers*. London: Kogan Page.

TISHER, R.P., FYFIELD, J. and TAYLOR, S. (1979) *Beginning to Teach*. Vol. 2. ERDC Report No. 20. Canberra: Australian Government Publishing Service.

YEAP, LAY LENG, KHOR, P., LUI, E., LAM, T.L., POH, S.H. and SOH, K.C. (1985) *An Experimental Study of Inter-rater Reliability of Teaching Practice Supervision (A Pilot Study)*. Singapore: Institute of Education.

YIP, KATHERINE (1982) Additional selection instrument: Phase one report. Unpublished report, Institute of Education, Singapore.

YIP, KATHERINE, LUI ELENA and SOH, K.C. (1986) *A Study of Three Methods of Assessing Core Education Assignments*. Singapore: Institute of Education.

Chapter 8

Research on Teacher Training in a Changing Society: The Case of Britain in the Late 1980s

David McNamara

Introduction

For the past two decades teacher training in the United Kingdom has been in a state of flux as successive governments have, on the one hand, introduced their own policies in order to cope with the fluctuations in teacher supply and demand occasioned by changes in demographic trends and, on the other hand, sought to restructure teacher training within a changing higher education system.[1] The present system which is under scrutiny provides for two major routes into the teaching profession. The 'concurrent' mode is based upon a four-year course for non-graduates who gained the requisite qualifications to enter the higher education system. The course provides for the advanced study of one or more of the academic subjects typically found on the school curriculum, professional training and at least twenty weeks of direct school experience and leads to the qualification of either the Bachelor of Education (BEd) or BA (Education) degree. In general this route is available for intending primary teachers or secondary teachers training for the more practically oriented areas of the curriculum such as physical education or home economics. The 'consecutive' mode provides for candidates who have graduated and whose degree course included subjects normally included within the school curriculum to take a one-year course leading to the qualification of Post Graduate Certificate in Education for either primary or secondary teaching. This professional course includes at least fifteen weeks of school-based experience. Both concurrent and consecutive modes are located in the 'university' or 'polytechnic and colleges' sectors of the British higher education system, although concurrent courses are more prominent in the polytechnic and colleges sector and consecutive courses in the university sector. There are, of course, many variations to the above scheme, such as part-time variants. While the majority of intending teachers commence their training directly upon completing their formal education, a substantial minority train as mature students. In addition, from September 1989 new Department of Education and Science regulations will enable untrained mature candidates with appropriate academic qualifications to enter schools directly as licensed and articled teachers and acquire their training while working as practising teachers.

With the passing of the Education Reform Act (1988) there is no question that there will be further significant developments within the system. The Act legislates for a National Curriculum, and at both the initial and in-service levels teacher training institutions are being mandated as to how they should prepare both student teachers and serving teachers to deliver (the word is used advisedly) the National Curriculum. In addition the Act will change significantly the way in which higher education institutions responsible for teacher training are both controlled and financed; these changes will affect both the nature and provision of teacher training. At the time of writing a keynote speech by the Secretary of State for Education (SEO, 1989) outlined a scenario in which local education authorities (which employ teachers and manage the education systems at local level) will play a much more prominent role in the initial and in-service training of teachers, which will become more school-based, while drawing upon rather than relying on the services of the teacher training institutions.

On the initial teacher training side a dramatic shift has been effected since 1984, as the government of the day has sought not only to control both the numbers and the distribution of student teacher training places within the higher education system, but also to prescribe the content of teacher training courses. The establishment of the Council for the Accreditation of Teacher Education was a radical move which enabled the Department of Education and Science (DES) to establish clear criteria by which teacher training courses must be judged prior to their formal approval by the Secretary of State for Education. More disturbingly and inconsistently, the very government which a few years ago laid down over thirty criteria which initial teacher training courses must adhere to is now advocating routes into teaching which do not require conventional forms of training.

On the in-service front there has been an equally dramatic shift in policy. The DES has implemented a system whereby it has shifted the money available for in-service teacher training away from the 'providing bodies', such as university or polytechnic departments of education and colleges of higher education (which used this resource so that they could staff and offer in-service awards ranging from short courses to the taught MA) and transferred this finance to the local education authorities (LEAs), which are the teachers' employers. As such, LEAs are required to establish in-service teacher training policies within their region in the light of their own and national priorities and the current training needs of their teaching force. Thus a 'market economy' has been created in which the employers, who have the financial resources for in-service teacher training, either make use of it themselves or turn to training institutions and ask them to mount courses which are relevant to their immediate needs. This policy has resulted in a drastic fall in the number of experienced teachers studying for award bearing courses such as Diplomas and Masters' degrees and a marked increase in the number of teachers taking short, school-focused courses which are seen to be directly relevant to changing classroom needs. The higher education system is responding in the main by modularizing its post-experience programs and introducing systems of credit transfer and accumulation. The aim is to provide a flexible structure which will enable serving teachers to attend a sequenced and structured program of modular courses which can be available either to meet their immediate professional needs or, over a period of time, provide credit accumulation leading to Advanced Diplomas or Masters' degrees.

While it will come as no surprise to the educational researcher, it must be a matter of regret and concern to report that these dramatic shifts in policy have been undertaken without reference to the available research on teacher training. Research may be alluded to on occasion if it justifies a policy decision which will be taken anyway. More disturbingly, the academic educationist or researcher may be denigrated in the most partial and unscholarly manner by the politically motivated commentator who pamphleteers in favour of a particular policy (cf. O'Hear, 1988).

The socio-political context has not provided a supportive environment for research into teacher training during the past few years. There have been few grants available from both public and private funding agencies, and the pattern is one of scattered, small-scale studies which have come about as a consequence of the conviction and ingenuity of individual scholars, rather than from a substantial national investment in research into teacher training.

Scope

This review updates and extends the other most recent surveys of the field (McNamara, 1984; Reid, 1985). The major conclusions which emerged from these reviews were that:

1 the available empirical studies were, in the main, small-scale exercises initiated by interested individual researchers using a variety of methodologies and without a clear substantive focus,

and that this corpus had yet to establish a secure knowledge base which could inform practice;

2   that the limited funds available for research on teacher training were increasingly controlled by the DES which directs funds to support policy-oriented studies or development projects which are in accord with government thinking;

3   that at a time when substantial changes were being planned for the structure and content of teacher training there was no indication that they would be monitored or evaluated or that any research findings would inform the debate;

4   that insofar as researchers had distinctive expertise or skill which could be of service to policy-makers they would, at best, be used to render teacher trainers accountable.

The review aims to cover all those studies which have a research base and which have been published in reasonably accessible formats in the United Kingdom since my previous review, which covered the decade from about 1973 to 1983. The many commentaries on teacher training, which probably exceed the number of empirical studies, are not included and no attempt is made to compete with reviews in specialist areas which have been published in the United Kingdom but which are based very much upon research undertaken overseas such as Boydell's (1986) review of teaching practice supervision research and the relevant articles in Dunkin (1986). The review does not claim to be definitive. A computer search of a well established, international database yielded only a couple of the studies reported. Most have been generated by scanning the appropriate journals and most likely sources.[2] The review is organized under a series of headings which reflect a somewhat stereotypic process model of teacher training, namely:

> student teacher selection and recruitment;
> the process of teacher training;
> school experience and supervision;
> school-based training;
> in-service training;
> institutional studies.

Student Selection and Recruitment

The Scottish Education Department sponsored a project which investigated selection procedures for student teachers in which Wilson and Mitchell (1985) used a team of trained assessors to observe potential students in a variety of situations. Seventy candidates for a four-year BEd course, the majority of whom were female, were interviewed and data were collected on their personal qualities, intellectual abilities and attitudes. Candidates were observed in leaderless discussion groups, given simulated teaching tasks and a traditional employment type of interview. The program demonstrated that it was feasible to establish a viable selection program but that its quality could be improved. This can only arise after long-term follow-up which provides feedback into the selection process.

Previous research has indicated that a teacher training institution's prospectus is an important factor which influences student choice. Hence McNamara (1986) undertook a content analysis of the pictorial information contained in the prospectuses of initial teacher training institutions. It was found that the image of teaching (namely, activity-oriented teaching in small groups in pleasant surroundings) conveyed by the prospectuses designed to recruit applicants on to initial teacher training courses was at variance with primary school practice as described by available survey evidence. It was suggested that teacher training institutions should include in their prospectuses pictorial information which portrays something of the huge variety and diversity of approaches to primary practice, and the challenges which are faced by teachers in today's schools.

The Process of Teacher Training

It is often advocated that student teachers should be exposed to different learning styles during their training. Meighan and Harber (1986) describe a case study in which students on a Post Graduate Certificate in Education course were given an opportunity to opt for different approaches to their learning. They could select one of the following approaches for their methods course: the authoritarian expert, in which the course was designed and directed by a tutor within a traditional mode; the authoritarian consultative, in which the course commenced with tutor direction but was modified in the light of feedback from students, with the gradual handing over of decision-making to them; and the democratic, in which course members organized a learning cooperative and devised and directed their own program of studies using tutors as a resource and as facilitators. The experience of implementing the democratic approach was described and evaluated; both students and tutors were required to adjust to different models of learning. Evaluation suggested that students did not regret having chosen the democratic mode; they felt confident and learned to develop their existing skills and acquire new ones. They developed confidence in their own thinking and were highly motivated. Students were also able to cope with teaching in the authoritarian schools which they typically encountered and acquired a vision of possible alternatives which enabled them to challenge the status quo in situations in which this was possible.

A number of studies have sought to extend students' perceptions during training. In the area of gender awareness Skelton (1987) observed that initial teacher training programs do little to promote student teachers' awareness of discriminatory practices in the classroom. She researched a primary Post Graduate Certificate in Education course in a college of education. Her findings, based upon qualitative data, showed that student teachers tended to absorb messages which, rather than dismantle views about gender discrimination, actually promoted it. Student teachers learned, via the hidden curriculum, that they should expect to find differences in the capabilities, attitudes and behaviour of boys and girls in the primary classroom. This information reinforced their present commonsense knowledge about boys and girls. This study provides an indication of why gender discrimination continues to be a feature of primary education.

In a more prescriptive report Jayne (1987) describes how one college aimed to make teachers in training more knowledgeable and skilled in providing equal educational opportunities for boys and girls at classroom level. The requirement to rewrite a primary teacher training program provided the opportunity to focus on increasing awareness, skills and practices concerned with sexual equality. The task involved not only changing course syllabuses but also implementing a program of staff development and investigating how, within a dynamic context, change can be brought about within teacher training courses. Qualitative evaluation suggested that the initiative had been worthwhile and involved staff as well as students in new learning experiences.

Russell-Gebbett (1984) sought to expand the professional contacts of postgraduate student teachers by developing a course on 'Children in Trouble', which was also attended by trainee social workers. The rationale for the course was that social workers and school teachers working with the same children seldom communicate effectively with one another. Subsequently the course was evaluated using attitude tests. The evidence indicated that the workshop, through the challenge of critical argument and problem-solving, encouraged trainee teachers to assess more realistically their roles in handling children in trouble and to see the complementarity of their own work to that of others in the field. The course also enabled individuals entering two different professions to meet and exchange views before prejudices and stereotypes were formed.

School Experience and Supervision

There is no neat division in the literature between school experience and supervision, but the first few studies reported in this section stress experience and those that follow supervision.

In two surveys Lawes (1987a, 1987b) has investigated student teachers' ability to decode pupils' non-verbal signals and their beliefs about non-verbal activity in the classroom. In the first investigation fifty-seven student teachers were asked to decode pupils' non-verbal signals displayed on video. Analysis indicated that student teachers whose teaching competence was rated as low also tended to be those who were poor at decoding pupils' non-verbal signals. The study suggests that certain personality traits may confound attempts to train some students to improve their non-verbal decoding skills. In the second study eighty-one students' beliefs about non-verbal activity in the classroom were assessed together with their awareness of their own non-verbal behaviour. This study also indicated that student teachers rated as competent were more aware of the importance of pupils' non-verbal activity and their own non-verbal behaviour. On a similar theme St J. Neill, Fitzgerald and Jones (1983) compared ninety-two student teachers' and ninety probationer teachers' awareness of non-verbal communication in the classroom. Again teachers rated as effective were more likely to mention the importance of non-verbal communication and probationer teachers were more aware of the importance of non-verbal communication than were students.

The salience of student teachers' subject specialism has been investigated by Calderhead and Miller (1986) who undertook detailed case studies of eight students to explore the process whereby subject matter knowledge informed their classroom practice. It was found that the students themselves valued their own high-level subject matter knowledge and made use of it in their lesson planning. However, their practical teaching was hardly influenced by subject knowledge and was based more upon direct practical experience and observation of and discussion with other teachers.

In a qualitative study Calderhead (1987) followed ten students through their field experiences during their training year to investigate the importance of 'reflection' in learning to teach and the role of tutors in promoting it. The students' capacity to think reflectively about practice quickly reached a plateau and was constrained by situational factors in the classroom. This study has been followed up by Calderhead (1988) with an investigation of what twenty-seven student teachers learned from their introductory school experience. Substantial efforts were made by tutors and teachers to structure and standardize the school experience for all students but, even so, it took different forms offering qualitatively different types of professional learning. Factors contributing to the variety of experience included the student teachers' conceptions of professional learning and of their own role, their supervising teachers and tutors, and organizational features of the school.

Mansfield (1986) investigated the supervisor's role during school practice. Previous work in the institution in question indicated that there was a disjunction between supervisors' aims and what students actually practised in the schools. In particular, supervisors claimed that the critical analysis of lessons was important but it rarely occurred; there was a dearth of demonstrations of good practice by supervisors; and while supervisors stressed the importance of good practice, in fact they paid closer attention to class teaching situations. The study explored the potential for encouraging supervisors to become more involved with students in joint teaching so as to heighten consideration of pedagogical issues. In the event, it was found that supervisors were constrained by the lack of clear frameworks for developing students' pedagogic skills and their efforts were hampered by the difficulties of presenting students with critical information in the emotionally charged situation of the practice classroom.

The transatlantic reader may be interested in surveys of American students acquiring school experience in Britain. Mahan and Stachowski (1987) investigated a project which places American students in English, Scottish and Irish schools for school practice. They obtained survey information from thirty course directors responsible for the scheme. In general, the professional strengths of the American student teachers were seen to be that they were socially adept and developed good relationships with pupils and school staff. They were pleasant, friendly, polite and outgoing. They were usually mature and capable individuals who were seen to be confident, adaptable and to have enthusiasm and keenness. However, there were sometimes problems with language differences and a lack of cultural sensitivity or understanding of the host educational system. The evidence indicates that the program is successful in promoting insight, sensitivity and understanding between the USA and the host country. Barnes and Hunter (1985) report an investigation in which successive cohorts of students from an American university undertook supervised teaching practice in schools in northern England over a five-year period. The essential finding was that for the American students there was a dichotomy between the child-centred education they encountered in schools and their wish to control children through behaviour modification. It was suggested that the students' own experience of American schools and their professional training socialized them into accepting an ideology of competitive individualism supported by psychological theories of behaviourism.

Smith and Tomlinson (1984) evaluated novel procedures for tutors to assist trainee teachers during actual teaching activity. Radio Assisted Practice (RAP) involves the use of miniature radio transmitters and receivers to enable a tutor to communicate directly with a student while he or she is practising in the classroom. The paper describes the methodology and the theoretical approach which underpins it, and a pilot study based upon work with eight students. RAP is seen as a flexible technique whose central contribution to teacher training is the integration of insight and action in the enhancement of intelligent skills. It enables tutors to intervene directly so as to help the trainee to develop skills actively. Students responded very positively to this approach.

School-based Training

The hiatus between theory and practice is an enduring issue for teacher trainers and a few institutions have established innovatory school-based teacher training programs in an attempt to reconcile training and school-based competence.

The DES, which is particularly interested in this model of training, sponsored four training institutions to enable them to cooperate with local education authorities to develop school-based, one-year professional courses. They were all given the freedom to decide what 'school-based' meant and to devise their own courses. The innovations and the evaluation research associated with the project are reported by Furlong, Hirst, Pocklington and Miles (1988). The initial aim of the evaluation was to compare the school-based courses with conventional approaches, but during the course of the research the brief changed and became one in which the research team sought to clarify the principles of school-based training. Rather than generate comparative, evaluative date, the study is used to explore the policy implications of school-based training for schools and training institutions. The authors make a distinction between four levels of training, namely:

Level (a) 'Direct practice' — practical training through direct experience in schools and classrooms;

Level (b) 'Indirect practice' — detached training in practical matters usually conducted in classes or workshops in training institutions;

Level (c) 'Practical principles' — the critical study of the principles of practice and their use;

Level (d) 'Disciplinary theory' — the critical study of practice and its principles in the light of fundamental theory and research.

It is claimed that traditionally teacher training courses have provided students with instruction in levels (b), (c) and (d) before they entered the schools to undertake (a). It is proposed that, in future, if beginning teachers are to become reflective practitioners, level (a) training must be at the heart of their preparation and the other levels of training used increasingly to develop informed critical reflection so that they may develop as effective practitioners. Training must start from classroom practice set within a context which ensures that theoretical training is accorded its proper professional significance. (At the time of writing this approach is generating considerable interest among all parties associated with teacher training.)

A report which attracted considerable interest because of its implications for policy is Maclennan and Seadon's (1988) evaluation of a one-year teacher training program in which fifteen students were all based in a comprehensive school for the year. The experience and evaluation of this school-based model led the sponsors to abandon the scheme after one year. The students were placed in an ambiguous position; they were neither students nor 'real' teachers. The demands upon the supervising teachers were such that they felt unable to repeat the experiment. The logistics of running the course were too complex and students missed the initial security and support of a university-based course.

Tickle (1987), in one of the few studies located in a coherent theoretical framework, conjectured that practical knowledge is at the heart of the teaching enterprise and the key to professional credibility. In order that this notion could be treated in a serious manner to effect improvements in teacher training, he devised a predominantly school-based training course. Students were considered to be self-motivated learners and they worked with supervisors and serving teachers who continued to enhance their own professional competence through school-based research. The practical product stemming from this research is the development of a 'professional preparation document' which sets out the characteristics of professional development which are considered important in the work of student teachers. The document has a diagnostic and formative purpose and it clarifies and makes explicit what is expected of student teachers so as to aid discussion with them about their practice.

In-service Training

During the late 1980s the most substantial and adequately funded surveys of in-service training have been associated with educational initiatives sponsored by a government agency, the Manpower Services Commission, which in a word have attempted to introduce vocationally oriented curricula into secondary schools based upon methods of active learning. A substantial corpus of literature has been produced but its value for an international audience may be limited. A useful entree for the general enquirer is the Manpower Services Commission (1987) report. Within this corpus Eraut, Pennychick and Radnor (1988), which describes a meta-evaluation, may be of particular value to the researcher who is interested in the methodology of evaluation research and McIntyre and Jenkins' (1988) and Hall and Oldroyd's (1988) reports on the development of individual teachers, the management of professional development and the application of the findings derived from the innovations may be of some interest to those who have to devise and manage in-service programs. (see also Oldroyd and Hall, 1988).

Smaller-scale studies include Lynch and Burn's (1984) comparison between serving teachers who did or did not attend in-service courses. The main reasons why teachers were not prepared to attend in-service courses were that they did not wish to give up their own time, they had little opportunity for doing so, it was too tiring after school, they lacked financial support or time, and there was no incentive or encouragement. A particularly worrying finding was the large number of teachers who claimed that they did not need in-service education. The main reasons for attending in-service courses were to improve promotion prospects, a desire to improve knowledge or enhance self-esteem, improve teaching skills, and financial motivation.

Hargreaves and Grey (1983) evaluated a part-time, in-service degree which was committed to heightening teachers' awareness and consciousness about their professional activities. An essential aim was to enable teachers to become critical and carry out research into their own classroom practices so as to find effective solutions. However, the evaluation indicated that teachers did not make particular use of the processes and perspectives they acquired on the degree course.

Miller (1988) surveyed 250 science teachers who did not have qualifications in physics but who taught this subject. He aimed to identify their perceptions of their difficulties in teaching physics so as to identify priorities for in-service training. His findings led him to propose that in-service physics courses should be school-based and grounded in a constructivist model of pupils' learning in schools.

Institutional Studies

This section includes those studies which have taken a broader view and studied teacher training within an institutional context or related teacher training to subsequent professional activity. The first four studies described were funded by the only substantial allocation of grants to teacher training research during the past few years when in 1985 the Economic and Social Research Council (ESRC) made available £250,000 as part of a teacher training initiative.[3]

Nias (1987) investigated why and how headteachers and non-teaching staff in medium-sized primary schools worked productively together, paying particular attention to leadership characteristics, formal and informal roles and structures, the nature and process of the staff group and the culture of the school. The aim was to acquire insights which could be incorporated into the content and pedagogy of initial and in-service teacher education programs. The research was based upon case studies in five schools. Leadership was identified as the crucial variable, and the findings of this research have implications for the professional education of all staff at both the initial and in-service levels which, in brief, are that promoting effective, educational practice requires head-teachers to develop a 'culture of collaboration' in which individual teachers should be treated as valued members of a professional group which is open and fosters the exchange of ideas and which also respects the security of the individual.

Poppleton (1987) investigated teacher professional satisfaction and its implications for secondary education and teacher training in a survey which acquired quantitative data from 1200 teachers in twenty schools, supplemented with qualitative data based upon group interviews with 150 teachers in the sample schools. The study researched the perceptions of a sample of teachers in comprehensive schools with reference to the factors contributing to their sense of professional satisfaction. These included: working conditions, work activities, relationships with pupils, colleagues and relevant social and professional groups. Particular attention was paid to the experience and perceptions of two subgroups of teachers: those in the first five years of their careers and those who were working in social priority schools. The implications for initial teacher training of drawing schools and teachers more closely into the whole process of training were examined. A general conclusion was that the concepts and practices of partnership in teacher education have not been delivered to teachers in forms which carry conviction, and that teachers' contractual arrangements need to be reassessed if teachers are to be convinced that they have a vital role to play in professional preparation.

Booth (1987) investigated two interrelated areas, the first being the theoretical understanding of the teaching and learning of history within institutions concerned with training specialist secondary teachers, and the second being the secondary school-based experience and training that students receive in teaching methods. Case studies were undertaken of two history methods courses and data were collected through semi-structured interviews and observations. Observations were also made of students and tutors working together in schools. In addition there was a questionnaire study. Major themes emerging were that a crucial factor was evaluation and reflection on classroom practice and that students were unable to develop professional expertise without regular supervision which focused primarily on pupils' learning. The research showed, however, that school supervisors, who were largely responsible for students for at least one-third of the course, varied greatly in the perceptions which they had of their role. There is a strong recommendation that there is a need for supervisors in schools and tutors in training institutions to receive training themselves in student supervision.

Patrick (1987) studied the aims of teaching history in secondary schools. The project focused on the nature of the history teaching to which students were introduced during their training. Although most students had a background of fairly traditional history teaching, by the end of the course most expressed approval for the 'new' history and for using a variety of teaching methods. A questionnaire survey was also undertaken of schools where history students were located for teaching practice. The majority of students were placed in schools where teachers were broadly sympathetic to the views of students. An observation study undertaken while working on case studies was used for designing a systematic observation schedule for analyzing history lessons. It is suggested that it could become a useful tool for teachers and students wishing to analyze their practice.

A significant proportion of British teacher training is located within voluntary church colleges of higher education which are governed by and, in part, funded by religious foundations. Given that (1) the state provides the greater proportion of the funding; (2) the proportion provided by the churches is a considerable drain upon their limited resources; and (3) some church colleges have been absorbed within other higher education institutions in recent years, the contribution of the voluntary colleges has been under scrutiny of late. On this matter Gay, Kay, Perry and Lazenby (1986) report a substantial research program into teacher training in institutions supported by the Church of England which addressed the question: 'what justification can validly be put forward for the retention of the Anglican colleges in the 1980s and beyond?' The research is premised upon a theological rationale for the future of the Anglican colleges, and is located within sociological models of institutions. A huge data set was acquired from some 760 individuals working in Anglican colleges including principals, staff and students. The report describes the institutions and their work; provides information about students and their expections and experiences, and academic staff, their training, background and future expectations; and considers the colleges' roles and their objectives, with particular reference to teacher education. The report concludes by proposing that what differentiates the Anglican colleges from other training institutions is the nature of their foundation and the expectation that they should display certain Christian qualities and fulfil a Christian role.

Discussion

The studies reviewed in this chapter amount to a somewhat eclectic corpus which demonstrates no distinctive theoretical or methodological trends or substantive focus for investigation, beyond a methodological emphasis on case studies employing qualitative methodologies and, on the substantive side, a disposition to investigate the relationship between teacher training and subsequent classroom practice so as to generate recommendations which will foster reflective practice. The impetus for many of the reported studies seems to be the individual interests and concerns of the investigators. A striking instance is the studies which received substantial grants from the ESRC. The major proportion of the funding went to two teams investigating history teaching in secondary schools. There is no doubt that history teaching is important, but it is not at present, with the advent of the National Curriculum, at the forefront of the educational agenda. Hence it is hardly surprising to report that there is no indication that national policy on teacher training is being informed by research findings. At best, protagonists for or against a particular policy invoke research evidence ex post facto in order to support their case.

There is another reason why research has not and indeed will not have an impact upon policy and practice. It is now appreciated by educationists in general (Desforges and McNamara, 1979) that if research is to inform educational practice, it must recognize and be located within the context of the real time constraints in which teaching and learning take place. This is equally true for teacher training research. Teacher educators are busy people with demanding and time-consuming workloads. If research is to inform their practice, it must produce research which recognizes the 'real world' of teacher training and generate information and procedures which teacher trainers can use within that context.

Ironically, it must be reported that there is a group of publications which, while they do not constitute research in the accepted sense and, indeed, make no claim to do so, are having a substantial influence upon the direction of teacher training in Britain. These are the surveys under-taken by Her Majesty's Inspectors (HMI), which are based upon HMI visits to institutions and their collection of information. However, the reports tend to be partial in their approach, fail to reveal their databases, and appear to provide the information which policy-makers wish to hear. From the point of view of the researcher the most informative of these reports is the Department of Education and Science (1987) survey of twenty-six public sector teacher training institutions which provides a substantial amount of detailed statistical information about the institu-tions and describes the various ways in which student teachers are trained. A subsequent report on teacher training in the university sector (Department of Education and Science, 1988a) is more impressionistic and prescriptive. The relationships between initial teacher training and the first year of teaching are commented upon in another HMI survey (De-partment of Education and Science, 1988b). One must report, *sotto voce*, that the policy recommendations stemming from these surveys, the quali-ty of which has concerned educationists, have been endorsed by the Secretary of State for Education and commended to teacher training institutions. The American reader may be interested in the latest HMI report which is based upon a visit to New Jersey to examine the state's scheme for 'on-the-job' teacher training for graduates (Department of Education and Science, 1989). The Inspectorate manage to note aspects of this scheme which are convenient for policy-makers in this country anxious to cope with a shortfall in teacher supply, but fail to report what others may see as serious concerns about the quality of training.

In sum, if one poses the question: 'what has research on teacher training been about in Britain during the past few years?', the hard-headed answer must be: 'it has been about individual researchers, or small teams, pursuing themes which are of intellectual or professional interest to themselves and which they judge to be important.' The somewhat eclectic nature of this activity has not lent itself to the accretion of a sustained set of research findings which have informed policy. During the same period Her Majesty's Inspectors have visited teacher training institu-tions and acquired information and presented it in such a way that it is in tune with the beliefs of politicians and policy-makers and can be taken by them to legitimate teacher training policies which they wish to pursue.

The awkward question must, therefore, be faced: will educational researchers have a contribution to make concerning the future of teacher training or are they at best irritating critics and at worst redundant? It is suggested that there is a role for researchers if they are prepared to give their endeavours a different focus. Much of the British research on teacher training has been concerned with policy issues and shaped by social scientists who are interested in the structure, function and processes of institutions. These are, of course, important themes, but since researchers lack the effective authority necessary to change policy or institutions, they should recognize that their contribution on this front can be no more than that of the marginal critic. They should redirect their attention to the content of teacher training programs and the essential role of the teacher, which is to transmit knowledge and skills. At a time when the government is introducing a National Curriculum in order, it is claimed, to improve the quality of education but is, at the same time, silent on how the aforesaid National Curriculum will, in fact, enhance the quality of teaching and learning in schools, there is a key remit for the researchers. Drawing upon recent work in the USA, which stresses the importance of investigating teachers' pedagogical competence within the context of teaching subject matter (see, for example, Shulman, 1987) and optimizing learning tasks (see, for example, Doyle 1986), there is a twofold agenda for the researcher: on the one hand, to investigate how teacher training can be improved so as to enhance the ability of students to transmit their own understanding of subject matter into effective classroom practices; and, on the other hand, to act as social critics and evaluate the impact of an imposed National Curriculum upon the quality of children's education and also upon the morale and practices of teachers and the nature of the preparation they receive in training institutions.

Notes

1 Throughout this chapter 'teacher training' should be taken to embrace 'teacher training and education'.
2 Grateful thanks are due to the University of Durham Library staff who have provided valuable bibliographic support.
3 The major published accounts of this corpus of research are only now in the process of becoming available.

References

BARNES, L.R. and HUNTER, J.K. (1985) American students teach in English primary schools: A conflict of educational ideologies? *Journal of Education for Teaching*, 11, 1, 77–91.
BOOTH, M.B. (1987) *ESRC End of Award Report. Reference No. C0925 0005.* Available from ESRC.
BOYDELL, D. (1986) Issues in teaching practice supervision research: A review of the literature. *Teaching and Teacher Education*, 2, 2, 115–125.
CALDERHEAD, J. (1987) The quality of reflection in student teachers' professional learning. *European Journal of Teacher Education*, 10, 3, 269–278.

CALDERHEAD, J. (1988) Learning from introductory school experience. *Journal of Education for Teaching*, 14, 1, 75–83.

CALDERHEAD, J. and MILLER, E. (1986) *The Integration of Subject Matter Knowledge in Student Teachers Classroom Practice*. Research Monograph Series. Lancaster: University of Lancaster, School of Education.

Department of Education and Science (1987) *Quality in Schools: The Initial Training of Teachers. A Survey of Initial Teacher Training in the Public Sector in England, Northern Ireland and Wales, Carried Out by H.M.I. and the Inspectorate in Northern Ireland*. London: HMSO.

Department of Education and Science (1988a) *Education Observed 7: Initial Teacher Training in Universities in England, Northern Ireland and Wales*. London: HMSO.

Department of Education and Science (1988b) *The New Teacher in School: A Survey by HM Inspectors in England and Wales, 1987*. London: HMSO.

Department of Education and Science (1989) 'The Provisional Teacher Program in New Jersey.' Paper by Her Majesty's Inspectorate. London: HMSO.

DESFORGES, C. and McNAMARA, D. (1979) Theory and practice: Methodological procedures for the objectification of craft knowledge. *British Journal of Teacher Education*, 5, 2, 145–152.

DOYLE, W. (1986) Content representation in teachers' definitions of academic work. *Journal of Curriculum Studies*, 18, 4, 365–379.

DUNKIN, M.J. (Ed.) (1986) *The International Encyclopedia of Teaching and Teacher Education*. Oxford: Pergamon Press.

Education Reform Act (1988) Chapter 40. London: HMSO.

ERAUT, M., PENNYCHICK, D. and RADNOR, H. (1988) *Local Evaluation of INSET: A Meta-Evaluation of TRIST Evaluations*. Bristol: Manpower Services Commission and National Development Centre for School Management Training.

FURLONG, V.J., HIRST, P.H., POCKLINGTON, K. and MILES, S. (1988) *Initial Teacher Training and the Role of the School*. Milton Keynes: Open University Press.

GAY, J., KAY, B., PERRY, G. and LAZENBY, D. (1986) *The Future of the Anglican Colleges: Final Report of the Church Colleges Research Project*. Abingdon, Oxfordshire: Culham College Institute. (Included in the *Report* are references to interim working papers and other papers referring to the future of the Anglican colleges.)

HALL, V., and OLDROYD, D. (1988) *Managing Inset in Local Education Authorities: Applying Conclusions from TRIST*. Bristol: Manpower Services Commission and National Development Centre for School Management Training.

HARGREAVES, J. and GREY, S. (1983) Changing teachers' practice: Innovation and ideology in a part-time B.Ed. course. *Journal of Education for Teaching*, 9, 2, 161–183.

JAYNE, E. (1987) A case study of implementing equal opportunities: Sex equity. *Journal of Education for Teaching*, 13, 2, 155–162.

LAWES, J.S. (1987a) Student teachers' awareness of pupils' non-verbal responses. *Journal of Education for Teaching*, 13, 3, 257–266.

LAWES, J.S. (1987b) The relationship between non-verbal awareness of self and teaching competence in student teachers. *Journal of Education for Teaching*, 13, 2, 147–154.

LYNCH, J. and BURNS, B. (1984) Non-attenders at INSET functions: Some comparisons with attenders. *Journal of Education for Teaching*, 10, 2, 164–177.

MCINTYRE, A. and JENKINS, C. (1988) *Recording and Accrediting the In-service Training and Development of Individual Teachers: Summary Research Report.* London: HMSO.

MACLENNAN, S. and SEADON, T. (1988) What price school based work? Reflections on a school sited PGCE method course. *Cambridge Journal of Education*, 18, 3, 387–403.

MCNAMARA, D. (1984) Research in teacher education: The past decade and future trends, in R.J. ALEXANDER *et al.* (Eds) *Change in Teacher Education: Context and Provision since Robbins.* London: Holt, Rinehart and Winston.

MCNAMARA, D. (1986) Prospectus for teaching: A misleading image, *Journal of Education for Teaching*, 11, 1, 25–33.

MAHAN, J.M. and STACHOWSKI, L.L. (1987) Feedback from British and Irish educators for improving overseas teaching experiences. *Journal of Education for Teaching*, 13, 1, 29–47.

Manpower Services Commission (1987) *Paper of National Interest 6: TRIST Regional Network, New Approaches to Teaching and Learning.* London: Technical Vocational Education Initiative Unit.

MANSFIELD, P.A. (1986) Patchwork pedagogy: A case study of supervisors' emphasis on pedagogy in post-lesson conference. *Journal of Education for Teaching*, 12, 3, 259–271.

MEIGHAN, R. and HARBER, C. (1986) Democratic learning in teacher education: A review of experience at one institution. *Journal of Education for Teaching*, 12, 2, 163–172.

MILLER, R. (1988) Teaching physics as a non-specialist: The in-service training of science teachers. *Journal of Education for Teaching*, 14, 1, 39–53.

NIAS, D.J. (1987) in *End of Award Report from ESRC Reference C0925 0003.* (Economic and Social Research Council, 160 Great Portland Street, London W1N 6Dt). (The research will be more comprehensively reported in J. NIAS and R. YEOMANS, forthcoming, *Understanding the Primary School as an Organisation*, to be published by Cassell.)

O'HEAR, A. (1988) *Who Teaches the Teachers?* Research Report 10. London: Social Affairs Unit.

OLDROYD, D. and HALL, V. (1988) *Managing Professional Development for INSET: A Handbook for Schools and Colleges.* Bristol: Manpower Services Commission and National Development Centre for School Management Training.

PATRICK, H. (1987) in *End of Award Report, Reference No. C0925 0006.* (A mimeographed report, Helen Patrick, 1987, *The Aims of Teaching History in Secondary Schools*, is published by the University of Leicester School of Education as an occasional paper.)

POPPLETON, P.K. (1987) in *End of Award Report. Reference No. C0925 0004.* (A book based upon the project is in preparation: P.K. POPPLETON and G.F. RISEBOROUGH, forthcoming, *The Social World of Teachers and Teaching: A Study of Teachers' Career Experiences*, to be published by Falmer Press.)

REID, K. (1985) Recent research and development in teacher education in England and Wales, in D. HOPKINS and K. REID (Eds) *Rethinking Teacher Education.* London: Croom Helm.

RUSSELL-GEBBETT, J. (1984) Working with children in trouble: An interprofessional approach to the training of teachers and social workers, *Journal of Education for Teaching*, 10, 1, 73–81.

St J. NEILL, S.R., FITZGERALD, J.M. and JONES, R. (1983) The relation between reported awareness of non-verbal communication and rated effectiveness in probationer and student teacher. *Journal of Education for Teaching*, 9, 1, 16–29.

SEO (1989) Managing the teaching force. *Education*, 173, 5, 105–107.

SHULMAN, L.S. (1987) Knowledge and teaching: Foundations of the new reform. *Harvard Educational Review*, 57, 1, 1–22.

SKELTON, C. (1987) A study of gender discrimination in a primary programme of teacher training. *Journal of Education for Teaching*, 13, 2, 163–175.

SMITH, R. and TOMLINSON, P. (1984) Radio-assisted practice: Preliminary investigations of a new technique in teacher education. *Journal of Education for Teaching*, 10, 2, 119–134.

TICKLE, L. (1987) *Learning Teaching, Teaching Teaching: A Study of Partnership in Teacher Education.* Lewes: Falmer Press.

WILSON, J.D. and MITCHELL, L (1985) Developing a programme for selecting primary teachers. *Journal of Education for Teaching*, 11, 3, 264–280.

Chapter 9

Indian Research in Teacher Education: A Review

R. Govinda and M.B. Buch

By its very nature the teacher education system must maintain a symbiotic relationship with the school system. However, this appears to be incompatible with what we see taking place. On the one hand, it should help in maintaining the school system by preparing teachers who can effectively discharge their duties within existing realities. On the other hand, teacher education should bring about desirable changes in the prevalent practices of pedagogy and school organization. For this, teacher education must train teachers who are creative, who can initiate innovative trends and transform the existing system of education in a progressive manner. Thus teacher education has simultaneously to operate in the real as well as the ideal world. It is not uncommon to come across criticisms of the teacher education system for its failure to prepare teachers for the actualities of schooling. But a program which is totally rooted in the existing realities of the school will be criticized as being non-progressive and hence adhering to the status quo. Teacher education in India is caught up in this tension of trying to achieve these apparently incompatible and contradictory goals. Obviously, researchers in the field of teacher education cannot escape the dilemma. They have to perform this difficult task of holding the real and the ideal in a state of countervailing balance.

As well as being entangled in this complex situation, educational research in India has a relatively recent origin. Yet the amount of educational research done is quite impressive, particularly in teacher education. This chapter analyzes the research in teacher education carried out in India during the last decade or so. The presentation is divided into three sections: a brief overview of the existing organizational set-up for teacher education in the country; a quantitative picture of research in teacher education suitably classified under different headings; and an attempt to draw the broad trends of findings and conclusions emerging from the research surveyed. A few final observations regarding the nature of research carried out conclude the chapter.

Teacher Education in India

The teacher education system in India has to serve more than 670,000 primary schools and about 65,000 secondary schools. Over 3.7 million teachers work in these schools. To cater for their trained manpower needs, India has about 1200 primary teacher education institutions and about 500 secondary teacher education institutions spread all over the country. But these institutions are not uniformly placed across different regions of the country. This creates a surplus of teachers in some areas, and shortages in others. The country also has a sizeable number of institutions which offer teacher training programs through correspondence; most of these programs are for those already teaching in secondary schools or aspiring to become secondary teachers.

Pre-service teacher education consists of two tiers. In the first tier institutions provide training to primary school teachers. These institutions normally admit those who have successfully completed ten years of schooling and passed the secondary school certificate examination. During the last few years, however, the entry requirement has been revised in many places and requires entrants to have completed twelve years of education and to possess a higher/senior secondary certificate. The course consists of two years of full-time training leading to a Diploma in Education/Primary Teachers Certificate. The program comprises coursework and teaching practice. Teacher training at the primary level does not involve any specialized areas of training. Normally all students go through the same set of courses. The second tier of teacher education provides pre-service training to potential secondary school teachers. In most places a bachelor's degree is required to enter these institutions. However, in reality a large number of entrants hold master's degrees as candidates have to face tough competition for admission to these institutions. The one-year training program provides graduates with a Bachelor of Education. The program consists of courses in the foundations of education, in teaching areas and optional courses. Students also have practice in teaching where they are required to give about twenty-five to thirty lessons to secondary school classes in their areas of subject specialization. While this is the general pattern adopted in almost all the institutions, a few institutions offer a four-year integrated program of secondary teacher training. These institutions admit qualified higher secondary students and offer a four-year degree of Bachelor of Education in special subject areas such as science, arts and technology.

The secondary teacher education program is considered a higher education program and is organized by the university system. The curricula for the courses are framed and degrees are given by the various universities. The primary teacher training program falls outside the purview of the university system.

While this suggests a fairly widespread network for pre-service teacher training, the situation is not particularly encouraging with respect to arrangements for in-service programs of teacher education. The institutional arrangement for in-service education is very fragile and hardly capable of meeting the continuing education needs of millions of teachers working in the schools at different levels. To meet the needs of primary teachers, a network of Continuing Education Centres has been created. The number of teachers that each Centre services, however, is so large that they meet neither their demands nor the financial requirements that ensue. Currently a way around these problems is being made by creating District Institutes of Education and Training which can more effectively handle the task of providing in-service training to primary school teachers.

The situation with respect to in-service education facilities for secondary school teachers is no better. The existing arrangement is a relatively small number of Extension Services Units located within some of the secondary teacher education institutions. As a follow-up of the National Policy on Education adopted in 1986, attempts are afoot to create a better mechanism for the in-service training of secondary school teachers as well.

The following review of research on teacher education highlights the trends observed in the studies completed during the last decade. While the observations have been derived from a close examination of more than 100 studies conducted during this period, they do not make explicit reference to all these studies. The review is based on two types of studies, namely, institution-based research projects and doctoral research studies conducted by individual scholars. Abstracts of all these studies can be found in the volumes on research in education edited by Buch.[1]

A Quantitative Overview

Nearly 150 studies on teacher education have been conducted during the last decade. Surprisingly, more than four-fifths of these address teacher education at the secondary level. Only sixteen studies focus exclusively on the training of primary school teachers. A few others deal with both primary and secondary teacher education. Only eighteen of these studies have in-service teacher education as their main concern. The situation obviously represents a lack of balance in perspective and priorities considering the nature of the problems that teacher education is now facing. Very likely the reason for this emphasis is that most of the researchers are teachers and scholars attached to secondary teacher education institutions. The immediate possibility of easy access to data sources could have prompted them to take up studies on secondary teacher education.

Regarding topic, the studies fall into four subject areas. About one-third of the studies have teaching as their main focus. Even among these most deal with micro-teaching and teaching skills within the broad framework of behaviour modification technology. A small number attempt to carry out comparative and cross-sectional analysis of the system of practice-in-teaching adopted in different parts of the country. The second set of studies, roughly about 30 per cent, can be called system-level studies focused on a broad spectrum analysis of the programs of teacher education prevalent in different parts of the country. Though quite sizeable, they do not represent a cogent perspective because of their variety. A third set of studies, constituting about 20 per cent, analyzes the characteristics of student teachers. They use a largely socio-psychological framework and many try to study the interrelationship among different characteristics including academic performance. The fourth set includes institutional studies which deal with topics such as organizational climate and innovative practices, with a few studies on such topics as admission procedures, evaluation techniques and institutional case studies. This group comprises about 15 per cent of the research efforts.

Methodological Dimensions

A variety of methods and techniques has been used by the researchers even though a few of them have been adopted more often than others. Obviously, the methodology adopted is closely linked with the nature of the topic being studied. A fairly large number of studies have used experimental techniques. A closer look at these shows that many are experiments carried out in real classroom conditions rather than under simulated conditions. Several of these experiments are concerned with comparing the effectiveness of micro-teaching or different models of teaching or different approaches to integration of teaching skills with the conventional method of training (Lalitha, 1981; Passi, Singh and Sansanwal, 1986a, 1986b; Dave, 1987). It should be noted, however, that the ideas of skill-based teaching, micro-teaching techniques for training of teachers, or different models of teaching, have been conceived within the parameters of particular theoretical paradigms. Unfortunately, many of the researchers, in their enthusiasm for experimental comparisons, have lost sight of these basic theoretical considerations. Consequently, their interpretation of results, both in methodological rigour and conceptual perspective, tends to be weak.

Survey studies constitute a second type of research. Among these two categories can be identified. One category of studies consists of questionnaire-based surveys such as those conducted by M. Sharma (1982), Hemambujam (1983), Misra (1986) and Mohanty (1984), wherein the questionnaires have been prepared by the researchers themselves according to the objectives of the study. The other category of survey studies (e.g., Aggarwal, 1980; Raina, 1981; Patil, 1984; and Laverne, 1985), which focuses on student characteristics, institutional climate or the personality of teacher educators, depends on standardized instruments on personality, intelligence, teacher morale, organizational climate and so on. A few studies try to adopt such techniques as content analysis, case studies or a historical method. But these are very few and far between; they depend mostly on secondary courses and are confined to chronological and quantitative analyses.

Two major observations can be made regarding the methods of research adopted by scholars in the field of teacher education. The first relates to the use of statistical techniques of data analysis. One finds that researchers in education have invariably adopted sophisticated techniques of analysis such as multiple regression, analysis of variance or factor analysis. But in analyzing the nature of the problems explored, it seems doubtful whether the use of sophisticated techniques has really produced greater insight into the subjects under investigation. The second observation, which follows from the first, is the neglect of qualitative methods of research in studies of teacher education. Teacher education provides ample opportunities for using such qualitative methods as content analysis, participant observation and case study techniques. It appears to be time that educational researchers grew out of their dependence on a limited set of quantitative techniques and broadened their horizons by adopting relevant qualitative approaches to data analysis.

Trends of Findings and Conclusions

Though the lack of studies conducted in different areas precludes un-
equivocal answers to the questions explored, this section attempts to
identify the broad trends from the more than 100 studies reviewed.

Status of Teacher Education Programs

Several researchers have tried to analyze the overall status of teacher
education in the country — its growth and development, current status,
and problems and issues involved. Some of these have traced the development of the system through a historical perspective, but generally the
emphasis has been to survey the current status. Goyal and Chopra (1979)
analyzed the program in relation to the school curriculum, and found that
the teacher education program failed to reflect the changes and revisions
introduced in the school curriculum. Even though physical education,
health and art education were considered to form an integral part of the
school curriculum, they were not properly reflected in the teacher education program. Pathak (1979) made an analytical survey of a large number
of teacher education institutions and revealed that more than 80 per cent
of teacher educators were males and that the proportion of women
students from rural areas was less than 30 per cent. Many studies have
shown that the absence of women teachers has a negative impact on the
attendance of girls in rural schools. Pathak also reported that, by and
large, teacher educators did not hold favourable attitudes towards the
teaching profession. Mohan (1980) conducted a survey of twelve teacher
education institutions and identified several problems affecting the functioning of the teacher education program. On average, the institutions
functioned for only 118 days, partly because admission procedures were
too complex, taking more than two months of the academic year. Dubey
(1981) pointed out that the fieldwork component was underemphasized
in the teacher education program. Also development of skills related to
out-of-class activities and school management needed greater attention.
M. Sharma (1982) studied the course content of the teacher education
program followed in different universities of the country, and observed
considerable diversity in the stated objectives of the program as well as in
its theoretical and practical components.

    Hemambujam (1983) conducted a critical analysis of the teacher
education program at the secondary level in the state of Tamilnadu, a
relatively advanced area in terms of educational development; he found
the lack of coordination among practising schools and colleges of education the major problem. Whereas the course inputs were considered

appropriate for developing professional skills particularly related to classroom instruction, they did not adequately help in strengthening the content mastery of the student teachers in teaching subjects. The course organization did not provide adequate time to the teacher educators for interacting with their students or give necessary guidance to them. Kakkad (1983) analyzed the syllabi prescribed for pre-service teacher education in twenty-four different universities along with the framework suggested by the Indian Association of Teacher Educators and the National Council of Teacher Education. Opinions were collected from teacher educators for the construction of a revised program based on the analysis. They considered that an internship program of three months was necessary to make the component of practice teaching effective; student teachers should be required to specialize in teaching two school subjects; and suitable training should be given for carrying out action research projects in real classroom settings so that innovative practices learned during the pre-service program are put to use and suitably adapted in their future work.

A large-scale survey for three consecutive years covering 3863 student teachers was conducted by Pillai and Mohan (1985) with a view to discovering the factors that motivated student teachers to take up teaching. However, an objective analysis of the responses to the questionnaire would make one feel that the responses were guided more by concern for social acceptability than by real intentions. It would have been more apt to adopt a qualitative approach, involving interviews and participatory discussions, to find out the real motivating factors. Gupta (1985) conducted a survey covering forty-seven colleges of education and reported that in terms of facilities and problems involved relative uniformity existed among all the colleges surveyed.

A few researchers have tried to analyze the system through institution-centred studies. For instance, Bhatnagar (1979) studied the organizational climate of secondary teacher education institutions and reported that they were characterized by a high level of hindrance, authoritarianism, high academic emphasis, low level of discipline and control, and lack of facilities. Jangira (1982) surveyed thirty-three teacher training institutions at the primary level, focusing on the social cohesion status of these institutions. It was reported that the institutions varied considerably on this aspect and also that social cohesion had a significant impact on student teacher achievement. The study by Kalla (1984) adopted a different approach for understanding the institutional dimensions. An in-depth case study of an institution of long standing was conducted which highlighted the dynamics involved in the institutional development process.

One finds very few studies which focus on the impact of teacher education programs. Sharma (1980) studied the effectiveness of pre-service teacher training at the elementary level by comparing the performance of 363 trained and 187 untrained teachers. A variety of techniques, including observation, was adopted for collecting the relevant data. It was concluded that trained teachers were superior to untrained ones in almost all aspects of their professional work. Particularly, untrained teachers were more prone to purely content-oriented interactions in their approach to teaching. Sinha (1982) also conducted a similar study and the findings confirmed these observations. Singh (1985) conducted a very significant study comparing the four-year integrated program of teacher training at the secondary level with the traditional model of one-year training following a basic bachelor's degree. No significant difference was observed in the attitude of the teachers who had undergone the two different models of training. However, it was found that the teachers who had undergone training through the integrated model scored higher in their teaching competence and in role performance. Across-subjects analysis showed that science students benefited significantly more by the integrated training approach compared to their counterparts from social science subjects.

On the whole, the studies conducted represent a descriptive survey approach for understanding the teacher education program. They have highlighted a number of serious problems affecting the teacher education system in the country. Although different researchers have explored the system operating in different regions, one observed considerable uniformity in their conclusions. These observations should provide some guidance to policy-makers and planners regarding future directions for action. But the observations are not derived from in-depth explorations into specific problems and longitudinal studies which could provide a diagnostic insight into the causes of the problem. However, certain findings such as that the total program is only operative for an unduly short period (118 days), or that more than two months are devoted to admission should alarm anyone concerned with teacher education in the country.

In summary, while a number of studies have dealt with the general problems and issues confronting teacher education, specific studies dealing with the curriculum dimension of the program are very few. A similar observation holds good for primary teacher training programs also, as most of the researchers deal only with secondary teacher education programs. One of the research studies has highlighted the positive value of integrated programs of teacher preparation over the traditional consecutive model. But this seems to have made no impact on the overall organization of teacher education programs in the country. Possibly many more researchers should tackle this question to make an impact on the overall position.

Development of Teaching Skills

Training in pedagogy is the mainstay of teacher education. Therefore, it is not surprising that a very large amount of research in teacher education deals with the topic of developing classroom teaching skills. Research on this topic began in the early 1970s. The objective of the initial studies was mainly to compare the relative effectiveness of micro-teaching techniques, or skill development strategies, with the conventional approach to training for classroom teaching. This trend seems to have continued during the present decade as well, in spite of the fact that micro-teaching has now become an integral part of the program of teacher training in almost all institutions of teacher education. For instance, Naik (1984) and Khan (1985) conducted experiments to compare micro-teaching with the conventional approach. Both concluded that micro-teaching proved to be more effective in terms of performance of learners on achievement tests. Naik concluded that subject-specific skills should be practised, whereas Khan focused on improvement in general teaching competence. While most studies on micro-teaching dealt with pre-service teacher education, Kalyanpurkar (1986) conducted a large-scale experiment involving thirty-six teachers and 720 pupils to explore the efficacy of micro-teaching as a tool for developing teaching skills in in-service teachers. The study, focusing on four teaching skills, namely, probing skills, reinforcement, explaining with examples, and stimulus variation, reported a positive impact of training in micro-teaching on the use of teaching skills and also on student learning.

Researchers have also tried to examine whether skill development through micro-teaching should be seen in a subject-specific manner. Pratap (1982), with the help of student teachers, identified three skills as specially important for the teaching of mathematics: problem-solving, formulating mathematical models, and blackboard work. Suitable instructional materials were developed for imparting these skills through micro-teaching, and were field tested. Oak (1986) made a critical study of micro-teaching in the context of three subjects, namely, science, mathematics, and mother tongue. Relevant skills were identified based on student teacher perceptions and also on direct observation. It was concluded that subject is an important variable in the process of teaching skill-development through micro-teaching. In spite of these observations, many researchers have continued to view effectiveness of micro-teaching with respect to general teaching competence only. Studying the relative effectiveness of different variations of micro-teaching procedures has also been the concern of several researchers. Studies by Das *et al.* (1982), Singh (1982) and Prabhune *et al.* (1984) belong to this category. Variations in effectiveness under different modes of feedback practices have been the concern of some of these researchers. Prabhune *et al.* (1984) experimented with three feedback practices: self-feedback through audio-cassette, peer feedback, and supervisor's feedback, and reported that the variations did not have any significant impact on the general teaching competence of the student teachers. As Das and Jangira (1987) point out, generalizability of the findings of many of these studies is limited since the definitions of teaching efficiency, teaching effectiveness or teaching competence are governed by the tools used by the investigators, which were not identical.

Considering the importance of questioning in the classroom teaching-learning process, some have experimented exclusively on development of questioning skill. Through field tryout, Kaur (1980) developed self-instructional material for this purpose in the form of audiocassettes. The study by Jangira and Dhoundiyal (1981) made a detailed analysis of the questioning behaviour of student teachers to identify the type of instructional inputs to be provided for improving their questioning skill. Yadav (1983) went a step further and studied the impact of training in questioning skills on student learning, and reported positive results.

With micro-teaching finding a permanent place in the student teaching program of many institutions, researchers have turned their attention to the effectiveness of different methods of integrating teaching skills developed through micro-teaching. The study by Ekbote (1987) is significant in this regard. The study, which was developmental as well as experimental in nature, was carried out in the normal conditions of a teacher training institution. The study resulted in a package of instructional material for integration of teaching skills through micro-teaching, whose effectiveness and feasibility had been established by trying it out as part of the student teaching program. Lalitha (1981) and Dave (1987) tried to compare the suitability of different approaches for integration of teaching skills. Dave's experiment involved the comparison of a summative model with a miniteaching approach. The latter was found to be more effective in terms of student achievement as well as attitude towards teaching.

The current trend in this area is to experiment with different models of teaching, largely those suggested by Bruce Joyce and Marsha Weil.[2] Joshi (1984) conducted an elaborate but meticulously designed experiment on development of teaching skills, studying the relative effectiveness of two models, the symbolic planning model and the behaviour perform-ance model. The experiment involved analysis of the transcripts of 318 micro-teaching lessons which focused on development of a cluster of three skills: reacting, questioning, and initiation. It was reported that the models did not differ in terms of changing teacher behaviour and teacher attitude. Passi *et al.* (1986a) studied the effect of the concept attainment model and the inquiry training model on classroom teaching-learning processes. A national-level cooperative study was carried out involving 321 student-teachers and about 2500 pupils from ten different institutions. A common experimental design was drawn jointly by the team of resear-chers so that the results could be meaningfully combined to draw gener-alizations. The significant observation of the study was that the inquiry teaching model changed the typical authoritarian teacher-dominated class-room into one characterized by high pupil initiative. The concept attain-ment model had the effect of transforming the usual symbolic passive learning sessions. In another study conducted on the same lines (Passi *et al.*, 1986b) the nature of peer feedback emerged as a significant factor influencing student teacher competence under both the models of teaching.

It will not be out of place to make two broad observations about the nature of the studies reviewed here. The fact that almost all the studies on teaching view teaching as consisting of trainable skills shows that Indian researchers have tended to consider teaching only from the behaviouristic angle. Not a single research study has attempted to analyze classroom teaching from a cognitive theoretical perspective, nor with an ethno-graphic approach. This narrow theoretical position adopted by resear-chers has painted a fragmented picture of teaching, as only an ensemble of otherwise independent skills. This is quite in contrast to the trend of studies being carried out in other parts of the world. Even studies carried out within the behaviouristic paradigm seem to suffer from a major limitation. Viewing teaching as a composite of skills in a meaningful way demands the identification and development of a comprehensive set of teaching skills which together form a composite whole. Unfortunately, none of the studies experimenting with the development of teaching competence through micro-teaching has dealt with such a comprehensive set. Ignoring this self-created limitation, the researchers have tried to assess the effectiveness of their strategy in terms of general teaching competence or even student learning outcomes. The studies on models of teaching represent a positive step to viewing teaching in a more holistic way. Does it indicate a move away from the narrow confines of a behaviouristic paradigm to a broader learning perspective?

Student Characteristics

Understanding the characteristics of students who are aspiring to enter the teaching profession has been the concern of many researchers. As noted earlier, these studies have used standardized tools of psychological measurement for collecting the relevant data. Most of the researchers have also tried to correlate these characteristics with academic performance. Gopalacharyulu (1984) conducted a survey in twelve secondary teacher education institutions and found that socio-economic status and attitude towards the teaching profession significantly influenced the academic performance of the student teachers, whereas their personality made no impact on achievement. Goyal, Sabharwal and Tewari (1984) surveyed the characteristics of 749 student teachers. On the basis of multiple regression analysis, it was reported that intelligence, attitude and personality factors were effective predictors of achievement; interestingly, previous teaching experience did not correlate significantly with achievement. Patil (1984) also found a significant correlation between academic performance of student teachers and their intelligence, attitude and interest. Katiyar (1982) administered the 16 Personality Factor Questionnaire and found that skill acquisition through micro-teaching had a significant positive correlation with ego strength, shrewdness, conservatism and dependence. The concern of Dutt (1983) was with the level of social cohesion in elementary teacher training institutions. Donga (1987) studied the adjustment patterns of student teachers. The findings indicated that adjustment level depended on socio-economic status, length of teaching experience and sex of the student teacher. The longer the teaching experience, the more difficulties were experienced in adjustment; females were better adjusted than their male counterparts. But adjustment level had no relationship with academic achievement.

As stated earlier, these studies have involved the use of sophisticated measuring instruments and techniques of analysis, but what bothers an objective reviewer of these studies is their apparent lack of relevance to teacher education. No one can doubt the importance of finding out the background characteristics of those aspiring to enter the teaching profession, but the goal of such studies should not be limited merely to a psychological analysis of the characteristics. Rather, the substantive concern of the studies should be to relate these findings with the admission procedures followed, curricular inputs provided, or the evaluation procedures adopted in teacher education programs. In the absence of such a concern, the studies have become mere academic exercises in psychological analysis. It may not be wrong to observe that most of the studies dealing with student teacher characteristics do not have teacher education as their main concern; the selection of student teachers as the subjects for study seems to have been guided more by expediency than by a conscious desire to understand teacher education in greater depth.

Research on Teaching Practice

A core component of all pre-service teacher education programs is the direct school experience given to prospective teachers through teaching practice sessions in real school settings. Considering that this is the main aspect of the teacher education program, questions related to this aspect should have been the central concern of a number of researchers. But, contrary to expectation, very few scholars have studied this vital aspect of teacher education.

Field surveys were conducted by Rai (1982), Mohanty (1984), Raj (1984) and Shah (1986) to understand the various dimensions of teaching practice programs, their organization and the problems involved. It was found that there were considerable variations across the country in the organization of teaching practice. Three main models were being followed. Some institutions adopted block practice teaching of the internship model for organizing the teaching practice program. Under this model student teachers were attached to particular schools on a full-time basis for a period ranging from two to six weeks, during which they were required to participate in all the activities of the school along with their practice lessons. In the second model student teachers attended theory classes, received guidance from their supervisors at the teacher training colleges, and participated in teaching practice at the school on alternate days. In the third approach, adopted by a small number of institutions, student teachers spent half of the day with their supervisors on the college premises and the remaining half at the practising schools. Two problems found to be generally affecting the teaching practice program were inadequate guidance and supervision by the teacher educators and lack of cooperation and coordination among the school and the college authorities. Mohanty (1984) further pointed out that the stress in the teaching practice program was only on the delivery of a prescribed number of lessons and not on providing feedback to student teachers for improving the quality of performance. Sohoni *et al.* (1977) focused on identifying the factors that helped in the development of teacher effectiveness during practice teaching. He reported that teacher effectiveness was influenced significantly in cases where subject experts observed the lessons and gave appropriate feedback to their students. The commonly observed elements of teacher effectiveness were ability to motivate the pupils, ability to communicate effectively, apt use of blackboard, and a certain level of personal maturity. Pande (1980) also reported that most of the colleges surveyed were not adequately equipped for providing necessary guidance for teaching practice at the college premises. Very few of them had practising schools attached to them, nor did some of the teacher educators possess adequate knowledge of the subject being taught at the schools.

The picture that emerges from the various research findings on the practice teaching program is quite dismal. This may partly be because of unprecedent growth in the number of teacher training institutions during the last two decades. Many of these institutions, it appears, do not have facilities for organizing the practice teaching program effectively. In many cases this disregard for quality has also affected the relationship between teacher training institutions and practising schools. As has been pointed out by Pande (1980), many school authorities look with suspicion at the value of allowing student teachers to practise in their schools. In a significant study by Kakkad (1983) the curricular practices adopted in twenty-four different universities were analyzed and it was concluded that an internship of three months was ideal for equipping prospective teachers with teaching capabilities. Also it was necessary to incorporate action research in classroom practices as part of the teacher education program to ensure that teachers remained alive to the demands of the classroom setting, and continued their efforts in tackling the problems involved.

Research on In-service Education

As has been pointed out earlier, the in-service education of teachers is the weakest link in the whole system of teacher education in India. One would have naturally expected scientific investigations into the training needs of teachers serving at different levels, existing facilities for in-service education of teachers, the nature of in-service programs currently being organized, and the scope for evolving alternative organizational designs for in-service education of teachers. Does the researcher in this area answer these questions satisfactorily?

Mama (1980) observed that the contents of in-service education programs mainly focused on four areas: subject matter, planning of tests, evaluation techniques, and the use of audiovisual aids. There was no involvement of teachers in planning, evaluation and follow-up of in-service education programs. The programs were generally conducted as weekend courses. It was observed that many heads of institutions were not favourably disposed towards the participation by their teachers in in-service education programs. The study by Gangaiah (1980) focused exclusively on the status of in-service education for English teachers. It was concluded that often the programs were not needs-based and the periods of training were too inadequate to improve the competence of participants in English teaching. The State Council of Educational Research and Training (1981) in Andhra Pradesh conducted an investigation and identified a number of problems related to the in-service education of teachers at the primary stage. It was found that very few of the teachers got any opportunity to participate in such programs. Moreover, the programs were highly academic and lacked relationship with the practical situations prevalent in the schools. Nagaraju (1982) conducted an evaluation of the experimental project of providing in-service education through radio correspondence. It was reported that there was no proper planning and implementation of the program. The project framework did not have any scope to utilize feedback from teachers who received the training. There was a need to establish better coordination between the production wing and the academic wing of the project. It was also suggested that the contact programs had to be of a longer duration, and arrangements should be made for periodical evaluation of the project components. J.P. Sharma (1982) studied the situation with respect to secondary teacher education and reported a declining trend in the status of in-service education of secondary teachers. It may be mentioned that initially these centres were receiving substantial grants from the national budget, but these were discontinued after their control and supervision were taken over by state governments. In many states the number of in-service education programs conducted by the centres seems to have decreased considerably since then. Butala (1987) made an extensive survey and found that the majority of teachers were not covered under any in-service program. Except for a few programs which dealt with such aspects as educational technology and educational management, the in-service programs mainly concentrated on knowledge upgrading in school subjects. Teachers felt that the programs were, in general, useful for their professional growth and that participation in in-service training programs should be given due consideration in deciding promotion to higher posts.

The studies reviewed here provide some reference point for assessing the present status of in-service teacher education programs. The situation is quite discouraging in terms of quantity as well as quality. Research studies should have provided an empirical base for assessing overall in-service education requirements at different levels. This base would have helped in the development of suitable logistics and delivery mechanisms. Studies should also be conducted to work out alternative models for organizing in-service education programs. For instance, considering the number of teachers involved, it should be worthwhile to examine the relevance and possibility of using distance education mechanisms for this purpose, through necessary field experimentation. Also the contents of the in-service programs in operation seem to be somewhat ad hoc. Researchers should possibly conduct a number of needs surveys to identify specific in-service education requirements of different target groups and evolve suitable programs.

Concluding Observations

There is a clearly increasing trend in the amount of research conducted on teacher education. The studies have been largely survey research except those on teaching skills and micro-teaching. The researchers have identified a number of problems and issues confronting the teacher education system in the country. Some of the findings are well known and even appear trivial, but, unfortunately, they have not been able to elicit necessary remedial action from policy-makers and administrators. This lack of action is partly because many of the studies turn out to be highly academic exercises which do not immediately hold any import for administrators. Moreover, most of the studies have been conducted by individual scholars working for their doctoral degrees and, therefore, fail to present the findings in a form that is readily translatable into action.

Most of the studies in teacher education seem to lack a proper theoretical framework. Researchers in teacher education seem to have consistently failed to give adequate attention to the conceptual underpinnings of the phenomenon being studied. The studies on teaching skills and micro-teaching bring this point to focus. The extra attention paid by researchers to these topics is understandable; but simply carrying out empirical studies, while ignoring the demands of the basic theoretical framework within which these concepts have evolved, does not increase understanding of the phenomenon, nor does it help improve teaching practices in a meaningful manner. Findings of empirical research can add to the existing knowledge and skill base only if they represent a coherent perspective.

The researchers have considered a number of variables related to teacher education. While this is welcome, the concern for analyzing these multiple variables should not push the concern for teacher education to backstage, which is what one observes in many of the studies analyzing student teacher characteristics and even studies dealing with institutional characteristics. Many of them seem to be mere exercises in psychological analysis, with little concern for their relevance to teacher education programs.

The studies have dealt with a number of topics related to teacher education, yet there are also glaring lacunae. As pointed out under the quantitative overview, a negligibly small number of studies have dealt with the teacher education program at the primary stage. It should be noted that teacher education is not simply another area of academic study. Rather, it deals with the practical work of the teacher. Therefore, research in teacher education should essentially be a problem-solving endeavour. If one accepts this position, an area which should be of great concern is the in-service education of teachers; unfortunately, this area has attracted very little attention from researchers. Another area which had been little explored is the curriculum of teacher education at different levels.

A number of studies in teacher education have adopted quite sophisticated statistical techniques. At the same time, several methods of investigation relevant to teacher education have not been adequately represented, in particular such methods as the case study, participant observation, ethnographic analysis, and historical and comparative studies. It is essential that educational researchers overcome their inhibitions and adopt qualitative techniques as well in their investigations.

The studies reviewed here, irrespective of many inherent limitations, have succeeded in highlighting several crucial problems facing the teacher education system in India. If research is to contribute to evolving solutions for these problems, two steps seem imperative. One is that studies in the area of teacher education should adopt a long-term perspective. It is essential that a coherent framework for action be developed, based on analysis of the existing system and a vision for future development in the field. What is required is to develop research programs instead of carrying out isolated empirical investigations. A second point, which is a corollary of the first, is that such research programs cannot be meaningfully pursued by individual scholars working for their academic degrees. It is necessary that interdisciplinary team work be encouraged in teacher education. Professionals in the field have to come together to work on a cooperative basis to find solutions to many of the fundamental questions in this area. Sporadic, one-time efforts will not do. The need is to launch research projects which deal with different aspects of teacher education in a comprehensive manner. It is urgent that professionals concerned with teacher education, in addition to the efforts of individual scholars, come together to inject an element of dynamism into the field through effective institutional-level research projects.

Notes

1 M.B. Buch (Ed.) *Third Survey of Research in Education: 1978–1983.* New Delhi: NCERT, 1987; and M.B. Buch (Ed.) (in press) *Fourth Survey of Research in Education: 1984–1987.* New Delhi: NCERT.
2 B. Joyce and M. Weil (1985) *Models of Teaching.* New Delhi: Prentice Hall, India.

References

AGGARWAL, Y.P. (1980) Motivational factors in the choice of teaching as profession and its relationship with other variables. Kurukshetra University, Department of Education.

BHATNAGAR, M.A. (1979) A study of organisational climate of the teacher training institutions of Uttar Pradesh and its relationship with their effectiveness. PhD Edu, Meerut University.

BUTALA, M. (1987) A critical inquiry into inservice educational programmes conducted by secondary teachers training colleges of Gujarat State. PhD Edu, Gujarat University.

DAS, R.C. and JANGIRA, N.K. (1987) Teacher education: A trend report, in M.B. BUCH (Ed.) *Third Survey of Research in Education.* New Delhi: NCERT.

DAS, R.C., PASSI, B.K., JANGIRA, N.K. and SINGH, A. (1982) Effectiveness of different strategies of integration of teaching skills in developing general teaching competencies of student teachers. NCERT, Department of Teacher Education.

DAVE, C.S. (1987) Relative effectiveness of microteaching having summative model of integration versus miniteaching model in terms of general teaching competence, teacher attitude towards teaching, pupil liking and pupil achievement. PhD Edu, Devi Ahilya Vishwa Vidyalay.

DONGA, N.S. (1987) A study of the adjustment of trainees of teachers training colleges of Gujarat. PhD Edu, Saurashtra University.

DUBEY, T.B. (1981) A comparative study of secondary teacher education in Madhya Pradesh and Maharashtra. PhD Edu, Saugar University.

DUTT, R. (1983) A study of social cohesion in the elementary teacher training institutions and its relationships with attitude and adjustment of student-teachers. PhD Edu, Meerut University.

EKBOTE, E.R. (1987) Development of a strategy for integration of skills in teacher training. PhD Edu, MS University of Baroda.

GANGAIAH, N. (1980) A critical study of English teacher education in Andhra Pradesh. PhD Edu, Karnatak University.

GOPALACHARYULU, R.V.V. (1984) A study of relationship between certain psychological factors and achievement of student teachers in teacher training institutes of Andhra Pradesh. PhD Edu, Sri Venkateshwara University.

GOYAL, J.C. and CHOPRA, R.K. (1979) A study of the problems bearing on teacher education in the context of the 10+2 pattern. NCERT, Department of Teacher Education, New Delhi.

GOYAL, J.C., SABHARWAL, N. and TEWARI, A.D. (1984) Developing tools for admission to secondary teacher training institutions in India. NCERT, New Delhi.

HEMAMBUJAM, K. (1983) A critical study of teacher education at the secondary level in Tamil Nadu. PhD Edu, Karnatak University.

JANGIRA, N.K. (1982) A study of social cohesion in elementary teacher training institutions and its relationship with their efficiency. NCERT, Department of Teacher Education, New Delhi.

JANGIRA, N.K. and DHOUNDIYAL, N.C. (1981) Effect of Classroom Behaviour Training (CBT) on the classroom questioning behaviour of teachers. NCERT, New Delhi.

JOSHI, A.N. (1984) A study of developing performance criteria and testing their efficacy in training student teachers in a teaching skill cluster. PhD Edu, Poona University.

KAKKAD, G.M. (1983) Secondary teacher education curricula: an analytical study and developing teacher education programme. PhD Edu, Nagpur University.

KALLA, A.S. (1984) Gandhi Shikshan Bhavan: An experiment in education — A case study. PhD Edu, Bombay University.

KALYANPURKAR, S. (1986) The effect of microteaching on the teaching competence of inservice teachers and its impact on pupils' attainment and pupils' liking. PhD Edu, Devi Ahilya Vishwa Vidyalay.

KATIYAR, B.L. (1982) Personality traits and attainment of skills through microteaching. PhD Edu, Banaras Hindu University.

KAUR, R., (1980) An enquiry into the effectiveness of self-instructional audio-cassettes in developing teaching skills among student-teachers in a three-phased study. PhD Edu, Punjab University.

KHAN, A.H. (1985) Effectiveness of microteaching technique in terms of student achievement. PhD Edu, Avadh University.

LALITHA, M.S. (1981) Effectiveness of a strategy of training for integrating teaching skills on teaching competence of student teachers. Mysore University, Department of Post-Graduate Studies and Research in Education.

LAVERNE, M.R. (1985) A study of some personality components of creative student teachers in relation to their competence towards teaching. PhD Edu, Lucknow University.

MAMA, K. (1980) A study of the impact of in-service education on teachers in the State of Maharashtra. PhD Edu, Bombay University.

MISRA, A. (1986) Growth of teacher education for women and problems thereof with special reference to UP. PhD Edu, Gorakpur University.

MOHAN, K. (1980) Effectiveness of teacher training programmes. PhD Edu, Avadh University.

MOHANTY, S.B. (1984) A study of student teaching programmes in colleges of education with special reference to innovation. PhD Edu, MS University of Baroda.

NAGARAJU, C.S. (1982) Evaluation of radio correspondence-cum-contact in-service teacher training programme in Kerala. Institute for Social and Economic Change, Bangalore.

NAIK, V.V. (1984) A comparative study of the effect of microteaching and conventional approaches of teacher training upon pupils' achievement, pupils' perception and general teaching competence of preservice student teachers. PhD Edu, Bombay University.

OAK, A.W. (1986) A critical study of microteaching techniques with a view to suggest improvement in its implementation in colleges of education. SNDT University, Department of Post-Graduate Education and Research.

PANDE, S.M. (1980) A critical study of supervision practices. PhD Edu, Avadh University.

PASSI, B.K., SINGH, L.C. and SANSANWAL, D.N. (1986a) Adopting training strategy and studying effectiveness of different variations in components of training strategy for concept attainment model/inquiry training model in terms of understanding competence, reactions and pupil liking. Devi Ahilya Viswa Vidyalaya, Department of Education.

PASSI, B.K., SINGH, L.C. and SANSANWAL, D.N. (1986b) Implementing training strategy and studying effectiveness of different variations in components of training strategy for concept attainment model/inquiry training model in terms of understanding, competence, reactions and willingness of student teachers. Devi Ahilya Viswa Vidyalaya, Department of Education.

PATHAK, V.B. (1979) Teacher education in Eastern UP: A quantitative and qualitative analysis. PhD Edu, Banaras Hindu University.

PATIL, G.G. (1984) A differential study of intelligence, interest and attitudes of the BEd college students as contributory factors towards their achievement in the compulsory subjects. PhD Edu, Nagpur University.

PILLAI, J.K. and MOHAN, S. (1985) Why graduates choose to teach: A survey. Madurai Kamaraj University, Department of Education.

PRABHUNE, P.P., MARATHE, A.H. and COHANI, G.R. (1984) An experimental study to measure the effect of microteaching skills and different strategies of feedback on the student-teachers' performance with respect to teaching. State Institute Education, Pune.

PRATAP, D. (1982) The effectiveness of micro-teaching for development of skills specific to the teaching of modern mathematics. PhD Edu, Panjab University.

RAI, V.K. (1982) A survey of the problems of teachers' training colleges with regard to practising schools. PhD Edu, Gujarat University.

RAINA, V.K. (1981) A factorial study of the personalities, attitudes to teaching and creativity of inservice and student-teachers belonging to three subject areas. PhD Edu, MS University of Baroda.

RAJ, T. (1984) A study of the organisation and administration of student teaching programmes in the secondary teacher education institutions. PhD Edu, Agra University.

SHAH, M.M. (1986) A survey of management of student teaching in India. MS University of Baroda, Centre of Advanced Study in Education.

SHARMA, J.P. (1982) Growth and development of in-service education for secondary school teachers in the State of Bihar since 1955. PhD Edu, Patne University.

SHARMA, M. (1982) Progress and problems of teacher education in India. PhD Edu, Patna University.

SHARMA, V.S. (1980) Effectiveness of pre-service teacher training programme at elementary level in Rajasthan. State Council of Educational Research and Training, Udaipur.

SINGH, G. (1982) Comparative study of different strategies of integration of teaching skills. PhD Edu, Banaras Hindu University.

SINGH, N. (1985) A comparative study of teachers trained through integrated and traditional methods in terms of attitude towards teaching, teaching competence and role performance. PhD Edu, Banaras Hindu University.

SINHA, P. (1982) An evaluative study of teacher education in Bihar. PhD Edu, Patna University.

SOHONI, B.K. *et al.* (1977) A study of the development of teacher effectiveness through teaching practice. SNDT College of Education for Women, Pune.

State Council of Educational Research and Training, Andhra Pradesh (1981) *Evaluation of Inservice Training Programme for Primary School Teachers in the Selected Government and Aided Teacher Training Institutions.* Hyderabad: SCERT.

YADAV, R.A. (1983) A study of the effect of training for classroom questioning behaviour on teaching competence and pupil achievement, PhD Edu, Meerut University.

Chapter 10

Scholarly Inquiry into Teacher Education in the United States

Nancy L. Zimpher and Kenneth R. Howey

This chapter reviews discernible evolving lines of inquiry into teacher preparation in the United States. At present there are no full-blown programs of research. Nonetheless, there are a few major national studies underway, and some first-class conceptual and investigatory work by a growing number of individual scholars. Six major themes or lines of inquiry in the literature have been identified. Research into:

1 learning to teach;
2 the purposes, structure and character of *programs* of teacher preparation;
3 specific contexts and modalities for learning to teach;
4 education faculty and students;
5 clinical teacher education; and
6 the induction and socialization of beginning teachers.

These categories emerged from a thorough review of the literature, especially that of the last five years. Though hardly exhaustive, and though others could be added, they did seem to be the major foci for study. Neither does one exclude the other; understandable overlap in the categories exists. For example, studies of learning to teach cut across several of the other categories, but each of the categories embraces studies of a variety of other types as well. Space prohibits even nominal interpretation and assessment of most of this work. Our contribution is rather to illustrate where and in some instances why a number of studies inform us about the preparation of teachers in the United States and to provide multiple references to this scholarship. At the close of the chapter we briefly note some of the major issues we see as attached to research into teacher education in this country and where more and better inquiry is needed. The overview is limited to pre-service teacher education with some attention to induction, as this appears a needed and logical extension of pre-service.

Research into Learning to Teach

The mental life of the teacher has become a central topic in studies of teaching in the United States and has signalled the transition to studies of learning to teach rather than studies of teaching as such. Studies concerned with unravelling teacher thinking processes, particularly in the area of planning, have been conducted for some time. Other studies have been more concerned with 'thinking-in-action', employing 'thinking-aloud' strategies, wherein teachers reconstructed their thought processes as they were engaged in critical events of teaching. Studies of teachers' preactive and interactive thought were summarized by Clark and Peterson in 1986.

The research agenda of the National Center for Research on Teacher Education (NCRTE) at Michigan State University addresses the question of what various programs of teacher education contribute to the learning of teachers.

> Learning to teach occurs unevenly over time. Prospective teachers, for example, come to higher education with ideas about what teachers do. While in the university they acquire knowledge and skills in their subject matter areas. Formal studies shape their ideas about teaching as well as their commitments and orientations. When they begin to teach, they continue to learn — about teaching, pupils, and subject matter. Our interest in teacher learning requires that we pay attention to changes that occur separately in teachers' knowledge, skills, and dispositions as well as changes in how they bring these ingredients together in their teaching. (National Center, 1989, p. 29)

The longitudinal design of the Center is to examine teacher changes in knowledge, skills and dispositions as teacher candidates move through teacher education into independent teaching. The Center focuses on learning to teach mathematics and writing, since both of those content areas are taught throughout the twelve years of schooling. They see understanding the phenomenon of learning to teach as a major challenge; as Barnes (1989) observes, 'teaching is seen as ambiguous and complex work requiring judgement, action, and the capacity to reflect and revise decisions on the basis of one's observations and insights' (p. 3).

As study in this domain, largely in its infancy, begins to unfold, one can discern the following variations on the theme which Barnes outlined. First, learning to teach is being studied as a function, in part, of what beginning teachers think they already know about learning to teach; that is, what they have learned through their own years of experience as 'teacher watchers' (McDiarmid, Feiman-Nemser, Melnick and Parker, 1987; Brousseau, Book and Byers, 1988; and Lortie, 1975).

Second, others are studying the ways that teachers not only come to understand their discipline but also acquire content-specific pedagogy or pedagogical content knowledge which allows them to transform this knowledge so that it is understandable to others (Shulman and Ringstaff, 1986; Shulman, 1987; and Wilson and Shulman, 1987).

Third, several scholars are concerned with the schemata or cognitive structures of prospective teachers and the metacognitive strategies they can be taught and the implications of these for learning to teach (Wittrock, 1986; Doyle, 1986; and Weinstein and Mayer, 1986).

Fourth, the question of timing, what one does when in teaching, is critically important. Certain scholars postulate that 'practical knowledge is stored in specific systems and then one decides what knowledge to use at a given time by reviewing one's repertoire of knowledge', which relates to how experts and novices use knowledge differently. Differences in thinking between expert and novice teachers explain key differences in classroom effectiveness which are not easily discernible by observation of teaching. The need for structured and protracted discourse about teaching between more and less experienced teachers, an uncommon occurrence now, becomes essential as a matter of learning to teach. Scardamelia and Bereiter (1987) define this domain of expert-novice knowledge in terms of the process whereby 'expert teachers confront core problems whereas inexpert teachers avoid them.' Studies in this domain allow us to look at teaching developmentally as teachers become increasingly more expert and thus more integrative and more reflective (Carter, Sabers, Cushing, Pinnegar and Berliner, 1987; and Carter, Cushing, Sabers, Stein and Berliner, 1988). Berliner (1988) has tentatively identified stages of pedagogical knowledge which categorize teachers first as novices, then as advanced beginners and then as competent, proficient and finally expert. Still others are concerned with teacher reasoning and thinking-in-action as these relate to various conceptions of reflectivity (Clift, Houston, and Pugach, in press).

Fifth, the critical link between teaching and learning is treated by studies wherein the teacher attempts to step inside the student's mind and look at the way content knowledge evolves. In this pioneer work 'the teacher involves students more actively and consciously in building knowledge and skills and in advancing in their own development' (Scardamelia and Bereiter, 1989, p. 37). This process of learning how to teach develops from a cognitive mediational point of view wherein interrelated propositions drive the nature of teaching and learning. As Anderson (1987) states:

> To learn to teach requires that teachers understand that students need to recognize links among main ideas..., the role of scaffolded dialogue..., the importance of tasks and their social context..., and the ways that the larger social environment affects students' motivation.... (p. 111)

Research into the Purposes, Structures and Character of Teacher Education Programs

Assumptions about the general quality of teacher preparation programs, the faculty attached to them, and students enrolled in them are obviously at the root of the current debate about needed reform in teacher education in the United States. Critics vary regarding their assessment of the current quality of these programs, and in terms of how they should be changed. Thoughtful advocates argue for both what are basically baccalaureate as well as extensive post-baccalaureate approaches to teacher preparation. Many see no compelling reason to make any major changes in current practice. Others take the position that teacher preparation should be more realistic regarding what can be done initially, and suggest that phases in the career of a teacher call for more powerful teacher education interventions spread out over a longer time. Still others view the likely impact of teacher education as problematic as long as the basic conditions of schooling militate against effective teacher practice. Thus some have embedded their advocacy in a process of transferring the process of teacher education more properly to elementary and secondary schools.

A fundamental constraint to the dialogue and debate, however, is the lack of a clear understanding of the nature and quality of various programs of teacher education. Little is known in a fine-grained manner about the nature of teacher preparation curricula, the instructional activities of faculty attached to these curricula, and the frequency, timeliness and quality of opportunities which prospective teachers have for learning how to teach. Some scholars, such as Evertson, Hawley and Zlotnik (1985), reviewed studies which compare provisionally certificated and regularly certificated teachers as a very general assessment of the effects of teacher preparation. They observed:

It seems clear that teachers who participate in preservice teacher preparation programs are more likely to be, or even to be seen to be by supervisors and other trained observers, more effective than teachers who have little or no formal training before they teach. And, efforts to teach preservice teachers specific capabilities and knowledge invariably appear to be effective, at least in the short-run. (p. 9)

Their analysis was limited to a comparison of thirteen studies, which focused largely on supervisor assessment of beginning teacher competence. They found the conceptual, methodological and practical problems attached to examining the effects of programs to be considerable. Koehler (1985) questioned follow-up studies of students in teacher education programs:

Given the extreme conceptual and technical difficulties in attributing a teacher's behavior, attitudes and/or beliefs to a teacher education program, these studies often say more about practising teachers than about the quality of their preservice programs. (p. 24)

We briefly share four efforts to address the challenge and to describe and assess aspects or attributes of teacher education programs in the U.S. The first of these is the study of the education of educators undertaken by John Goodlad and his colleagues at the University of Washington. They generated a set of twenty-two axioms or postulates about the nature of teacher education programs. They visited twenty-nine institutions across the U.S. to review documents and interview faculty and students in order to formulate perspectives on both extant and ideal practices. A report on the conceptualization of the study and the data collection and site visitation strategies is available (Goodlad, 1988; and Sirotnik, 1988).

A second study, framed by the Center for Research on Teacher Education at Michigan State and noted above, concerned the central question of what teacher education programs contributed to teachers' learning. The Center defines program as 'a deliberate educational intervention designed to foster learning'. They examine among other factors: the organization of components in the program; standards for entry and exit; the content and rationale of the program; the nature of the learning tasks in the program; and learning opportunity dimensions, particularly processes that facilitate learning how to teach. The Center's design includes case studies of teacher education programs combined with longitudinal studies of teachers' learnings. As in the education of educators study, data sources include program documents, accompanied by periodic interviews and surveys of program directors, teacher educators and students. Through the selection of eleven sites across the country the Center is looking at pre-service programs, entry-year and beginning-year assistance programs and in-service programs. More traditional as well as alternative certification strategies are being examined.

A primary goal of the Center is 'to uncover the reasoning behind *different* ways of helping teachers learn to teach and describe their impact on teachers' knowledge, skills and dispositions' (National Center, 1989). To this point, a series of reports from the Center has been generated concerned with definitional and conceptual problems as well as some baseline data generated during the site selection period of the design.

A third study provided comparative cases of elementary teacher education programs housed in different types of institutions, ranging from a small liberal arts college to major research-oriented institutions. Howey and Zimpher (1989) selected programs for their curricular innovation and program variation to serve as a basis for providing a more in-depth picture than currently exists of how teachers are prepared in pre-service programs. These case studies, as with the National Center studies, examined the nature and quality of curricula through program documentation, observations and repeated rounds of interviews with critical participants in these programs. Relatively in-depth descriptions of these programs have resulted wherein the programs are described by the professors, students and cooperating teachers. A cross-site analysis of the six programs is also provided. As in the 'effective' schools literature, the investigators have identified fourteen attributes which they hypothesize provide coherence and potency to a program.

A companion study, more broad-based and longitudinal in nature, is being conducted by the American Association of Colleges for Teacher Education's (AACTE) committee on Research about Teacher Education, now referred to as the RATE studies. A team of researchers from member institutions of AACTE is in the fourth year of data collection from a nationally stratified random sample of AACTE member institutions to provide information on the nature of programs and institutional context, including the reactions, observations and perceptions of faculty and students and, as of this fourth year, participating cooperating teachers. The authors of this chapter have been members of the research team from its inception. The national stratified random sample includes slightly less than 100 institutions, two-thirds of which are retained annually for successive iterations of data collection. Through trained research representatives at each of the campuses, this study also acquires difficult to obtain institutional data. In successive rounds, data have been collected regarding the nature of programs from the perspective of those engaged in

secondary methods courses; philosophical, historical and social foundations courses; elementary methods courses and field experiences; and
those primarily responsible for student teaching. Two summative technical reports are available from the American Association of Colleges for
Teacher Education (AACTE)/RATE (1987, 1988). As the longitudinal
research agenda of the RATE project emerges, working hypotheses designed in the companion case studies by Howey and Zimpher (1989) can
be tested in the surveys directed to RATE's sample of teacher education
institutions. While AACTE data reveal concerns, they also portray
teacher education as a viable, changing enterprise. The RATE project is a
long-term venture to establish a reliable database for analyzing trends
in teacher education and providing essential information for intelligent
decision-making.

A few other studies bear brief mention as well. Zeichner (1988),
representing the National Center for Research on Teacher Education,
correlated findings from the RATE study with the initial baseline data
collected by the National Center in order to understand the character and
quality of the academic and professional components of teacher education, particularly looking at the degree of rigor in the teacher education
programs he studied. While the Center's definition of rigor is more
differentiated than that posed by the RATE study, nevertheless, both
portray a more positive picture of student perceptions of rigor in their
education courses than might be expected.

Additional studies, some conceptual in nature, which inform us
about the nature of programs include Tom's (1985) definitional treatment
of inquiry-oriented programs; Champion's (1984) study on the use of
research in pre-service programs; studies of how programs of teacher
education evolve (McCaleb, Borko, Arends, Garner and Mauro, 1987);
studies on approaches to planning and problem-solving and on the use
of practical arguments in pre-service programs (Neely, 1986; Morine-
Dershimer, 1988); descriptive analyses of education courses (Goodman,
1986) and programs (Kluender, 1984); and standards for comparing more
traditional certification programs with alternative route programs (Galluzzo and Ritter, 1986; and Huling-Austin, 1986).

Research into Specific Contexts and Modalities
for Learning to Teach

Conceptions of how teachers learn to teach are understandably constrained when decontextualized. Programs of teacher education are
embedded in contextual layers. For example, different schools, colleges

and departments of education must be understood in the larger context of the universities in which they reside. Physical environment is, of course, important as well. The very buildings, structures and technologies that are provided for students to acquire knowledge about and ability in teaching are critical variables. Social interaction and social relationships of the student and the professor outside the classroom can be important and provide another example of context.

We begin with studies of institutional and organizational variation. As Bok (1986) observes, 'professional schools serve many different callings and come in many sizes and shapes.' It is important to look at institutional hallmarks and variations peculiar to schools, colleges and departments of education, since there is no guarantee that organizational structures in higher education are isomophoric to them. Those who have studied organizational functioning and climate have identified a number of factors which inform us in terms of administration, faculty and student behavior (Clark and Guba, 1980; Dill, 1980; Baldridge, 1971; McCarty and Reyes, 1987). Organizations in schools and colleges of education reflect bureaucratic models and 'organized anarchy'. Obviously the nature of the organization affects the degree of professorial autonomy, the interaction of faculty with administrative leaders, the degree of collegiality and flexibility necessary to create and recreate programs of teacher preparation and the interaction of faculty with students.

A second important contextual variable which has been the attention of some study is the nature of student and faculty interaction in the broader university environment. Astin (1977), for example, studied institutions in order to learn what aspects of the broader student experience might promote positive effects on students generally. The 1988 RATE study, for example, reported that foundations faculty in bachelors granting institutions reported almost ten hours per week reserved for office hours. One faculty member's sentiment, which follows, was typical in many interviews conducted in the Howey and Zimpher (1989) case studies:

> We're not investing in a program, we're investing in the students
> in a very, very personal way. I don't think there's a single student
> that goes through our program that doesn't have a friend on the
> faculty. I'm not saying that some wouldn't have two or three
> friends on the faculty, but they choose somebody they can go to
> and can cry on a shoulder and they can share the things they do
> and get advice....And they come to me as a person, not as a
> professor — certainly not as one of their major professors —
> simply because we hit it off. We can interact in that way. But

everybody is the same way and there are people that come to them. (p. 120)

It is also important to look at the interaction patterns of students regarding their own social class affiliation and opportunities for more broadening experiences during the course of their academic education. Both the RATE studies and the Howey and Zimpher case studies revealed limited opportunities for students to expand their rather parochial orientations.

A third way to look at context focuses more precisely on the specific on-campus modalities employed in learning to teach, especially on-site laboratory and clinical facilities. Berliner (1986) advised that scientific laboratory components be developed for teacher education programs. The possibilities here are myriad including: live students with whom to teach concepts where expert teachers can observe and provide critiques of lessons with structured recall of thinking about critical events; using videocassettes for dozens of hours of analysis of key dimensions of teaching and learning through category systems representing different conceptual focuses; practising in simulated classroom environments; analyzing videotaped teaching protocols; problem-solving through the use of interactive computers and engaging in what has been increasingly reported in the literature, analyzing or developing cases. The reviews of the literature by Gliessman (1984) on laboratory training and Joyce and Showers (1983) on the problems of adaptation from laboratory training to the classroom context are both informative in this regard.

The development and use of cases in teacher education is now reflected in the work of a number of scholars, particularly Carter and Unklesbay (1988) and Doyle (1986) at the University of Arizona, and through a number of the projects funded by the U.S. Office of Educational Research and Improvement (Waxman, Freiberg, Vaughan and Weil, 1988). Judy Shulman at the Far West Laboratory has engaged in case development for mentor and intern teachers (Shulman and Colbert, 1987, 1988). We can look forward to further cases being developed in the 'wisdom of practice studies', which form a large part of the work of Lee Shulman and his colleagues as they attempt to develop protocols that will guide future assessments of teachers. Beyond case development, other scholars are developing and studying the technological capabilities of interactive videos as another aspect of laboratory experience (Strang, Badt and Kauffman, 1987; Stevens, 1983–84; Mathison, 1986; and Martin, 1987).

Some vision is evolving in terms of transforming the context of teacher preparation through the creation of a series of laboratory experiences. These distinctly different contexts will offer multiple opportunities for research. What should be considered in this line of inquiry is understandably open-ended and we need to hold a place for those who study the organizational context of institutions and the social/interpersonal interactions of those within that environment.

Research into Education Faculty and Students

Studies of education faculty and students were reviewed in Lanier and Little's (1986) chapter on research on teacher education, in that they composed two of the 'commonplaces' of teacher education with which they were concerned. That is, 'for teaching to occur, someone (a teacher) must be teaching someone (a student) about something (a curriculum) at some place and point in time (a milieu)' (Schwab, 1978). Their review covers a range of important issues related to faculty, including social class origins, differences in work responsibility, practical and non-academic aspects of faculty life, research productivity, the growth of interest in writing and publication, propensities toward abstract thought and decision-making and attempts to establish academic image among the educational professoriate.

The range of student variables in the Lanier and Little review dealt particularly with the general profile of career decision-making, testing and demographics, issues of supply and demand, the social orientation of students, their academic ability, prepotent variables related to what students entering teacher education programs believe they already know about teaching as a result of prior socialization, and ultimately the ability of students to counter negative socialization as they move from on-campus teacher education experiences to school experiences.

Studies on the education professoriate in the United States in the recent past were largely attributable to the work of Ducharme and Agne (1982). Now this community of scholars has broadened, and the work of several colleagues is reported in a forthcoming text edited by Wisniewski and Ducharme (1988).

The 'studies' available in the early part of the decade with regard to students were often not so much a product of intellectual inquiry as they were a function of political and reform concerns regarding the capabilities, or perhaps more accurately the lack of academic capability, of those people who constitute the prospective teaching force. The initiation of longitudinal studies through AACTE's RATE committee will lend substantially to the knowledge base on the nature of students (as well as faculty) in teacher education beyond their academic aptitude, and more fully on their formal and informal activities while being prepared as teachers.

The data being developed by the community of scholars coalesced by Wisniewski and Ducharme, the RATE Committee, Howey and Zimpher's case studies, and the two national studies (National Center for Research on Teacher Education and the Education of Educators Studies) will ultimately create a rich fabric for better understanding education faculty and students, their backgrounds, aspirations and expectations and how these are played out in their personal and professional lives. The authors have just completed a review of the literature on education professors and deans for the forthcoming *Handbook of Research on Teacher Education* (Houston, Sikula and Haberman, in press) and reviewed over 150 studies that informed them in this area.

With regard to research on teacher education students, a range of studies exists in the United States from which we have selected a few to represent the diversity. Studies, for example, have been conducted which link the effects of testing to minority recruitment (Smith, Miller and Joy, 1988; and Morehead, 1986), the effects of testing generally to recruitment (Aksamit, Mitchell and Pozehl, 1987), the quality of recruits who come from education versus non-education programs (Olsen, 1985; and Book, Freeman and Brousseau, 1985), performance in academic coursework (Nelli, 1984; Dobry, Murphy and Schmidt, 1985; Krockover, Mortlock and Johnson, 1987; Matczynski, Siler, McLaughlin and Smith, 1988; and Skipper and Quantz, 1987), comparisons of teacher candidates with classroom teachers (Nelli and Atwood, 1986; and Kowalski and Weaver, 1988), and students who select elementary versus secondary studies (Book and Freeman, 1986). Howey and Strom (1987) review an extensive literature on general human qualities which they posit would have predictive validity in terms of teaching effectiveness. Similar scholarship has been engaged in by Case *et al.*, 1988; Clark and Fishetti, 1987; Joseph and Green, 1986; Fisher and Feldman, 1984–85; Lyson and Falk, 1984; McCaleb, 1984; and Haberman, 1987.

Research into Clinical Teacher Education

Clinical teacher education, according to Griffin (1986), is defined as 'the set of learning opportunities that take place in ongoing "real world" classrooms and schools'. By definition then we include in this cluster of studies early field experiences and observation and participation experiences in school settings that accompany both general and special methods courses as well as a review of the literature on student teaching and internships, stopping short of entry year and induction programs.

Historically this was the focus for research into teacher preparation in this country. Guiding our understanding of field experience and student teaching were the seminal works of such people as Florence Stratemeyer and Margaret Lindsey (1958) and L.O. Andrews (1964). Many scholars have added to this database, including contributions to an understanding of political and legal issues of university/school collaboration (Hazard, 1976; Lang, Quick and Johnson, 1975). More recently we have witnessed attempts to review the accumulated research in various ways. The three-volume series, Advances in Teacher Education, has been most helpful in this regard. Reviews here include the effects of early experience (Waxman and Walberg, 1986; Applegate's (1987) analysis of early experience; Zeichner's (1987) view of the ecology of field experience; Watts' (1987) review of student teaching; and Zimpher's (1987) analysis of the role of university supervision in student teaching.

A major study of student teaching, conducted by the former Center for Research and Development into Teacher Education, led to Griffin and Edwards' (1981) comprehensive analysis of problems and promising practices in student teaching. Prior to this, conditions of student teaching were examined as part of the national survey undertaken by Yarger, Howey and Joyce (1977). Other large-scale studies in terms of student teaching include Johnson and Yates (1982) and McIntyre and Norris (1980). Burden (1986), Reyes (1987), Ross (1988) and Copeland (1987) have made contributions to this field by studying different aspects of student development, especially as teacher candidates confront the reality of practice. Yarger *et al.* (1977), Isam, Carter and Stribling (1981) and Solliday (1982) have studied role perceptions in terms of human relations in field supervision and the demonstration of caring tendencies. Others have documented the considerable confusion with regard to appropriate roles for both cooperating teachers and university supervisors in field experiences and student teaching (Griffin and Edwards, 1981; Koehler, 1984; Zimpher, deVoss and Nott, 1981).

Probably no other category has received as much attention in the research literature as have studies that seek to determine the influence of university supervisors and cooperating teachers in the development of student teachers. The McIntyre review (1983) was devoted almost exclusively to this topic. More multidimensional qualitative studies as conducted by Zeichner (1988) suggest that student teacher socialization is less a function of either the particular belief systems of the student or influence of cooperating teachers or university supervisors as much as it is the socialization which occurs at school sites. In all reviews of field experience and student teaching research in the past decades, more naturalistic studies are called for to account for the complexities of student teacher development. Now that we have begun to blend our research on event structured knowledge (Carter and Richardson-Koehler, 1986) and issues of learning to teach more fully with elements of field and clinical experiences, further research is likely to be more robust.

The impact of the teacher preparation curriculum on field and clinical experiences remains a critical concern. Zeichner and Tabachnick (1982) and Goodman (1983) concluded that diverse orientations and perspectives have an impact on curriculum implementation. As Griffin (1983) cautions, however, there is little evidence that program goals find their way into the nature of field experiences and student teaching or, as Zeichner (1987) observed, there abound program description entries, but these descriptive data are not interwoven into any sustained pattern of inquiry such that they reveal relationships between curricular content and field and student teaching experiences.

Nonetheless, progress is being made and we observe a distinct turn in the last five to six years of more in-depth qualitative study of particular aspects of field experiences. A potpourri of promising studies illustrate this. First, there are studies which take a close look at supervisory discourse from several different vantage points; a view of preferred supervising strategies (Zahorik, 1988); how supervisors convey knowledge of practice to student teachers (Rust, 1988); how to increase the interactions of all involved during student teaching (Shapiro and Sheehan, 1986); increased student teacher involvement (Christensen, 1988); the nature of supervising discourse (Zeichner and Liston, 1985); and the potential of group clinical supervision to improve practice (Buttery and Weller, 1988).

Other studies have focused on the impact of the student teaching experience on students through the case study method (Goodman, 1985) and through reflective journals (Shulman, 1987; and Borko *et al.*, 1987). Another set of studies has taken a closer look at socialization/professionalization, through analysis of barriers to effective practice (Richardson-Koehler, 1988), conceptions of professional role (Borko, 1986, Tabachnick and Zeichner, 1984; Magliaro and Borko, 1986), and the development of student teacher conception of role and how or whether student teachers come to value student teaching (Feiman-Nemser and Buchmann, 1987). Others have attempted to identify differences between elementary and secondary student teaching (Killian and McIntyre, 1988), the degree of stress encountered during student teaching (Kaunitz *et al.*, 1986), student teacher concern about classroom discipline (Wright, O'Hair and Alley, 1988), more effective ways to involve cooperating teachers in planning of student teaching experiences (Hollingsworth, 1988), and ways to involve pupils in providing feedback to student teachers (Martin, 1987). Still others have added substantially to our knowledge of perceptions of early field experience (Lasley and Applegate, 1985; Bischoff *et al.*, 1988).

Again, conclusions drawn from many of the studies identified here are that we need to delve in an even more fine-grained manner into the experiences of student teachers in practice and that we need to look more carefully at the interactions or discourse phenomena of cooperating teachers, student teachers and university supervisors in triadic and in dyadic situations. Zeichner (1987) provides an ecological framework for looking more intensively at the nature of field experiences including the relationship between program goals and conceptions of teaching and learning which undergird programs and their manifestations in field experiences; the retention of particular conceptual bases as students continue to engage in practice in field sites; our ability to prepare effectively and work collaboratively with cooperating teachers in structuring program and field experiences; and the degree to which there is evidence of professional and, more importantly, instructional analysis during the course of field experiences.

Research into the Induction and the Socialization of Beginning Teachers

The induction period of professional development is generally recognized as the beginning years of teaching and as a transition stage from pre-service teacher education to that of becoming an experienced classroom teacher. Data combined from studies which document the considerable problems of beginning teachers combined with data about those conditions necessary to maximize learning on the job make a powerful case for more formal induction. These latter conditions call for continuing discourse about the 'whys' and 'whens' of teaching with a more expert teacher. Thus the research on learning to teach strongly suggests that these formative first years be viewed more rightly as an extension of pre-service teacher preparation and not some peripheral nicety.

There is not space to review the many burgeoning studies that are now focusing on these critical first years of teaching. We would be remiss, however, if we did not acknowledge their importance, their obvious relationship to pre-service teacher preparation, and at least the conceptual frames which exist to guide further conceptual work and inquiry into these endeavours. Veenman (1984) not only provides us with his comprehensive synthesis of the problems of beginning teachers as a basis for designing induction programs; he also presents three perspectives on the development of beginning teachers as a basis for designing teacher induction programs. The first is the recognition of the existence of developmental stages of concern among beginning teachers (Fuller, 1969; Fuller and Bown, 1975). This perspective supports teachers going through stages of teacher concern, starting with survival concerns, moving to a focus on teaching strategies, and eventually to focusing on learner outcomes. The second perspective, the cognitive development framework, has several variations but fundamentally focuses on the content and thinking of teachers at different stages of their careers and lives. This perspective suggests a hierarchy from less to more complex cognitive abilities (Sprinthall and Theis-Sprinthall, 1983), and relies on ways of identifying levels of cognitive development to work more effectively with adult learners who differ in cognitive ability and to increase their cognitive complexity. The third framework, as noted earlier, is the teacher socialization framework and incorporates the work of such scholars as Gehrke (1976, 1981) and Zeichner and Tabachnick (1982). It focuses on how beginning teachers adapt to the role of teacher, the way they give meaning to their beliefs, and the way they adapt to the beliefs of others as they enter various school contexts from a variety of pre-service program structures.

These approaches constitute vital references for studying the thought patterns, the belief systems and behaviors of beginning teachers and how these are mediated, especially by the school context. They also pose frameworks for those interested in the development of programs to meet the demands of newly inducted teachers, as well as the study of these programs. There is a small but growing number of studies to consider in further conceptualizing such research, including documentation of the 'sink or swim' approach imposed on most new teachers (Lortie, 1975; Varah, Theune and Parker, 1986), recording the stresses and problems of first-year teachers (Ryan, 1980; Howey and Bents, 1979), issues related to first-year teacher expectations (Weinstein, 1988; Marso and Pigge, 1987), first-year teacher performance (Emmer, 1986; Hitz and Roper, 1986; Hidalgo, 1986–87; Mark and Anderson, 1985), and student perceptions of support (Odell, 1986; Huffman and Leak, 1986). The monograph prepared by the Association of Teacher Educators (Brooks, 1987) on the beginning years of teaching makes a substantial contribution to our knowledge of the phenomenon of entry-year transition.

An intensive study of two state mandated induction programs through which teachers must pass before receiving certification is reported in detail by Hoffman and Edwards (1986) in *Reality and Reform in*

Clinical Teacher Education. Findings from this study point to policy implications and to the difficulties in design and implementation of entry-year or induction programs. They also provide a framework to answer the major question, how to determine the potential impact of these programs (Griffin, 1985; Hawk, 1986–87). The fact that ten of the twenty-nine Office of Educational Research and Improvement's federally funded projects, *Using Research to Improve Teacher Education Grants*, focused on the entry year suggests that we could have, in the near future in the United States, a more broad-based analysis of the nature of entry-year/induction programs, and some beginning data on the *efficacy* or *impact* of such programs as well.

Summary Thoughts

This analysis culminates with the acknowledgment that even identifying major lines of inquiry and providing representative sources in the space allotted was difficult. Nonetheless, it is hoped that the chapter is helpful in presenting more clearly major foci for inquiry in the U.S. While individual scholars continue to promulgate research findings, we have a long way to go in terms of scholarship into teacher preparation. There is a need for more and better policy-oriented research. Throughout this review important social issues have been uncovered by many of these studies: the absence of minority representation in the prospective teacher cohort, issues of academic ability, prospective teachers' parochial and culturally insular nature, proposals which provide misguided accountability, test bias, and policies more concerned over the structure of teacher preparation than its substance. Inquiry that points to more reasoned policy is badly needed.

At the same time we continue to conduct our scholarship into teacher preparation mostly by way of individual faculty and doctoral studies. It is to be hoped that the directions cited in the six clusters of research identified here will move forward to actual research programs and to more collaborative studies with more power. We need to move developmentally beyond the level of course analysis to looking more fully at programs as interventions. We need to look more fundamentally at the process of learning how to teach. A new world of case knowledge is opening up to us and we are improving our methods for collecting more qualitative and more fine-grained data and information.

In the United States, as we move from largely quantitative to more multidimensional qualitative methodologies, perhaps the next phase will be more research that assumes a critical perspective. Because of a growing educational underclass in this country, we need to look more toward research that critically examines hegemony. We need to move toward a more liberating inquiry which causes us in the sense of reflectivity not to take anything for granted. In a liberation orientation there is a basic concern over both the origin of the research and the tellers of the tale. We need study that not only addresses the major problems in our schools within this society but that more fully involves those who are the focus of the study, namely teachers.

The great majority of studies referenced herein largely codify more traditional forms of university-based research. On occasion studies are cited that involve a shared interest on the part of both university and school personnel. Even less frequently works are cited that have evolved from on-site action research, conducted primarily by teachers. As Carr and Kemmis (1983) remind us, certainly there are teachers who have historically made their own way toward the systematic study of their teaching. Instances of collaborative action research increasingly serve as examples of staff development and as examples of self-discovery in understanding beliefs and assumptions that undergird our notions of practical action (Oberg, 1985). However, for action research to fulfil its potential it must go beyond describing and interpreting classroom practices, and generate means for analyzing and improving practice. The rich history of researchers who have utilized collaborative action research is impressive (Jaccullo-Noto, 1985; Connelly and Clandinin, 1985; Buchmann, 1985; Ward, 1983; Griffin, Lieberman and Jaccullo-Noto, 1983; Tickunoff and Griffin, 1979; and Oja, 1982). Perhaps we will move in this direction as well, and in the not too distant future an overview of research such as this will include many more examples of such work.

Epilogue

Those familiar with the literature on teacher preparation in the United States over the last quarter-century could well infer that considerable ferment, if not major change, has occurred. The authors contend, however, that this literature reflects more exhortation for than evidence of change. From our perspective there were few fundamental changes in the mission and character of teacher preparation generally over this period. Certainly some diversity exists. The fact that over 1200 institutions of higher education in the U.S. prepare teachers ensures this. But while teachers can be prepared in a high quality manner in a variety of settings, the quality of teacher preparation across this mosaic of institutional contexts and cultures has been and remains uneven.

While exhortations for 'reform' during the 1960s, 1970s and into the 1980s were pervasive, several major deterrents to change were also readily documentable. For example, research into teaching, let alone into teacher preparation itself, has not historically provided much guidance for new directions. In the U.S. teacher preparation is typically an endeavour grossly underfunded resulting in, among other things, faculty who are generally overextended. The common procedure for the licensing of new teachers — program approval — can accurately be characterized as a case of the hens guarding the henhouse. Limited interest by the general public in teacher preparation, let alone scrutiny, has resulted in little external impetus for change. An extension of this is the cyclic demand for tens of thousands of new teachers for a basically conservative system of schooling which has repeatedly pre-empted movement in new directions. The collective body of teacher educators generally has been characterized by a commitment to people and practice rather than ideas and scholarship. The teachers' unions' basic posture toward the initial education of teachers has been one of benign neglect. Finally, there has been a fundamental lack of leadership, individually and collectively, intellectually and politically.

These constraints have not been fully acknowledged in a literature often approaching missionary zeal. It appears now that they are, and it is important to note them in interpreting present conditions, policy and practice relative to teacher preparation. If present practice is not what it should be, and it isn't, there has nonetheless recently been considerable movement forward from the above characterization. There are, in fact, conditions which suggest the late 1980s may well be a watershed in teacher preparation in the United States.

Discernible *lines* of inquiry and *programs* of research into teaching now provide considerable guidance to informed teacher educators. Recent insights from cognitive studies especially have considerably advanced our understanding not only of teaching and learning but also of *learning to teach*. In addition, well conceived naturalistic studies of classroom processes which examine the social and cultural as well as cognitive dimensions of classroom life provide general pedagogical knowledge to complement our growing understanding of pedagogical *content* knowledge. We are moving out of a neo-behavioristic era of teacher preparation.

Standards being evolved within the Holmes Group, some major revisions in national accreditation, and the promise of the voluntary credentialing of experienced teachers by the new National Board for Professional Teaching Standards all address what historically has been the largely political and self-serving nature of program approval. Beyond this there has been the major intrusion of teacher testing and not only state educational agencies but state legislatures into the initial education of teachers. Teacher preparation has become a public concern. Thus pressures calling for change, both internal and external to the profession, have come together with increased knowledge to guide those changes.

There are other notable changes as well. The relatively brief history of teacher unions in the U.S. understandably has focused on conditions of the teacher's workplace. Now, however, there is movement towards fuller professionalization. The unions' major involvement on the new National Standards Board, their support of Holmes, their involvement in several entry-year programs for new teachers, their experimentation with career ladders in limited instances — these are all evidence of this. There is, nonetheless, a considerable way to go and there is little doubt that union muscle must be brought more centrally to bear on matters pertaining to the support and extension of initial teacher preparation and to veteran teachers' expanded roles and responsibilities in clinical training for pre-service and beginning teachers.

There is, when one examines the longitudinal data in the aforementioned RATE studies, more evidence at this time of broader, programmatic changes in pre-service teacher preparation than at any time in the past. The Holmes Group, which among other things should properly be understood as a cross-institutional change strategy, has served as a major catalyst in this regard — not only for the some ninety research-oriented institutions within the Holmes Group. Many of those institutions not involved in the Holmes effort have taken considerable exception to the implications by some that their not being part of this national consortium suggests that they might be less than capable in terms of educating teachers or less than fully motivated to pursue this function in a self-renewing manner. Thus institutions have documented their change efforts, as have Holmes-related institutions.

Finally, when identifying recent conditions providing impetus for change, one needs to note the changing nature of the teacher education professoriate itself. For some time there has been a 'buyers' market' in terms of hiring new professors in education, given a relatively small turnover of faculty in most schools, colleges and departments of education (a situation which will shortly be dramatically reversed). This factor, combined with improved forms of scholarship, especially relative to teaching and teacher education and concomitant better graduate training, has resulted in a younger cohort of teacher education faculty concerned more with research and development than many of their counterparts historically. The ability to sustain and even expand and improve such scholarship, as large numbers of new faculty enter the ranks, will have much to say about the nature and success of future reform efforts.

In summary, we appear to have turned a major conceptual corner in terms of how we view learning to teach. There now exists ample pressure, external as well as internal, for alternatives to the status quo. These can be combined with considerably expanded knowledge about teacher preparation. Whether we have the collective resources and will to move forward boldly on the best of what we have learned is problematic, however. The armada of institutions preparing teachers has been turned from a long-standing course, but their future direction is still unclear.

References

AMERICAN ASSOCIATION OF COLLEGES FOR TEACHER EDUCATION (1987) *Teaching Teachers: Facts and Figures*. Washington: AACTE.

AMERICAN ASSOCIATION OF COLLEGES FOR TEACHER EDUCATION (1988) *Teaching Teachers: Facts and Figures*. Washington: AACTE.

AKSAMIT, D., MITCHELL, J. and POZEHL, B. (1987) Relationships between PPST and ACT scores and their implications for the basic skills testing of prospective teachers. *Journal of Teacher Education*, 38, 6, 48–52.

ANDERSON, L. (1987) Classroom instruction, in M. REYNOLDS (Ed.) *Knowledge Base for the Beginning Teacher*. Oxford: Pergamon Press.

ANDREWS, L. (1964) *Student Teaching*. New York: Center for Applied Research in Education.

APPLEGATE, J. (1987) Early field experiences: Three viewpoints, in M. HABERMAN and J. BACKUS (Eds) *Advances in Teacher Education*. Vol. 3, Norwood, N.J.: Ablex.

ASTIN, A. (1977) *Four Critical Years*. San Francisco, Calif.: Jossey-Bass.

BALDRIDGE, J. (1971) *Academic Governance*. Berkeley, Calif.: McCutchan.

BARNES, H. (1989) Structuring knowledge for beginning teaching, in M. REYNOLDS (Ed.) *Knowledge Base for the Beginning Teacher*. Oxford: Pergamon Press.

BERLINER, D. (1986) Laboratory settings and the study of teacher education. *Journal of Teacher Education*, 36, 6, 2–9.

BERLINER, D. (1988) *The Development of Expertise in Pedagogy*. Charles W. Hunt Memorial Lecture, presented at the annual meeting of the American Association of Colleges for Teacher Education, New Orleans.

BISCHOFF, J., FARRIS, P. and HENNINGER, M. (1988) Student perceptions of early clinical field experiences. *Action in Teacher Education*, 10, 3, 22–25.

BOK, D. (1986) *Higher Learning*. Cambridge, Mass.: Harvard University Press.

BOLIN, F. (1988) Helping student teachers think about teaching. *Journal of Teacher Education*, 39, 2, 48–54.

BOOK, C. and FREEMAN, D. (1986) Differences in entry characteristics of elementary and secondary teacher candidates. *Journal of Teacher Education*, 37, 2, 47–54.

BOOK, C., FREEMAN, D. and BROUSSEAU, B. (1985) Comparing academic backgrounds and career aspirations of education and non-education majors. *Journal of Teacher Education*, 36, 3, 27–30.

BOOK, H. (1986) Clinical teacher education: The induction years, in J. HOFFMAN and S. EDWARDS (Eds) *Reality and Reform in Clinical Teacher Education.* New York: Random House.

BORKO, H., LALIK, R. and TOMCHIN, E. (1987) Student teachers' understandings of successful and unsuccessful teaching. *Teaching and Teacher Education*, 3, 2, 77–90.

BROOKS, D. (Ed.) (1987) *Teacher Induction: A New Beginning.* Reston, Va.: Association of Teacher Educators.

BROUSSEAU, B., BOOK, C. and BYERS, J. (1988) Teacher beliefs and the cultures of teaching. *Journal of Teacher Education*, 39, 6, 33–39.

BUCHMANN, M. (1985) 'Improving education by keeping educational research and practice apart.' Paper presented at the Meadow Brook Research Symposium, Rochester, Mich.

BURDEN, P. (1986) Teacher development: Implications for teacher education, in J. RATHS and L. KATZ (Eds) *Advances in Teacher Education.* Vol. 2. Norwood, N.J.: Ablex.

BUTTERY, T. and WELLER, L. (1988) Group clinical supervision: A paradigm for preservice instructional enhancement. *Action in Teacher Education*, 10, 1, 61–74.

CARR, W. and KEMMIS, S. (1983) *Becoming Critical: Knowing through Action Research.* Waurn Ponds, Vic.: Deakin University.

CARTER, K. and RICHARDSON-KOEHLER, V. (1986) The process and content of initial years of teaching programs, in G. GRIFFIN and S. MILLIES (Eds) *The First Years of Teaching: Background Papers and a Proposal.* Chicago, Ill.: University of Illinois at Chicago and Illinois State Board of Education.

CARTER, K. and UNKLESBAY, A. (1988) 'Case methods in teaching and law.' Paper presented at the annual meeting of the American Association of Colleges for Teacher Education, New Orleans.

CARTER, K., CUSHING, K., SABERS, D., STEIN, P. and BERLINER, D. (1988) Expert-novice differences in perceiving and processing visual classroom information. *Journal of Teacher Education*, 39, 3, 235–231.

CARTER, K., SABERS, D., CUSHING, K., PINNEGAR, S. and BERLINER, D. (1987) Processing and using information about students: A study of expert, novice, and postulant teachers. *Teaching and Teacher Education*, 3, 2, 147–157.

CASE, C., SHIVE, R.J., IBGEBRETSON, K. and SPIEGEL, V. (1988) Minority teacher education: Recruitment and retention. *Journal of Teacher Education*, 39, 4, 54–57.

CHAMPION, R. (1984) Faculty reported use of research in teacher preparation courses: Six instructional scenarios. *Journal of Teacher Education*, 35, 5, 9–12.

CHRISTENSEN, P. (1988) The nature of feedback student teachers receive in post-observation conferences with the university supervisor: A comparison with O'Neal's study of cooperating teacher feedback. *Teaching and Teacher Education*, 4, 3, 275–286.

CLARK, C. and PETERSON, P. (1986) Teachers' thought processes, in M.C. WITTROCK (Ed.) *Handbook of Research on Teaching.* 3rd ed. New York: Macmillan.

CLARK, D. and GUBA, E. (1980) Schools, colleges and departments of education: Demographic and contextual features, in D. GRIFFITHS and D. McCARTY (Eds) *The Dilemma of the Deanship.* Daneville, Ill.: Interstate Printers and Publishers.

CLARK, R. and FISCHETTI, J. (1987) Candidate selection in a fifth year teacher education recruitment model: A multi-stage partnership approach. *Journal of Teacher Education*, 38, 2, 26–30.

CLIFT, P., HOUSTON, R. and PUGACH, M. (in press) *Encouraging Reflective Practice: An Examination of Issues and Exemplars.* New York: Teachers College Press.

CONNELLY, F. and CLANDININ, J. (1985) 'Narrative history and the study of minded practice: Narratives of reference.' Paper presented at the Meadow Brook Research Symposium, Rochester, Mich.

COPELAND, W. (1987) Classroom management and student teachers' cognitive abilities: A relationship. *American Educational Research Journal*, 24, 2, 219–236.

DILL, D. (1980) Schools of education as complex organizations. in D. GRIFFITHS and D. McCARTHY (Eds) *The Dilemma of the Deanship.* Daneville, Ill.: Interstate Printers and Publishers.

DOBRY, A., MURPHY, P. and SCHMIDT, D. (1985) Predicting teacher competence. *Action in Teacher Education*, 7, 1–2, 69–74.

DOYLE, W. (1986) Classroom organization and management, in M. WITTROCK (Ed.) *Handbook of Research on Teaching.* 3rd ed. New York: Macmillan.

DUCHARME, E. and AGNE, R. (1982) The educational professoriate: A research-based perspective. *Journal of Teacher Education*, 33, 6, 30–36.

EMMER, E. (1986) Academic activities and tasks in first-year teachers' classrooms. *Teaching and Teacher Education*, 2, 3, 229–244.

EVERTSON, C., HAWLEY, W. and ZLOTNIK, M. (1985) Making a difference in educational quality through teacher education. *Journal of Teacher Education*, 36, 3, 2–12.

FEIMAN-NEMSER, S. and BUCHMANN, M. (1987) When is student teaching teacher education? *Teaching and Teacher Education*, 3, 4, 255–273.

FISHER, R. and FELDMAN, M. (1984–85) Trends in standards for admission to teacher education. *Action in Teacher Education*, 6, 4, 59–63.

FULLER, F. (1969) Concerns of teachers: A developmental conceptualization. *American Educational Research Journal*, 6, 207–226.

FULLER, F. and BOWN, O. (1975) Becoming a teacher, in K. RYAN (Ed.) *Teacher Education*, Chicago, Ill.: University of Chicago Press.

GALLUZZO, G. and RITTER, D. (1986) Identifying standards for evaluating alternate route programs. *Action in Teacher Education*, 8, 2, 59–65.

GEHRKE, N. (1976) The role personalization of beginning secondary teachers: A grounded theory study. Doctoral dissertation, Arizona State University.

GEHRKE, N. (1981) A grounded theory study of beginning teachers' role personalization through reference group relations. *Journal of Teacher Education*, 32, 6, 34–38.

GLIESSMAN, D. (1984) Changing teacher performance, in L. KATZ and J. RATHS (Eds) *Advances in Teacher Education.* Vol. 1. Norwood, N.J.: Ablex.

GOODLAD, J. (1988) Studying the education of educators: Values-driven inquiry. *Phi Delta Kappan*, 70, 2, 104–111.

GOODMAN, J. (1983) The seminar's role in the education of student teachers: A case study. *Journal of Teacher Education*, 34, 3, 44–49.

GOODMAN, J. (1985) What students learn from early field experiences: A case study and critical analysis. *Journal of Teacher Education*, 36, 6, 42–48.

GOODMAN, J. (1986) University education courses and the professional preparation of teachers: A descriptive analysis. *Teaching and Teacher Education*, 2, 4, 341–353.

GRIFFIN, G. (1983) *Student teaching and the commonplaces of schooling*. Austin, Tex.: University of Texas at Austin, R&D Center for Teacher Education, Research in Teacher Education Program.

GRIFFIN, G. (1985) Teacher induction: Research issues. *Journal of Teacher Education*, 37, 1, 42–46.

GRIFFIN, G. (1986) Issues in student teaching: A review, in J. RATHS and L. KATZ (Eds) *Advances in Teacher Education*. Vol. 2. Norwood, N.J.: Ablex.

GRIFFIN, G. and Edwards, S. (1981) *Student Teaching: Problems and Promising Practices*. Austin, Tex.: University of Texas at Austin, R&D Center for Teacher Education, Research in Teacher Education Program.

GRIFFIN, G., LIBERMAN, A. and JACULLO-NOTO, J. (1983) *Interactive Research and Development on Schooling: Executive Summary of the Final Report*. Austin, Tex.: University of Texas Research and Development Center for Teacher Education.

HABERMAN, M. (1987) *Recruiting and Selecting Teachers for Urban Schools*. New York: ERIC Clearinghouse on Urban Education, Teachers College Columbia University and Reston, Va.: Association of Teacher Educators.

HAWK, P. (1986–87) Beginning teacher programs: Benefits for the experienced educator. *Association of Teacher Educators*, 8, 4, 59–63.

HAZARD, W. (1976) *Student Teaching and the Law*. Washington, DC: ERIC Clearinghouse on Teacher Education.

HIDALGO, F. (1986–87) The evolving concerns of first-year junior high school teachers in difficult settings: Three case studies. *Action in Teacher Education*, 8, 4, 75–79.

HITZ, R. and ROPER, S. (1986) The teacher's first year: Implications for teacher educators. *Action in Teacher Education*, 8, 3, 65–71.

HOFFMAN, J. and EDWARDS, S. (Eds) (1986) *Reality and Reform in Clinical Teacher Education*. New York: Random House, Inc.

HOLLINGSWORTH, S. (1988) Making field-based programs work: A three-level approach to reading education. *Journal of Teacher Education*, 39, 4, 28–36.

HOUSTON, R., SIKULA, J. and Haberman, M. (in press) *Handbook of Research on Teacher Education*. New York: Macmillan.

HOWEY, K. and BENTS, R. (1979) *Toward Meeting the Needs of the Beginning Teacher*. St Paul, Minn. Midwest Teacher Corps Network and the University of Minnesota.

HOWEY, K. and STROM, S. (1987) Teacher selection reconsidered, in M. HABERMAN and J. BACKUS (Eds) *Advances in Teacher Education*. Vol. 3, Norwood, N.J.: Ablex.

HOWEY, K. and ZIMPHER, N. (1989) *Profiles of Preservice Teacher Education: Inquiry into the Nature of Programs*. Albany N.Y.: SUNY Press.

HUFFMAN, G. and LEAK, S. (1986) Beginning teachers' perceptions of mentors. *Journal of Teacher Education*, 37, 1, 22–25.

HULING-AUSTIN, L. (1986) Factors to consider in alternative certification programs: What can be learned from teacher induction research? *Association of Teacher Educators*, 8, 2, 51–58.

ISAM, M., CARTER, H. and STRIBLING, R. (1981) A study of the entry mechanisms of university-based teacher educators. Unpublished manuscript, University of Texas at Austin, Research and Development Center for Teacher Education.

JACCULLO-NOTO, J. (1985) 'Collaborative action research and staff development.' Paper presented at the Meadow Brook Research Symposium, Rochester, Mich.

JOHNSON, J. and YATES, J. (1982) *A National Survey of Student Teaching Programs.* Dekalb, Ill.: Northern Illinois University.

JOSEPH, P. and GREEN, N. (1986) Perspectives on reasons for becoming teachers. *Journal of Teacher Education*, 37, 6, 28–33.

JOYCE, B. and SHOWERS, B. (1983) *Power in Staff Development through Research on Training.* Alexandria, Va.: Association for Supervision and Curriculum Development.

KAUNITZ, N., SPOKANE, A., LISSITZ, R. and STREIN, W. (1986) Stress in student teachers: A multidimensional scaling analysis of elicited stressful situations. *Teaching and Teacher Education*, 2, 2, 169–180.

KILLIAN, J. and McINTYRE, D. (1988) Grade level as a factor in participation during early field experiences. *Journal of Teacher Education*, 39, 2, 36–41.

KLUENDER, M. (1984) Teacher education programs in the 1980s: Some selected characteristics. *Journal of Teacher Education*, 35, 4, 33–35.

KOEHLER, V. (1984) 'University supervision of student teaching.' Paper presented at the annual meeting of the American Educational Research Association, New Orleans, April.

KOEHLER, V. (1985) Research on preservice teacher education. *Journal of Teacher Education*, 36, 1, 23–30.

KOWALSKI, T. and WEAVER, R. (1988) Characteristics of outstanding teachers: An academic and social involvement profile. *Action in Teacher Education*, 10, 2, 93–100.

KROCKOVER, G., MORTLOCK, H. and JOHNSON, B. (1987) Comparing success predictors and common core course performance. *Action in Teacher Education*, 9, 1, 61–65.

LANG, D., QUICK, A. and JOHNSON, J. (1975) *The Supervision of Student Teachers.* Mt Pleasant, Minn.: The Great Lakes Publishing Co.

LANIER, J. and LITTLE, J. (1986) Research on teacher education, in M.C. WITTROCK (Ed.) *Handbook of Research on Teaching.* 3rd ed. New York: Macmillan.

LASLEY, T. and APPLEGATE, J. (1985) Problems of early field experience students of teaching. *Teaching and Teacher Education*, 1, 3, 221–227.

LORTIE, D. (1975) *School Teacher: A Sociological Study.* Chicago, Ill.: University of Chicago Press.

LYSON, T. and FALK, W. (1984) Recruitment to school teaching: The relationship between high school plans and early adult attainments. *American Educational Research Journal*, 21, 1, 181–193.

McCALEB, J. (1984) Selecting a measure of oral communication as a predictor of teaching performance. *Journal of Teacher Education*, 35, 5, 33–38.

McCALEB, J., BORKO, H., ARENDS, R., GARNER, R. and MAURO, L. (1987) Innovation in teacher education: The evolution of a program. *Journal of Teacher Education*, 38, 4, 57–64.

McCARTY, D. and REYES, P. (1987) Organizational modes of governance: Academic deans' decision-making styles. *Journal of Teacher Education*, 35, 5, 2–9.

McDiarmid, W., Felman-Nemser, S., Melnick, S. and Parker, M. (1987) 'Changing conceptions of beginning teacher education students: A study of an introductory education course.' Paper presented at the annual meeting of the American Educational Research Association, Washington, DC.

McIntyre, D. (1983) *Field Experience in Teacher Education*. Washington, DC: Foundation for Excellence in Teacher Education and the ERIC Clearinghouse on Teacher Education.

McIntyre, D. and Norris, W. (1980) The state of the art of preservice teacher education programs and supervision of field experiences. *Action in Teacher Education*, 2, 3, 67–69.

Magliaro, S. and Borko, H. (1986) A naturalistic investigation of experienced teachers' and student teachers' instructional practices. *Teaching and Teacher Education*, 2, 2, 127–137.

Mark, J. and Anderson, B. (1985) Teacher survival rates in St. Louis, 1969–1982. *American Educational Research Journal*, 22, 3, 413–421.

Marso, R. and Pigge, F. (1987) Differences between self-perceived job expectations and job realities of beginning teachers. *Journal of Teacher Education*, 38, 6, 53–56.

Martin, D. (1987) Use of stimulated recall in videotape analysis of student teacher performance. *Action in Teacher Education*, 9, 3, 71–83.

Matczynski, T., Siler, E., McLaughlin, M. and Smith, J. (1988) A comparative analysis of achievement in arts and science courses by teacher education and non-teacher education graduates. *Journal of Teacher Education*, 39, 3, 32–36.

Mathison, C. (1986) Teacher training in educational technology: What student teachers want to know. *Action in Teacher Education*, 8, 3, 79–86.

Morehead, M. (1986) Minorities and admission to teacher education. *Action in Teacher Education*, 8, 1, 61–64.

Morine-Dershimer, G. (1988) Premises in the practical arguments of preservice teachers. *Teaching and Teacher Education*, 4, 3, 215–229.

National Center for Research on Teacher Education (1989) Teacher education and learning to teach: A research agenda. *Journal of Teacher Education*, 39, 6, 27–32.

Neely, A. (1986) Planning and problem solving in teacher education. *Journal of Teacher Education*, 37, 3, 29–33.

Nelli, E. (1984) A research-based response to allegations that education students are academically inferior. *Action in Teacher Education*, 6, 3, 73–80.

Nelli, E. and Atwood, V. (1986) Teacher education students and classroom teachers: A comparison of conative levels. *Journal of Teacher Education*, 37, 3, 46–50.

Oberg, A. (1985) 'The personal knowledge of the practitioner.' Paper presented at the Meadow Brook Research Symposium, Rochester, Mich.

Odell, S. (1986) Induction support of new teachers: A functional approach. *Journal of Teacher Education*, 37, 1, 26–29.

Oja, S. (1982) *A Two-year Study of Teacher Stages of Development in Relation to Collaborative Action Research in School*: Final Report. Durham, N.H.: University of New Hampshire, Collaborative Action Research Project Office.

Olsen, D. (1985) The quality of prospective teachers: Education vs. noneducation graduates. *Journal of Teacher Education*, 36, 5, 56–59.

REYES, D. (1987) Cognitive development of teacher candidates: An analysis. *Journal of Teacher Education*, 38, 2, 18–21.

RICHARDSON-KOEHLER, V. (1988) Barriers to the effective supervision of student teaching: A field study. *Journal of Teacher Education*, 39, 2, 28–34.

ROSS, E.W. (1988) Becoming a teacher: The development of preservice teacher perspectives. *Action in Teacher Education*, 10, 2, 101–109.

RUST, F.O. (1988) How supervisors think about teaching. *Journal of Teacher Education*, 39, 2, 56–64.

RYAN, K. (Ed.) (1980) *Biting the Apple: Accounts of First-year Teachers*. New York: Longman.

SCARDAMELIA, M. and BEREITER, C. (1987) Conceptions of teaching and approaches to core problems, in M. REYNOLDS (Ed.) *Knowledge Base for the Beginning Teacher*. Oxford: Pergamon Press.

SCHWAB, J. (1978) *Science, Curriculum and Liberal Education: Selected Essays*. Chicago, Ill.: University of Chicago Press.

SHAPIRO, P. and Sheehan, A. (1986) The supervision of student teachers: A new diagnostic tool. *Journal of Teacher Education*, 37, 6, 35–39.

SHULMAN, J. (1987) From veteran parent to novice teacher: A case study of a student teacher. *Teaching and Teacher Education*, 3, 1, 13–27.

SHULMAN, J. and COLBERT, J. (1987) *The Mentor Teacher Casebook*. San Francisco, Calif.: Far West Laboratory for Educational Research and Development and Eugene, Ore.: ERIC Clearinghouse for Educational Management.

SHULMAN, J. and COLBERT, J. (1988) *The Intern Teacher Casebook*. San Francisco, Calif.: Far West Laboratory for Educational Research and Development and Eugene, Ore.: ERIC Clearinghouse for Educational Management.

SHULMAN, L. and RINGSTAFF, C. (1986) Current research in the psychology of learning and teaching, in H. WEINSTOCK (Ed.) *Learning Physics and Mathematics via Computers*. Berlin: Sprenger.

SIROTNIK, K. (1988) Studying the education of educators: Methodology. *Phi Delta Kappan*, 70, 3, 241–247.

SKIPPER, C. and QUANTZ, R. (1987) Changes in educational attitudes of education and arts and science students during four years of college. *Journal of Teacher Education*, 38, 3, 39–44.

SMITH, G., MILLER, M. and JOY, J. (1988) A case study of the impact of performance-based testing on the supply of minority teachers. *Journal of Teacher Education*, 39, 4, 45–53.

SOLLIDAY, M. (1982) The university supervisor: A double image. *Teacher Educator*, 18, 3, 11–15.

SPRINTHALL, N. and THEIS-SPRINTHALL, L. (1983) The teacher as an adult learner: A cognitive-developmental view, in G. GRIFFIN (Ed.) *Staff Development: The Eighty-second Yearbook of NSSE*. Part 2. Chicago, Ill.: University of Chicago Press.

STEVENS, D. (1983–84) Microcomputers: An educational alternative. *Association of Teacher Educators*, 5, 4, 53–37.

STRANG, M., BADT, K. and KAUFFMAN, J. (1987) Microcomputer-based simulations for training fundamental teaching skills. *Journal of Teacher Education*, 38, 1, 20–27.

STRATMEYER, F. and LINDSAY, M. (1958) *Working with Student Teachers*. New York: Columbia University, Teachers College, Bureau of Publications.

TABACHNICK, B.R. and ZEICHNER, K. (1984) The impact of the student teaching experience on the development of teacher perspectives. *Journal of Teacher Education*, 35, 6, 28–36.

TICKUNOFF, W. and GRIFFIN, G. (1979) *Interactive Research and Development on Teaching Study: Final Report*. (IR & DT 379–11). San Francisco, Calif.: Far West Regional Laboratory for Educational Research and Development.

TOM, A. (1985) Inquiring into inquiry-oriented teacher education. *Journal of Teacher Education*, 36, 5, 35–44.

VARAH, L., THEUNE, W. and PARKER, L. (1986) Beginning teachers: Sink or swim? *Journal of Teacher Education*, 37, 1, 30–34.

VEENMAN, S. (1984) Perceived problems of beginning teachers. *Review of Educational Research*, 54, 2, 143–178.

WARD, B. (1983) 'Collaborative action research: An avenue for the reform of preservice teacher education?' Paper presented at the Meadow Brook Research Symposium, Rochester, Mich.

WATTS, D. (1987) Student teaching, in M. HABERMAN and J. BACKUS (Eds) *Advances in Teacher Education*. Vol. 3, Norwood, N.J.: Ablex.

WAXMAN, H. and WALBERG, H. (1986) Effects of early field experiences, in J. RATHS and L. KATZ (Eds) *Advances in Teacher Education*. Vol. 2. Norwood, N.J.: Ablex.

WAXMAN, H., FREIBERG, J., VAUGHAN, J. and WEIL, M. (1988) *Images of Reflections in Teacher Education*. Reston, Va.: Association of Teacher Educators.

WEINSTEIN, C. (1988) Preservice teachers' expectations about the first year of teaching. *Teaching and Teacher Education*, 4, 1, 31–40.

WEINSTEIN, C. and MAYER, R. (1986) The teaching of learning strategies, in M. WITTROCK (Ed.) *Handbook of Research on Teaching*. 3rd ed. New York: Macmillan.

WILSON, S. and SHULMAN, L. (1987) 150 different ways of knowing: Representations of knowledge in teaching, in J. CALDERHEAD (Ed.) *Exploring Teachers' Thinking*. London: Cassell Educational.

WISNIEWSKI, R. and DUCHARME, E. (Eds) (1988) *The Professors of Teaching: An Inquiry*. Albany, N.Y.: SUNY Press.

WITTROCK, M. (1986) Students' thought processes, in M. WITTROCK (Ed.) *Handbook of Research on Teaching*. 3rd ed. New York: Macmillan, pp. 297–314.

WRIGHT, R., O'HAIR, M. and ALLEY, R. (1988) Student teachers examine and rate classroom discipline factors: Help for the supervisor. *Action in Teacher Education*, 10, 2, 85–92.

YARGER, S., HOWEY, K. and JOYCE, J. (1977) Reflections on preservice preparation: Impressions from the national survey. *Journal of Teacher Education*, 28, 2, 34–37.

ZAHORIK, J. (1988) The observing-conferencing role of university supervisors. *Journal of Teacher Education*, 39, 2, 9–16.

ZEICHNER, K. (1987) The ecology of field experience: Toward an understanding of the role of field experiences in teacher development, in M. HABERMAN and J. BACKUS (Eds) *Advances in Teacher Education*. Vol. 3. Norwood, N.J.: Ablex.

ZEICHNER, K. (1988) *Understanding the Character and Quality of the Academic and Professional Components of Teacher Education* (Research Report 88–1). East Lansing, Mich.: National Center for Research on Teacher Education.

ZEICHNER, K. and LISTON, D. (1985) Varieties of discourse in supervisory conferences. *Teaching and Teacher Education*, 1, 2, 155–174.

ZEICHNER, K. and TABACHNICK, B. (1982) The belief system of university supervisors in an elementary student teaching program. *Journal of Education for Teaching*, 8, 2, 34–54.

ZIMPHER, N. (1987) Current trends on university supervision of student teaching, in M. HABERMAN and J. BACKUS (Eds) *Advances in Teacher Education*. 3rd ed. Norwood, N.J.: Ablex.

ZIMPHER, N., DEVOSS, G. and NOTT, D. (1981) A closer look at university student teacher supervision. *Journal of Teacher Education*, 31, 4, 11–51.

Chapter 11

Research on Swedish Teacher Training

Bertil Gran

Background: School Reforms in Sweden

In 1950 the Swedish parliament introduced an integrated and non-streamed compulsory nine-year school for all children between 7 and 16 years of age. At that time Sweden was educationally underdeveloped. Most children completed only seven years of schooling in an old-fashioned school system, and only about 10 per cent completed secondary education. Fewer than 5 per cent attended universities and professional colleges. In 1962 a comprehensive school was introduced throughout the country, followed in 1968 by a new organization for upper secondary education (the gymnasium), which integrates theoretical and vocational programs.

Today nearly 100 per cent of Swedish children complete eleven years of schooling. This expansion, occurring in that short period during the 1960s and 1970s, resulted in the appointment of many new teachers and a corresponding expansion of the organization for teacher training. Consequently, the typical Swedish school teacher today is about 50 years old, and in the near future there will be the need for further expansion of teacher training.

School reforms are part of social reforms to develop social and economic welfare, equal opportunities and democracy. The reforms also aim to avoid early differentiation by developing comprehensive schools, and integrating all pupils in the same class (Gran, 1986). Integration has dealt also with mentally, socially and physically handicapped children. The compulsory, comprehensive school system has seen the term 'failed' removed from school terminology, with the focus shifting from test results to the teacher's counselling work.

Other reforms include a coordination of theoretical and practical work, new relationships between subjects with a more thematic structure, teachers working together in 'work units' for common planning, priority given to the development of the whole personality of the child, a school more open to society with an effort to establish cooperation between school and leisure activities and life outside the school.

A very important political aim has been to decentralize decisions and shift responsibilities to the local community and the local school. Although centrally steered by goal descriptions from the parliament and the government, teaching teams within schools retain responsibility for planning and finding solutions to school problems. This has dramatically changed the teacher's functions from a single person's job steered by central regulations towards cooperative responsibility in teams.

This reform work has had an impact on pre-service and in-service teacher training, and has also been the focus for research on teacher training (Lundgren, 1987).

The Structure of Teacher Education in Sweden

Far-reaching reforms of Swedish higher education in 1977 resulted in the creation of a single, coherent system for all types of post-secondary education called 'hogskola', which encompasses not only traditional university studies but also those of the various professional colleges. All teacher education became a part of university organization, but with variations from one university to another. A central curriculum is prescribed (by the Chancellor for the Universities — UHÄ) for all teacher training with common aims and a range of different subjects. All teacher training includes theory and subject studies alternating with practice in schools. Several reforms in teacher education occurred, paralleling reforms in the schools, but the organizational structure of teacher education was not clearly coordinated with the school system until 1988. Now initial teacher training is organized in three main groups (Council of Europe, 1987):

> study programs for pre-school teachers and teachers for leisure activities;
>
> teacher training for the nine-year compulsory school but with two different specializations: one for teaching in grades 1–7, one for grades 4–9. Teacher training for grades 1–7 occupies three and a half years and the training for grades 4–9, four and a half years;
>
> teacher training for upper secondary schools which consists of studies in two academic subjects coordinated with practical educational training. Teachers of technical and vocational subjects complete

several years of practical vocational experiences and teacher training during one to one and a half years.

A Transitional Period in Research on Teacher Training

Swedish governmental committees have a very important function in developing the school system, and often carry out surveys or research programs related to their function. Researchers from education have been members of these committees or have worked as experts connected to them. A fruitful dialogue has developed between politicians and researchers, and this has meant that research programs have focused on the reforms. The programs have been of immediate interest, but have been limited in the choice of problems.

In 1962 the National Board of Education (NBE), using a special grant from parliament, established a section for educational research and development. The Board was given responsibility for research within the school sector, and teacher training was also under its jurisdiction until 1977. Consequently, high priority was given to research on teacher training, and during the 1960s and 1970s much research in teacher education occurred.

Gran (1977), who was commissioned to analyze the teacher education research, found research occurring in six areas:

teacher characteristics with an emphasis on individual traits and competencies for success in the profession;

study success during teacher training with a focus on exams and the control system, where institutional and structural factors were of importance;

goals and aims of teacher education, where the competencies and functions in the teacher's profession were stressed;

the structure of the training system, e.g., the relation between studies in pedagogics, academic subjects and teaching practice;

the educational process in teacher training, including tutoring, educational technology, micro-teaching, teachers' cooperation and team work, student democracy and pedagogical drama; and

in-service training including views of professional needs and the structure of the in-service program.

Further details of the extensive research findings in the decade preceding 1977 are given in reports by Gran (1977) and Marklund and Gran (1974, 1975).

Since 1977 the situation has altered markedly. 'For the last ten years no exhaustive research projects have been carried out. The resources allocated have been used for several minor research and development projects covering most teacher training institutions' (Council of Europe, 1987, p. 183). These changes had different causes.

Resources were allocated to smaller colleges without a research organization of their own who used them to develop local programs. An aim was to engage as many persons as possible at the local level in developmental work instead of researching for systematic knowledge of national interest.

The integration of teacher education into the university organization with varying local structures made it difficult to single out teacher training from other academic studies.

The division of teacher training into specializations with many different schemes highlighted differential aspects rather than common problems.

No separate faculty of teacher education exists in Sweden, thus research on educational matters occurs in different disciplines. Interest in educational research within these traditional academic disciplines develops slowly; only now is there a growing interest in such research.

Also some argue that the teacher's knowledge is derived more from tradition and practical experience than from research (Bergendal, 1983).

The Impact of Research of the 1970s on Reforms of the 1980s

Extensive research findings during the 1960s and early 1970s had an impact on the reforms of the 1980s for two reasons. First, many researchers worked, as was mentioned earlier, within state committees or in close contact with central planning boards. Although it is difficult to trace a particular decision about teacher training to a particular research finding, the reforms were fashioned through fruitful dialogue with researchers. Second, research findings have entered teacher training by a personal linkage channel: researchers have also been employed as teachers in teacher training departments.

Illustrations of early studies which affected the reforms of the 1980s are those in the areas of teachers' aptitudes and success, teacher functions, and means and methods of teaching training.

Research into *the aptitudes and the success of teachers* has a long tradition in Sweden, but one problem has been the definition of criteria to measure teachers' success. Marklund (1968) analyzed the relations between different criteria and developed an evaluation model for the process from the beginning of teacher training to the teacher's work in the classroom after qualification. Using the model, Sundgren (1970) followed a group of trainee teachers during their training and for two years after their entry to teaching. Relations were established between changes in the pupils' classroom behaviour and teachers' personal scores during teacher training. An authoritarian attitude and an achievement orientation were related to increased knowledge among the pupils. They were also related to emotional instability and negative social development among the pupils. A more human teacher attitude was found to yield the opposite results, but it was impossible to make individual prognosis based on test results. From the study Sundgren concluded that teacher training must stress student guidance and allow for tutors to advise certain trainees not to enter the teaching profession. Today Swedish teacher training contains a practice period early in the training to allow students to test their attitudes, aptitudes and likely successes in the teaching profession.

The research of the 1960s and 1970s drew attention to the school milieu as stimulating learning environments were desired, and research interests shifted from training issues to milieu factors, including teacher stress (Löfgren, 1981). Now the pendulum has swung back as decentralization of the school system has produced renewed interest in teachers' competencies and consequently in teacher training and research on it.

The *functions of the teacher* were studied through text analyses, interviews and questionnaires by Gran (1973), Fritzell (1974, 1981) and Löfqvist (1971). They conceptualized the functions as falling into five categories, namely:

a *social-emotional factor* describing the tasks of the teacher in promoting the social and emotional development of the pupil;

a *cognitive factor* related to the pupil's knowledge;

a *method-material factor* related to the teaching methods;

a *collaboration factor* describing the teacher's work together with other adults; and

a *development factor* related to the teacher's own or the school's educational development.

The gap between what was expected of the teacher and what resulted from teacher training was the greatest for the social-emotional and the collaboration factors. These findings had implications for reforms in teacher education.

The research on the *means and methods of teacher training* also changed teacher training. Studies by Bierschenk (1972) and Brusling (1974) on self-confrontation and micro-teaching stimulated the use of closed circuit television in training programs. Wiechel's (1976) work on group dynamics and role play gave an impetus to the use of pedagogical drama to foster students' communication, and Idman's (1972) research on student democracy and participation in planning programs provoked discussions about the role of students on planning committees. Today students are members of central and local planning boards.

The preceding discussion contains only a few examples of the relationship between research and reform work. Though research in teacher training has been meagre during the last ten years, a new interest has occurred which may have important effects on teacher training in the 1990s. Because many of these recent research projects remain ongoing, the rest of the chapter will focus more on designs and methods than on results and conclusions.

Recent Research on the Structure of Teacher Training

A distinction is made here between the structure of an educational system and its functions. In analyzing schools, Lundgren (1972) and Svingby (1978) have used frame factor theories to stress the importance of constitutional frames such as laws and regulations, organizational frames such as the largeness of pupil groups, time schedules and the distribution of time, and physical frames such as buildings and equipment. They regarded traditions and the teachers' attitudes to improvements as more or less hidden frames important for planning work in classrooms. These structural factors have also been the focus in research on teacher training.

As indicated earlier, the higher education reforms of 1977 led to a decentralization of pedagogical and organizational decision-making and control. Askling (1983) studied what happened in the new decentralized system at the various local teacher training units. Overall, although frames were widened, including wider possibilities for planning programs according to local interests and priorities, nothing happened. The content and organization of local programs remained as they had been in a more centrally planned teacher education. Locally people acted with regard to study programs as if the previous frames were still there. The local program committees seemed to find it difficult to exercise any kind of steering and controlling functions. Askling's study also showed that despite attempts to integrate within programs a 'collection code' still operated, that is, different subjects and study courses were planned separately from each other and collected together into a program. A set of common values was not particularly obvious. Askling concluded that it was important for teacher training not to be isolated from schools. New programs for teacher training now aim for closer contact between theoretical studies and practical training.

In another study Askling (1988) widened her interest to the university system, and concluded that during the implementation of the education reforms of 1977 more internal struggles than changes occurred.

With respect to a local teacher education study program based on students' needs in projects, Kussak and Linné (1980) found, as Askling had, little program integration. A high proportion of it still consisted of collections of separate components. The contradictions and goal conflict that occur in the central study plans provide an explanation for this.

The 1977 reform aimed to foster links between initial teacher training and educational research. Using documents and interviews and analyses presented to institutions, Gran (1982) attempted to gain a picture of what occurred using system-analytic and dialectical-humanistic perspectives. The study indicated that more teacher educators than previously were engaging in research and development, local conditions were being affected, personal competencies were fostered more than general knowledge, and student involvement in local activities was low.

Several colleges and universities have coordinated the training for pre-school and comprehensive school teachers with an aim to foster common attitudes to education in both groups. Johansson (1985) analyzed this coordination from the point of view of Lortie's (1975) assumption that teacher training develops a more individual teaching than a general professional role. Johansson could not confirm this assumption in the Swedish setting. On the contrary, the coordinated teacher training developed collectionistic professional roles in both groups of trainees. Johansson's studies also suggest that students' attitudes to their own teaching role are mostly developed by experiences before and outside teacher training.

To recapitulate: decentralization and integration are two of the structural characteristics of Swedish teacher education, but as we mentioned earlier, persons in this decentralized system tend to act in the way they did in the early central authoritarian system. Traditions then act as real, if hidden, frames to the system structure. In the institutions special parts of knowledge are collected together, thereby hindering integration; that is, a collectionistic code predominates and conflicts arise. This seems to be more apparent in local institutions which provide a sense of security for their members. Consequently, local actions and decisions may not be conducive to large-scale structural reforms. However, the intention of the reforms in higher education is to place more responsibilities for programs, and freedom to decide their nature, on local institutions.

Research on Professional Socialization

One can infer from the studies already discussed that teaching practice remains of great importance in the professional socialization of trainee teachers. You can't learn to swim without water! Consequently, the content of the tutoring that occurs and its organization are important in the socialization of students into the profession.

By tradition teaching practice in Sweden is a large proportion of the teacher training program — at least half to one and a half years (or 20–40 per cent of the total program), although this has shrunk in the last reforms. The practice periods are coordinated with the subject studies. Research has focused on how this rather expensive part of teacher training can be an integral part of professional socialization. Certain studies in the 1970s (e.g. Angel, 1974) showed that, what in German is called the 'praxis-shock', gave rise to more authoritarian and less child-centred attitudes, contrary to the aims of teacher education. These findings emphasize the importance of the tutoring process in practice teaching, the close coordination between teaching practice and theoretical studies, and a follow-up on trainees' experiences after a practice period.

In a study of the training of subject teachers Jonsson (1982) and Jonsson and Ahlström (1988) have examined the content of the tutoring process: what is treated in discussion with the trainee. In a first stage of the research the belief systems of individual teacher educators were determined by following them on their visits to the classrooms. They then recorded and analyzed the discussions between the teacher educators and the student teachers. Varying supervisory styles emerged. These, together with specific episodes from lessons, were examined in a series of interviews with each tutor, and individual profiles were constructed. They were discussed in a second interview. According to these studies the lecturers from the school of education stressed the specialized rather than the common and general aspects of teaching, and developed a more technocratic than integrated professional role. Consequently, the students learn a rather traditional teaching role which emphasizes the cognitive aims of the school with little regard to more superior goals such as democracy, equal opportunities, internationalism and preparedness for the future.

Jonsson and Ahlstrom have also presented different tutoring profiles, which can, according to Björndahl (1987), be classified as rational, behaviour control and reconstructionistic. The rational model is predicated upon a strong belief in the individual, and the reconstructive model is concerned with human interactions as the teacher's role primarily consists of guiding pupils. The individual Swedish teacher educators presented different tutoring profiles and were more or less ideological strangers to one another, which may cause problems in teacher education.

Brusling (1974) conducted a very intensive case study of the tutoring process with a few students, and classified tutors (teachers in schools, responsible for the daily tutoring of students' practical teaching) and tutoring into four models or categories:

a *clinical model* as described by Goldhammer (1969). Here tutors extract some frequently recurring structure in the students' teaching in the classroom and tutoring follows a step-by-step strategy;

an *ideosyncratic model* where tutors try to reveal to the students their own 'practical theory' of rationale for behaving;

a *behavioristic model* where the intention is to train an accepted set of teaching competencies;

inquiry-oriented teaching (Zeichner, 1981) which emphasizes reflective thinking by students.

From his studies Brusling drew the conclusion that students adapt themselves to the culture and traditions in the local school and to the tutors' way of teaching. He noted that there were no strict models in the empirical material comparable to the theoretical categories, and contextual factors in the local school situation dominated practice and tutoring.

Arfwedson (1984) drew the same conclusions about the influence of context-bound factors and local codes in practice schools, which he found to be obstacles for developing a more general professional code. About 130 teacher-students answering a questionnaire indicated that teacher training provided little uniformity in their way of thinking about school and society. A common code existed only to their thinking about their own training. According to Arfwedson, teacher training must make visible to the students the context-bound factors in education within schools and outside the school.

Thus the research findings have pointed to many factors producing difficulties in professional socialization into the official teaching roles which accord to the school reforms. The new curricula for teacher training have taken further steps to integrate theory and practice by prescribing that subject studies will have a didactic orientation and be planned in cooperation with persons responsible for pedagogical and practical training. Also a new practice organization has been worked out based on work units in the schools instead of individual tutors.

Kroksmark (1988) also indicates that difficulties in developing a professional role are due in part to the separation of theoretical subject studies from practice-based tutoring. He assumed that by developing professional self-reflection students may study their own learning processes as a basis for their professional competencies. The research on this point is still ongoing. In other studies Edqvist (1986) highlights the value of self-reflection among remedial teachers to ensure well thought out ecological teaching strategies in non-structured classes, and Björnhagen (1982) documents the difficulties pre-school teachers have in surmounting the huge gap in training between theory and practice.

The research projects dealing with the professional socialization of teachers points to some common factors and difficulties, namely:

A segregation exists between theoretical and practical studies which leads to difficulties for the professional socialization of students. This segregation has a negative effect on theoretical studies and practical training.

Tutors stress the special and technical aspects of teachers' work which leads to difficulties in fostering a general professional role.

Local contextual factors have a dominant influence on practice teaching, but students are not trained to manage these contextual frame factors.

No visible strategy exists for tutoring; consequently students are subject to different influences and do not develop a common set of values about teaching.

No training or time exists for self-reflection by students about their own learning and their own professional socialization.

Attempts are being made in the new teacher education reforms to counteract these features.

Curriculum and Educational Control

Some research has examined the curriculum and educational control in teacher education. Skog-Östlin (1984) examined the development of the national system of teacher training and found that training is part of the social context. When the school, more so than the church, became responsible for transferring norms from one generation to another, so too did teacher education become a key feature in this role. In Sweden teacher education is normative in nature and its aims and program frames are established by the government and parliament.

Norms and values are also affected by prior experiences. Linné (1982) has shown how curricular conflicts occur in teacher education between the academic and comprehensive education traditions. Her finding that these curricular conflicts can be lessened when trainees have some prior work experience has implications for recruitment and the teacher education curriculum.

The views that teacher educators have of professional knowledge also affect the teacher education curriculum. Dahlgren (1981) has identified one group of educators who believe this knowledge is external to trainees, and another group who believe it is internal and becomes internalized by trainees. These two views lead to two quite different teacher education curricula.

This research on curriculum and educational control points to

the normative nature of the curriculum and the role of the state in setting aims;

the role to be played by work experience in shaping student views of teacher education curricula;

the effect on teacher education curricula of teacher trainers' views about professional knowledge.

Perhaps it also implies that the pragmatic way to develop a teacher education curriculum is through a three-part agreement between state, teacher educators and teacher trainees.

In-service Teacher Training

The first part of the 1980s has seen few new teachers entering the schools; yet this period has also been characterized by far-reaching educational reforms and rapid development in technology and in social conditions. Consequently, in-service training has been given priority and about 1000 million Swedish crowns have been spent every year on in-service and on local developmental work.

The organizational and structural questions linked to in-service training have been studied using questionnaires and interviews with teachers, administrators and local politicians (Gran and Nilsson, 1985; Holmström, 1984). The results from these studies are mostly of national interest, and will not be reported here. However, in one study Gran (1985) examined whether in-service training improves the school. It was shown that while values and norms of the parliament and government were easily transferred to local community level and to school leaders, they did not transfer to the teachers who had other priorities concerning the needs for in-service training than those of school leaders. The perception of problems was not the same among the teachers as within the National Board of Education. It was concluded that normative in-service training must occur in a dialectic setting and not as one-way communication. The study also showed that success in in-service training is only partly due to the content of the training program. The 'receiving apparatus', the structure of the school is of utmost importance. Thus a lot of in-service training has to be carried out close to the practical teaching situation and through team work among the teachers.

In-service training also depends on characteristic factors, e.g., participatory democracy in a decentralized system (Wallin, 1983), and may be conducted in different ways (Alexandersson and Öhlund, 1984). One approach is of a compensatory nature to fill in the gaps in the teacher's knowledge, another is directed more to future development. Gran found the same kind of differences in approaches he called 'reactive' and 'active'. The active approaches were characterized by an evolutionary training paradigm: the training presented knowledge as well as producing new knowledge.

In another series of studies on the in-service training of pre-school teachers Gran (1987) found new evidence that institutional factors in the pre-school were of utmost importance to both the content and the structure of in-service training. It was also shown to be fruitful to distinguish between a more individual competency-based training on one hand and a training to develop the activities and organization of an institution on the other.

The results from these studies on in-service training have strong feedback to initial training of teachers by pointing out essential functions for professional socialization. The planning of new programs for pre-school teachers, for example, has been strongly influenced by results from research on in-service training.

Summary and Concluding Comments

During the 1960s and first half of the 1970s the Swedish compulsory schools were changed into a comprehensive non-streamed school system and great quantitative expansion took place, which resulted in a need for new teachers, trained for the new teaching conditions. This aroused a great interest in research on teacher training. This research focused mainly on six areas: teacher characteristics, study success, the goals of teacher education, the structure of the training system, the educational process and in-service training. The experiences of these six research areas influenced reform work in two main ways: several persons from the research area were working as experts in state committees and other researchers were employed as lecturers in teacher training departments.

During the last ten years a low production rate of new teachers has been accompanied by little research on teacher training. The research during these years focused on the structure of teacher training in a decentralized system and tutoring in the practicum. But there are difficulties in changing from a centralized planning system to a more decentralized one, partly because decentralization means there must be a more 'integrative code' with transformations to a more thematic structure and more collective planning.

Research on the tutoring process during practical training and on professional socialization shows that very few models exist for tutoring and that students are exposed to several conflicting ideas. Tutoring is directed to special functions and techniques in the teacher's profession more than to general professional characteristics. Practical training is also dependent on the structure of the local school, and students are given rather scanty knowledge about this. The new teacher training reforms pay attention to these research results.

During this period of rather low input of teachers into the schools but intensive reform, attention has been directed to in-service training and to research on in-service training. These studies consider structural factors in the schools in order to obtain successful in-service.

In 1988 new teacher education reforms were implemented, and at the same time there was an expanding need for new teachers. These have resulted in the planning of a nation-wide program for evaluation of the reforms and for a concentration on research on teacher education.

References

ALEXANDERSSON, M. and ÖHLUND, U. (1984) *Den nya personalfortbildningen för skolväsendet*. En utvärderings-rapport. Göteborg: Göteborgs Universitet, Fortbildningsavdelningen.

ANGEL, B. (1974) Praktikterminen i lågstadierlärarutbildningen: En undersökning av personlighets- och attitydförändringar under utbildningstiden [Practical teacher training for class teachers: A study of personality and attitude development during the training period]. *Pedagogisk- psykologiska problem*, Nr 257. Malmö, School of Education.

ARFWEDSSON, G. (1984) *Det är inte lärarutbildarnas fel*. Forskningsgruppen för läroplansteori och kultur-reproduktion. Högskolan för Lärarutbildning i Stockholm, Rapport 7.

ASKLING, B. (1983) *Utbildningsplanering i en lärar-utbildning.* Studies in Curriculum Theory and Cultural Reproduction, No. 6, Stockholm Institute of Education, Department of Educational Research.

ASKLING, B. (1988) *Decentralization and Quality Control.* Working Paper No. 1 from the Examination and Evaluation in Professional Higher Education Project. Stockholm: UHÄ.

BERGENDAL, G. (1983) (Ed.) *Knowledge and Higher Education.* A series of colloquia. Stockholm: National Board of Universities and Colleges.

BIERSCHENK, B. (1972) *Självkonfrontation via intern television i lärarutbildningen.* [Self-confrontation via Closed Circuit Television in Teacher Training]. Studia Psychologica et Peadagogica, Seires Altera IVIII. Lund: Gleerup. (With an English digest).

BJÖRNDAHL, B. (1987) On teachers' evaluations of pedagogic theory systems, in Å. STRÖMNES and N. SÖVIK (Eds) *Teachers' Thinking: Perspectives and Research.* Oslo: Tapir Publ, pp. 8–50.

BJÖRNHAGEN, E. (1982) *Praktiken i förskollärarutbildningen.* En intervjustudie och en historisk tillbakablick kring förhållandet teori och praktik. Rapport Nr 6/1982. Stockholm: Högskolan för Lärarutbildning, Institutionen för pedagogik.

BRUSLING, C. (1974) *Microteaching: A Concept in Development.* Göteborgs Studies in Educational Sciences. Göteborg: Acta Universitatis Gothoburgensis.

Council of Europe (1987) *New Challenges for Teachers and Their Education: National Reports on Teacher Education.* Standing Conference of European Ministers of Education. Strasbourg: Council of Europe.

DAHLGREN, L.O. (1981) Kunskapssyn och ämnessyn i lärarutbildningen, in T. LINDBLAD and S. STUKAT (Eds) *Kunskapssyn och ämnessyn i klasslärarutbildningen.* En konferensredovisning. Rapport Nr 111. Göteborg: Göteborgs Universitet, Institutionen för Praktisk Pedagogik, pp. 19–33.

EDQVIST, T. (1986) Två rapporter om speciallärar-utbildning. Specialläraren under utbildning och i arbete. Speciallärarutbildning igår, idag och kanske i morgon. *Arbetsrappirter från Pedagogiska institutionen, Umeå universitet,* Nr 28.

FRITZELL, C. (1974) The teacher's occupational functions. *Scandinavian Journal of Educational Research,* 18, 151–182.

FRITZELL, C. (1981) *Teaching, Science and Ideology: A Critical Inquiry into the Sociology of Pedagogy.* Studia Psychologica et Paedagogica. Lund: CWK Gleerup.

GOLDHAMMER, R. (1969) *Clinical Supervision.* New York: Holt, Rinehart and Winston.

GRAN, B. (1973) Med PIL för bättre lärarutbildning [With PIL for better teacher education]. *Pedagogiska Meddelanden,* 10, 7, 38–40.

GRAN, B. (1977) *Lärarutbildning- svenska erfarenheter och internationella utvecklingslinjer* [*Teacher Training: Swedish Experiences and International Trends*]. DsU. 21. Stockholm: Utbildningsdepartementet.

GRAN, B. (1982) *Forskningsanknytning av grundläggande högskoleutbildning.* Erfarengeter från verksamheten inom Lund/Malmö högskoleregion. [The relation between research and basic teacher training]. Rapport från Styrelsen för Lund/Malmö högskoleregion, Nr 9. Lund: Regionstyrelsen.

GRAN, B. (1985) *Är personalfortbildning ett bra sätt att förbättra skolan?* [*Is In-service Training of Teachers a Good Means to Improve the School?*] Stockholm: Skolöverstyrelsen.

GRAN, B. (1986) The comprehensive schools in Sweden: From primary to secondary education, in W. WIELEMANS (Ed.) *Vernieuwingen in het secundair undervwijs.* Leuven: Acco, pp. 81–91.

GRAN, B. (1987) *Forbildning av personal inom barnomsorgen.* [*In-service Training of Pre-school Staff*]. PM 168/87. Stockholm: Socialstyrelsen.

GRAN, B. and NILSSON, B. (1985) *Skolans personalutbildning ur högskolans perspektiv. En strukturstudie inom högskolesystemet. Del IV: Syntes och analys.* UHÄ-rapport 1985: 19. Stockholm: Universitets- och högskoleämbetet.

HOLMSTRÖM, L-G. (1984) *Fortbildning av skolans personal i Uppsala högskoleregion.* Rapport Nr 92. Uppsala: Uppsala Universitet, Pedagogiska Institutionen.

IDMAN, P. (1972) *Equality and Democracy: Studies of Teacher Training.* Studia Psychologica of Paedagogica, Series Altera XXIII. Lund: CWK Gleerup.

JONSSON, M. (1982) Handledarens syn på sin roll och ämneslärarpraktiken. *Arbetsrapporter från Pedagogiska institutionen,* Nr 58. Uppsala: Uppsala Universitet.

JONSSON, M. and AHLSTRÖM, K-G. (1988) *Educational Belief Systems among Teacher Educators.* Uppsala: Uppsala University, Department of Education.

JOHANSSON, J-E. (1985) Gemensam utbildning av fritidspedagoger, förskollärare och lågstadielärare i Härnösand 1978–1980. En utvärdering samt en diskussion av lärares yrkesroller. *Arbetsrapporter från Pedagogiska institutionen,* Nr 96. Uppsala: Uppsala Universitet.

KROKSMARK, T. (1988) *Lärarkompetens. Att lära andra lära sig.* Stencil. Göteborgs Universitet, Institutionen for Metodik i Lärarutbildningen.

KUSSAK, Å. and LINNÉ, A. (1980) *Ett lokalt läroplans-arbete.* Om framväxten av kursplaner vid klasslärarlinjerna i Stockholm i samband med 1977 års högskolereform. Stockholm: Högskolan för Lärarutbildning.

LINNÉ, A. (1982) Arbetslivserfarenhet och klasslärarutbildning. *Högskolan för lärarutbildning i Stockholm.* Rapport Nr 17.

LÖFGREN, H. (1981) Arbetsmiljön i skolan. En undersökning av kommunalt anställda inom skolväsendet i Malmö kommun [Work environment in school]. *Pedagogiska uppsatser,* 7. Lund: Pedagogiska Institutionen. (With an English abstract).

LÖFQVIST, G. (1971) Arbets- och utbildningskrav för ämneslärarkandidater [What demands are made on the subject teacher in the school situation, and how should these demands influence pre-service training programs?] *Pedagogisk-psykologiska problem,* Nr 156. Malmö: School of Education.

LORTIE, D. (1975) *Schoolteacher,* Chicago, Ill.: University of Chicago Press.

LUNDGREN, U.P. (1972) *Frame Factors and the Teaching Process: A Contribution to Curriculum Theory and Theory of Teaching.* Stockholm: Almqvist and Wiksell.

LUNDGREN, U.P. (1987) *New Challenges for Teachers and Their Education.* Strasbourg: Council of Europe, Standing Conference of European Ministers of Education.

MARKLUND, S. (1968) *Lärarlämplighet: Problem och propåer.* Stockholm: Liber.

MARKLUND, S. and GRAN, B. (1974) Research and innovation in Swedish teacher training, in *New Patterns of Teacher Education and Tasks: Country Experience, Sweden.* Paris: OECD, pp. 15–80.

MARKLUND, S. and GRAN, B. (1975) Research and innovation in Swedish teacher training. *Educational and Psychological Interactions*, No. 53. Malmö: School of Education.

SKOG-ÖSTLIN, K. (1984) *Pedagogisk kontroll och auktoritet: En studie av den offentliga lärarutbildningens uppgifter*. Studies in Education and Psychology, No. 14. Stockholm: Gleerup. (With an English summary).

SUNDGREN, P. (1970) Lärarpersonlighet och lärarlämplighet. En undersökning av klasslärarkandidater. *Pedagogisk-psykologiska problem*, Nr 121. Malmö: School of Education.

SVINGBY, G. (1978) *Läroplaner som styrmedal för svensk obligatorisk skola. Teoretisk analys och ett empiriskt bidrag*. Göteborgs Studies in Educational Sciences 26. Göteborg: Acta Universitatis Gothoburgensis.

WALLIN, E. (1983) Main organizational factors affecting in-service training of teachers, in W-P. TESCHNER, T. HARBO, B. GRAN and H. HAFT (Eds) *In-service Teacher Training: Models, Methods and Criteria of Its Evaluation*. Strasbourg: Council of Europe, pp. 179–190.

WIECHEL, L. (1976) *Roller och rollspel* [Roles and Role Playing]. Lund: Gleerup. (With an English digest).

ZEICHNER, K. (1981) Reflective teaching and fieldbased experience in teacher education. *Interchange*, 12, 4, pp. 1–22.

Chapter 12

Research on Teacher Education in Israel: Topics, Methods and Findings

Miriam Ben-Peretz

Teacher education provides a crucial part of the link between generations. Whether we view education as a reproductive force in society, or as the vehicle for social transformation, teachers fulfil a vital role. Teacher education prepares future teachers for their role. Some claim that teacher education is not very successful in fulfilling this function. Such a claim may be based on impressions, hearsay, anecdotal evidence or on research evidence. Questions arise about the nature of research on teacher education in certain cultural contexts. Is it mainly evaluative? Is it decision-oriented, aiming at change and improvement, or is it conclusion-oriented, attempting to provide insights into the phenomenon of teacher education? What are the questions and who asks them? What methodologies are used to find answers? What are some of the main findings? Additional questions are: what, if any, comprehensive frameworks guide research on teacher education? Which issues receive scant attention and why? And, last but not least, what, if any, is the impact of research on teacher education policies? Some answers to these questions appear in this chapter, which focuses on research on pre-service teacher education in Israel in the last fifteen years.

The chapter discusses the foci of the research, conceptual frameworks and methodologies, major findings and neglected areas. The social context of teacher education, and its bearing on choice of research questions, constitute a major theme in relation to the various studies.

Background: A Brief Description of the Nature of Teacher Education in Israel

Teacher education in Israel is carried out at two sites:

1 *colleges of teacher education.* These colleges, which prepare teachers

for K–6 and 7–9 grades, serve different purposes and address different audiences. They include general teacher education colleges, vocational colleges (e.g., for physical education), religious colleges and colleges of the kibbutz movement. All have special programs for early childhood education, accept students with a high school diploma, offer two-, three- or four-year training programs and include subject matter studies, foundation disciplines of education, methods courses and practicum. Some teacher education colleges in Israel grant the BEd degree, others grant only a diploma. These diplomas constitute the necessary credentials for working as teachers in kindergarten, elementary and junior high schools.

2 *departments of teacher education in universities.* These departments educate teachers for junior and senior high schools. Students are usually accepted in the third year of their studies towards a BA or BSc degree in the various disciplines. From this third year onward students study concurrently in the department of their chosen discipline, e.g., geography or history, and in the department of teacher education. Usually students choose two subject matter domains, so that at the end of their studies they are qualified to teach these in secondary schools. Studies in the departments of teacher education usually last two years and include foundation disciplines, method courses in each of the subject matter areas chosen by the student and practicum. Students receive a teaching diploma which is acknowledged by the Ministry of Education, and a BA or BSc in their respective subject matter areas. They start working as accredited teachers after receiving their academic degree and their teaching diploma.

Departments of teacher education at universities may offer two additional programs: a one-year program for postgraduate students, and a three-year program leading to a BA in teaching. Students participating in the three-year program study only one subject matter domain.

Methodology for the Review

Information on the nature of research on teacher education in Israel during the last fifteen years came from journals, a number of 'in-house' reports from colleges, universities or the Ministry of Education, and a few higher degree theses. One book (Zak and Horowitz, 1985) was also included. Forty articles and reports were consulted, and thirty-four are included in the present review. Of these, five (15 per cent) were published in 1971–1976, thirteen (38 per cent) in 1977–1981, and sixteen (47 per cent) in 1982–1986. Six sources (16 per cent) were higher degree theses. These figures suggest a growing interest among scholars in research on teacher education. A majority of the studies (60 per cent) deal with programs for elementary trainees, about 30 per cent with high school teachers and the remainder (10 per cent) with programs for vocational teachers. About 60 per cent of the projects sampled students in teacher education colleges and 40 per cent students in departments of teacher education in universities.

Within the framework proposed by Katz and Raths (1985), the studies tend to fall into six clusters:

1	characteristics of student-teachers	11 sources (one a comprehensive book)
2	characteristics of staff	3 sources
3	content of programs (the body of knowledge)	9 sources
4	modes of teaching and evaluation in programs	4 sources
5	interaction between student characteristics and program features	4 sources
6	evaluation of programs	4 sources[1]

Each of these clusters will be discussed in turn.

Characteristics of Student-teachers in Israel

Thirty-two per cent of the sources included in this review focus on the characteristics of candidates, the preferred research topic in Israel. One reason may be the pressing societal needs in a small country facing manifold problems and difficulties. The small population of the country, about four and a half million, creates a situation of 'competition' for gifted and dedicated candidates for a large variety of professions and occupations, including teaching. Consequently, researchers are interested in the characteristics of teacher candidates. Another reason for this interest stems from the view that teaching as a caring profession depends, to a large extent, on the personal qualities of teachers.

The characteristics of student-teachers that provide the focus of research in Israel include background, motives for entering teaching, attitudes towards education, and expectations of teacher training programs.

Most studies deal with only one or two specific characteristics, although one (Zak and Horowitz, 1985) tried to create a comprehensive profile of beginning teachers, and another (Ben-Peretz, Giladi and Kurtz, 1983) dealt simultaneously with three characteristics: personality, attitudes towards education and knowledge about teaching.

Let us turn to some of the specific findings: what motivates candidates to choose teaching? Marmer (1980) identified the motives of 220 female student-teachers studying at four teacher education colleges. They responded to a questionnaire dealing with motives of income, self-actualization, and service to society. Most students claimed service to society as their most important motive for choosing teaching. Perhaps this result reflects the social desirability for this kind of response in Israel. Other differences exist among subgroups, however. For example, high level of parents' education correlated with high emphasis on self-actualization motive, while lower socio-economic background of new immigrant parents correlated with high emphasis on the income motive. These findings can be interpreted to indicate that daughters of new immigrant parents perceive teaching as a route for upward social mobility, and when that has occurred, as in the case of professional families, self-actualization comes to the fore.

Personality questionnaires, self-concept scales, dogmatism tests, attitude scales and self-evaluation instruments have been used to study student-teachers' characteristics (Zak, 1976; Milgram and Milgram, 1976), and to develop composite profiles about them (Ben-Peretz and Tamir, 1983; Kremer and Hoffman, 1979). Surveys indicated that students in elementary and pre-school programs were more conforming and less open than those preparing for junior high teaching; high school trainees had a higher self-concept than their colleagues in elementary and special education programs; all trainees rated high on 'responsibility'. All believed that the 'ideal' teacher excelled on cognitive characteristics including the skill to explain and the 'bad' teacher was one who offended pupils. Trainees had little knowledge of educational concepts. A favoured profile of an effective teacher was a cognitive orientation to class teaching, an internal locus of control and an open belief system. These findings of the favoured profile (Kremer and Hoffman, 1979) and differences in conforming and openness (Zak, 1976, 1981) imply that selection procedures and criteria should be reconsidered. The findings related to high self-concept, which correlated with the level of schooling, were accounted for in terms of the higher qualifications required for high school teaching, the demanding nature of the teacher's role, and the perceived status of the high school in Israeli society. Milgram and

Milgram (1976) postulated a reciprocal relationship between a teacher's concept of self and school status.

Other trainee characteristics that researchers have deemed worthy of study on educational grounds include professional identification (Shafir, 1979), perceived competence to meet the needs of school pupils (Ullman, 1979) and concepts of the ideal teacher (Giladi and Ben–Peretz, 1981). Data from questionnaires, including the semantic differential technique, administered to student teachers, most of whom were in the early stages of their pre-service education, indicated that (1) students expected training programs to sensitize them to pupils' needs, but they only judged their competence in terms of unitary traits such as 'monitoring learning'; (2) those who chose teaching early in their university career had a higher level of professional identification; (3) practice teaching did not affect professional identification to a great extent; and (4) the ideal elementary teacher rated high on interpersonal characteristics and the ideal high school teacher rated high on cognitive characteristics.

The researchers pointed out that the Israeli experience shows that most teachers do not possess the abilities or dispositions to diagnose pupils' needs and to individualize teaching, and teacher education programs contribute minimally to balancing and developing trainees' interpersonal and cognitive characteristics. The finding related to the effect of the practicum on role identification challenges our usual assumptions about the role of the practicum and its impact. It also implies that we should consider other ways through which role identification may be fostered.

Characteristics of Staff

Only three studies deal with different roles of staff members. Ben–Peretz and Tamir (1983) replicated a USA study (Katz *et al.*, 1982), investigating the professional image and reputation of teacher educators. Teacher educators, university faculty members not involved in teacher education, student-teachers and practising teachers participated in the project which showed that the characteristics of credibility, knowledge and expertise, effectiveness and prestige constituted the professional image. No differences were perceived between the effectiveness of teacher educators and other members of faculty. Teacher educators in Israel appear to enjoy a reputation comparable to that of other university teachers.

In a recent study (Kremer–Hayon, 1986) of professional perspectives of supervision, twelve teacher education college supervisors discussed and evaluated their own activities. Protocols indicated that supervisors sought a body of knowledge to guide their professional work.

A third study (Lazarowitz, Dreyfus and Jungwirth, 1986) examined the match between cooperating secondary school biology teachers and the student-teachers assigned to them. Two questionnaires dealing with nine categories of teaching skills were administered to determine whether cooperating teachers were perceived as experts in the skills, and whether they possessed diagnostic abilities. All respondents were asked to rate how much each category of teaching skill should ideally be used. The performance of cooperating teachers was rated by the teachers and the trainees as approaching the ideal. Discrepancies existed, however, between the way student-teachers rated themselves and how they were rated by cooperating teachers. For example, cooperating teachers rated students as 'strong' in content, whereas the student teachers rated themselves as 'weak'. Disagreement occurred on a high proportion of items. The researchers interpreted this as a lack of diagnostic ability among teachers and poor communication between them and their student-teachers. These areas require further study because it is highly likely that discrepancies between student-teachers' perceptions of their skills, and the perceptions teachers have of them, can create barriers to communication and difficulties in enhancing teaching skills.

Content of Programs (the Body of Knowledge)

Defining the basic body of knowledge which is appropriate and necessary for the professional education of teachers is a difficult and problematic task. Some of the research efforts in Israel are directed to the issue. Elbaz *et al.* (1986) used conceptual mapping to identify and represent changes in the knowledge structures of student-teachers in various subject matter areas. The framework guiding the study distinguished between declarative and procedural knowledge and assumed three interacting factors: the kind of knowledge, the location in which it develops (university or school), and the role of teacher and student-teacher. They found that concepts significant for experts in the field were also significant for student-teachers, and misconceptions and changes in understandings existed. This suggests that concept mapping may be a useful procedure for identifying changes in knowledge structures related to teacher education, and to the roles teachers and student-teachers play in teaching-learning situations.

Another study (Tamir and Ben-Peretz, 1981) focused on the nature of learning materials which served as sources of knowledge in teacher education programs. Data derived from responses of teacher educators to interviews and questionnaires, and from analyses of bibliographies, syllabi and worksheets used in teacher education courses, found students required to read a variety of books and articles in Hebrew and English, with no common theoretical and professional core servicing teacher education programs, and no common body of knowledge transmitted to prospective teachers. Topics such as teaching by inquiry, individualization of instruction and action-oriented learning were included in many, but not all, courses. The situation supports Lortie's (1975) claim that teachers lack a shared culture of their profession. We believe that teacher education programs which are widely divergent in their choices of content and experiences cannot provide prospective teachers with a sense of a shared body of knowledge — the basis for the shared culture of the profession.

Several studies have dealt with specific teaching-learning strategies that are part of the nature of teacher education programs. These studies share a common experimental design, namely, introduction of some novel teaching strategies into teacher education programs, and the evaluation of their impact on student-teachers. Kremer and Perlberg (1979), for instance, organized special workshops for training teachers in developing and improving pupils' abilities to learn independently. Teachers' classroom behaviour changed as a result of the intensive workshop experience.

Two further studies dealt with improving the abilities of teacher candidates to guide classroom discussions (Kremer, 1974) and the development of moral reasoning (Kremer, 1984). In the first Kremer investigated the impact of micro-teaching experiences. Data obtained using the Verbal Interaction Category System (VICS) indicated that the learning experiences had a positive impact. In the second study he administered an instrument to identify stages of moral reasoning to teachers' college students who participated in value clarification workshops, and found the workshops to have a positive impact. Lazarowitz and Tamir (1980) studied student-teachers' attitudes toward teaching science by inquiry. Using an attitude instrument, they found that student-teachers in scientific disciplines had more positive attitudes toward inquiry learning than university teachers, and were closer to the attitudes of experienced school teachers.

Notwithstanding the positive results from these projects, the studies stimulate us to ask how a variety of learning experiences develop components of the 'body of knowledge' which serves teacher education.

A subcategory of the 'body of knowledge' includes 'curriculum studies'. These involve studies about modes of curriculum development and implementation, basic concepts of curriculum theories, and in-depth interpretation of curriculum materials. Silberstein and Tamir (1986) assessed the treatment of curriculum studies in twenty-three teacher education colleges and six university teacher education departments, and found that in general teacher educators appreciated the potential of curriculum studies to develop teaching abilities. Still, few teacher education courses devote significant time to these studies. Furthermore, colleges tend to focus on the content of curriculum materials and universities on problems of implementation.

In the colleges about half the teacher educators believe insufficient instructional materials dealing with curriculum studies exist (Silberstein, 1984), but those who have participated in in-service programs indicate they become aware of the role these studies play in helping teachers become more autonomous.

From these findings one can argue that curriculum studies should be accorded a higher priority in pre-service teacher education programs than they are now, because of their importance in developing teacher auto-nomy. Instructional materials dealing with curriculum issues should be prepared, especially for pre-service programs. In passing it should be noted that this has already begun in Israel (Silberstein, 1985).

Finally, the ways in which first- and third-year student teachers interpret curricula and sort curriculum items were investigated in a study (Ben-Peretz, Katz and Silberstein, 1982) which used Kelly's (1955) theory of personal constructs in its theoretical framework. The data indicated that third-year students used different and more elaborate personal con-structs than their first-year counterparts to interpret and sort curriculum items — a finding which was taken to show that pre-service programs have an impact on professional thinking of student-teachers. Curriculum interpretation exercises, based on Kelly's theory, could become a regular component in teacher education programs.

Modes of Teaching and Evaluation in Teacher Education Programs

The modes of teaching and evaluation experienced by student-teachers in their courses contribute to the climate, or ethos, of their programs. What student-teachers experience has an impact on their future practices as teachers. I turn therefore to a discussion of studies of modes of teaching and evaluation in teacher education programs.

The modes of teaching, and the strategies of evaluation, used in teacher education programs may be regarded as 'models of practice', but if a large gap exists between what is 'preached' as ideal practice, for instance, the importance of cooperative learning in schools, and what is actually done in the teacher education program, then a disservice is done to the implementation of innovation in schools. It is often claimed in Israel that the traditional modes of teaching, such as expository lecturing, and traditional evaluations of students, such as written tests, which are common in Israeli teacher education programs, serve to reproduce these modes in schools. Therefore, it seems crucial that research on teacher education should assess the modes of teaching and evaluation that characterize the programs.

Modes of teaching may, for instance, be based on different educational orientations such as progressive approaches leading to 'open' schools, or traditional approaches favouring highly structured school environments. According to Jackson (1986), we can differentiate between 'mimetic' and 'transformative' traditions within educational thought and practice. The mimetic tradition emphasizes the transmission of factual and procedural knowledge from one generation to the other, through an essentially imitative process. The transformative tradition stresses the achievement of qualitative changes in the person being taught. These features have been studied in two projects (Kremer-Hayon and Moore, 1985; Nevat, 1984), where student–teachers were tutored in a supervisory style congruent with their scores on a dogmatism scale. Student–teachers expressed more satisfaction when the orientation of the supervision style matched their own personality, for instance, when high scorers on dogmatism were matched with a closed style of supervision. These results suggest a call for the individualization of teacher training by matching personality traits of student–teachers with the teaching styles in the program.

Workshops are another preference mode of teaching and their informal settings are considered to provide many opportunities for cooperative learning with non-threatening feedback. Their short- and long-term effects and their value as a mode in teacher education to develop teaching skills have been examined in a training program for medical educators (Mahler and Benor, 1984). The positive findings from the study suggest the advisability of including workshops in teacher education programs as they have a long-term impact and they act as exemplars for later teaching practice.

Evaluation practices in teacher education programs were identified by Tamir and Ben-Peretz (1983) by administering three questionnaires to 110 teacher educators in five universities and five teacher education colleges, to seventy-five practising teachers, and to sixty-eight student–teachers. Findings showed that evaluation strategies used in schools and teacher education programs were similar, based mainly on written examinations and grading of papers. About half the teacher educators also stated that evaluation practices were not taught in their courses, and only a quarter of the student–teachers were satisfied with the way they were evaluated. We believe that varied approaches to evaluation need to be introduced into Israeli teacher education, so that student-teachers will become more knowledgeable about this important aspect of teaching.

Interaction between Student Characteristics and Program Features

According to Katz and Raths (1985), insights into teacher education can be gained by studying the effects of interactions between the nature of programs and student-teacher characteristics. Several Israeli projects have focused on these interactions. Zmora (1979) deals with the interaction of the belief systems of 110 student-teachers and the nature of their college's teacher education program. The more dogmatic students did not change their orientations toward education, or their teaching behaviour, but a change toward a more progressive orientation to teaching was noted in the less dogmatic students studying in the same program. In another project Milgram and Milgram (1978) studied the effects of the interaction between students' cognitive and personal-social characteristics, and the nature of the program, on students' success in practice teaching. The study showed that success in practice teaching was related more to cognitive than other personality characteristics. Danieli (1982) examined the relationship between the SES of student-teachers participating in different teacher education programs and changes in their attitudes toward disadvantaged pupils. Three hundred and seventeen student-teachers, in different stages of their studies, participated in this research project. The findings indicated that students of lower SES had more positive attitudes toward disadvantaged pupils than middle-class students. Also different teacher education programs led to different outcomes: students in kindergarten programs showed a decline in traditional orientations, whereas students in elementary programs showed a growth in traditional orientations at the end of their first year of studies.

These findings suggest that the interactions between students' characteristics and the nature of teacher education programs have to be considered by program planners. But the implications of these Israeli studies are not quite clear. Do they indicate a need for more individualized modes of teacher education, or suggest conclusions about admission policies? Or should teacher educators regard the results as part of the general phenomenon of differential outcomes from any educational program? It seems that in spite of their inherent interest the studies will have little impact on policies of teacher education. For example, it does not seem feasible to screen applicants to specific teacher education programs according to a variety of personality criteria. Individualized programs require resources which are not available at present. A valid and defensible approach to the interactions between student-teachers' characteristics and program features may be to provide student-teachers with a wide range of educational experiences during their pre- and in-service programs. Establishing a multifaceted educational environment for student-teachers may offer each one the most appropriate opportunities for professional growth.

Evaluation of Programs

Teacher education programs, like other educational programs, may be evaluated from time to time, but in the Israeli research literature only three evaluation reports and one description of the development and validation of an evaluation instrument (Fresko and Kfir, 1985) were found.

One evaluation study (Hoffman and Kraus, 1971) compared the progressive attitudes of university students after one year in different programs, another focused on student-teachers' perceptions of course goals and activities (Ehrlich, 1974), and the third (Kremer-Hayon and Ben-Peretz, 1986) dealt with beginning teachers' views of the nature and value of their pre-service education. The data from these evaluation studies indicated that university student-teachers as well as social science students developed progressive attitudes. These studies evaluate program goals of teacher education more highly than program activities and experiences; they see college teachers as presenting an unrealistic picture of teaching; and they perceive pre-service education, especially practical aspects such as practice teaching, as inadequate.

The educational system, particularly teacher education, has not responded and changed in reaction to studies such as these. This may be one reason that such studies are relatively scarce. Another reason may reside in the framework in which such studies are conducted. Present efforts focus on specific elements and lack a comprehensive framework for judging teacher education programs. I return to the issue of frameworks for research in the summary comments.

The main themes of the studies referred to in this chapter are summarized in Table 1.

Review and Discussion

Research on teacher education in Israel involves a rather small number of researchers. This may be a natural state of affairs in a small country, but it

Table 1 Summary of Studies of Teacher Education

	Topic of research	Number of sources	Methodology	Major findings	Possible implications for:
1	Characteristics of student-teachers, e.g. motives for choosing teaching, personality traits, professional identification	11	Personality tests Questionnaires Semantic differential	Most student teachers state that intrinsic motives, such as 'service to society', determine their choice of teaching. Personality traits discriminate between student-teachers in different programs. Earlier choice of career correlated with stronger professional identification.	Entry requirements Timing of programs
2	Characteristics of staff, e.g. professional image and reputation, professional perspectives, matching of cooperative teachers and student-teachers	3	Questionnaires and interviews	Reputation of teacher educators similar to that of other faculty members. Supervisors search for a body of knowledge to guide their work. Some discrepancies between cooperative teachers and student-teachers.	Status of teacher education programs Matching of teacher educators and students

	Topic	No.	Methods	Findings	Future research
3	Content of teacher education programs, e.g. knowledge base, instructional materials, specific strategies, curriculum studies	9	Questionnaires Interviews Content analysis Verbal interaction analysis Experimentation Repertory grid tests Conceptual mapping	No common body of knowledge incorporated in different teacher education programs. Workshops and value clarification experiences have positive impact on student-teacher. Little preparation in the curriculum domain.	Identification of legitimate body of knowledge for teacher education programs
4	Modes of teaching and evaluation, e.g. workshops, evaluation strategies	4	Questionnaires Classroom observation	Workshops have long-term impact. Significant effect of aptitude/teacher interaction on student-teachers' teaching behaviour and satisfaction. Similarity of evaluation practices in teacher education programs and schools.	Issues of individualization in teacher education programs Changes in instructional strategies and evaluation of student-teachers
5	Interaction between student characteristics and program features, e.g. belief system and program; SES and program; cognitive and socio-personal characteristics and practicum	4	Questionnaires IQ tests Verbal Interaction Category System	High and low levels of dogmatism and SES correlated to differential outcomes. Success in practicum related to cognitive characteristics.	Additional research
6	Evaluation of programs, e.g. student evaluation of courses, transition from teacher education to schools, educational attitudes	4	Questionnaires	Goals of teacher education evaluated higher than activities. General dissatisfaction with programs, especially with practice teaching.	Creation of framework for evaluation of programs Response of programs to evaluation outcomes

limits the scope of research. However, a steady growth in the number of studies has occurred over the years.

Research on teacher education in Israel is conducted mainly in universities by sociologists, psychologists and scholars in a variety of domains in education, such as curriculum or educational administration, who choose research questions which they consider important and relevant. Most of the research is funded by outside agencies, such as the Chief Scientist of the Ministry of Education and research foundations. This seems to ensure that the needs and priorities of the educational system in Israel are addressed. At present, for instance, the Chief Scientist of the Ministry of Education is sponsoring a research and development project at a teacher education college on teacher education for mastery learning.

To strengthen the research links between schools of education and colleges of teacher education, joint committees for research and publication have been established under the auspices of the Ministry of Education. The hope is that these committees will further research on teacher education, and promote its impact on educational policy in Israel.

The social context of Israel, with its strong emphasis on social and national issues, may account for the choice of many research topics. In our country, for example, we claim that 'the best' should choose teaching, so it is not surprising that many researchers turn to problems of selection of candidates for teachers' colleges, or try to determine the characteristics of candidates for the teaching profession. The effort expended may also explain why research on in-service programs is scarce.

Most research questions on student characteristics relate to a limited number of issues, such as 'incentives for choosing the profession', but a number of studies attempt to synthesize the findings to present a holistic view of candidates.

The results show that about 65 per cent of student-teachers claim that their professional choice was due to intrinsic motives, such as 'service to society'. This may be culture-dependent, as Israeli schools stress societal obligations, thereby creating high social desirability for this kind of response. Another finding on the level of professional identification shows it to be higher in student-teachers who choose to become teachers at an earlier, rather than later, stage of their university studies. This finding seems to imply that postgraduate studies in teacher education programs may lead to a weaker sense of professional identification. Of course, these findings and implications have to be viewed in the context of the Israeli system of teacher education. Most student-teachers in universities enter the teacher education program in their third year of BA or BSc studies, as a kind of 'insurance' that they will find appropriate employment after the completion of their studies. It seems plausible, therefore, that they will have a lower professional identification than their peers who chose teaching early as a first priority. Perhaps we need cross-cultural studies, at different stages of teacher education, to give us a better understanding of the association between the timing of professional choice and professional identification.

Advocates argue for a national selection system for candidates. Such a system may serve to enhance the quality of teachers. National and longitudinal studies are needed to examine its impact (Nevo, 1984).

Other major themes of research on teacher education in Israel relate to the content of programs, modes of instruction and student evaluation in the programs. These themes may be central for comparative studies on teacher education in different cultures, and several issues may be raised in relation to them. The Israeli studies found no common theoretical core serving teacher education programs, and no common body of knowledge transmitted to prospective teachers. If this is corroborated by international studies, we believe questions must then be asked regarding the nature of teaching as a profession.

It was suggested above that studies about teaching and evaluation are related to the ethos of these teacher education programs. This relationship provides another fruitful avenue for international comparative studies. The Israeli results suggest that modes of teaching and evaluation in teacher education programs may affect the practices of future teachers, and create obstacles for the introduction of innovations in schools. Comparative studies may, therefore, provide clearer implications for planning and implementing teacher education programs.

Research questions and methodology, as well as the interpretation of data, will be affected by the theoretical orientations favoured by researchers. Thus those favouring theories of personality will use them to structure their research on teacher education. Research on teacher education in Israel, however, is rather fragmented due largely to the fact that no comprehensive conceptual framework exists, and, considering the present studies, it is hard to envisage that a comprehensive framework will emerge.

In Israel the predominant research methodology has been the survey, using questionnaires and structured interviews. Relatively few studies have used ethnographic methods, or experimentation, though some employed experimental designs in order to evaluate innovative strategies in teacher education programs. Long-term research is not part of the present scene of research on teacher education in Israel, and without such longitudinal studies it is most difficult to evaluate and compare programs.

Experimentation with innovative strategies is evidence of a strong desire in Israel to contribute to the improvement of teacher education. This decision-oriented approach to research may also account for the relative scarcity of basic research, and for the few attempts to produce comprehensive theoretical frameworks.

Analytical or case descriptions of teacher education are also rare, which may be considered unfortunate, if Shulman's (1984) point of view about cases is accepted. He maintains that a case literature will present opportunities to learn from experiences which detail ways of dealing with concrete situations. It is to be hoped that a case literature in teacher education will develop in Israel.

Which teacher education issues are not 'covered' by present research efforts? Several of the parameters mentioned by Katz and Raths (1985), for example, goals, time and finances, receive scant attention. Only one study (Ehrlich, 1974) dealt with 'goals' and it found that student-teachers tended to evaluate program goals higher than the activities and experiences which were part of the program. This finding points to a possible lack of congruence between program goals and their expression in the program. This discrepancy is a perennial issue in the curriculum domain, and further studies are needed to clarify the relationship between goals and experiences in teacher education.

'Time' is another parameter to be studied at greater depth. The timing of teacher education was mentioned above, and it raises concerns which may have policy implications. At present too little is known about this issue in Israel.

Another perennial problem for teacher education is the nature of the knowledge base of teaching. Shulman (1984), who discusses the need to clarify and elaborate this base, states that 'to the extent that teaching is an art, its practice requires at least three forms of knowledge: knowledge of rules, knowledge of particular cases, and knowledge of ways to apply rules to cases' (Shulman, 1984, p. 191). It is suggested that research on teacher education should include an inquiry into the treatment of these forms of knowledge in teacher education programs.

Finally, it is suggested that intensifying international and comparative research on teacher education may provide useful and fruitful results for the growth of comprehensive and valid conceptualizations to guide further research efforts.

Note

1 One study appears in category 4 and in category 5.

References

BEN-PERETZ, M. and TAMIR, P. (1983) 'The professional image and reputation of teacher educators in Israel.' Paper presented at the Annual Conference of the American Educational Research Association, Montreal.

BEN-PERETZ, M., GILADI, M. and KURTZ, C. (1983) A multidimensional profile of prospective teachers. *Studies in Education*, 37, 193–202.

BEN-PERETZ, M., KATZ, S. and SILBERSTEIN, M. (1982) Curriculum interpretation and its place in teacher education programs. *Interchange*, 13, 4, 47–55.

DANIELI, D. (1982) Student teachers' attitudes to disadvantaged pupils. Summary of MA thesis, Bar Ilan University.

EHRLICH, M. (1974) Students' Perceptions of Study in the Department of Teacher Education. *Studies in Education*, 4, June, 45–64.

ELBAZ, F., HOZ, R., TOMER, Y., CHAYOT, R., MAHLER, S. and YEHESKEL, N. (1986) The use of concept mapping in the study of teachers' knowledge structures, in M. BEN-PERETZ, R. BROMME and R. HALKE (Eds) *Advances of Research on Teacher Thinking*, Lisse: Svets and Zeitlinger.

FRESKO, B. and KFIR, D. (1985) Introducing course evaluation in a teachers' college. *Higher Education in Europe*, 10, 2, 52–59.

GILADI, M. and BEN-PERETZ, M. (1981) The ideal teacher as perceived by students in teacher education programs. *Studies in Education*, 30, 5–14.

HOFFMAN, I. and KRAUS, U. (1971) Teacher education programs and their impact on educational orientation. *Magamot*, 18, 6, 254–260.

JACKSON, P.W. (1986) *The Practice of Teaching*, New York: Teachers College Press.

KATZ, L.G. and Raths, J.D. (1985) A framework for research on teacher education programs. *Journal of Teacher Education*, 36, 6, 9–15.

KATZ, L.G., RATHS, J.D., IRVING, J., KURASHI, A., MOHANTY, C. and SANI, M. (1982) 'Reputations of teacher educators among members of their role set.' Paper presented at the annual conference of the American Educational Research Association, New York.

KELLY, G. (1955) *The Psychology of Personal Constructs*, New York: Norton.

KREMER, L. (1974) Problems and issues in teacher education: Research on improving competencies in learning classroom discussions, in *Theory and Practice*, Ministry of Education and Culture, Jerusalem, and Gordon's Teacher College, pp. 75–92.

KREMER, L. (1984) Value clarification: A tool in developing value judgment. *Journal of Instructional Psychology*, 11, 1, 52–58.

KREMER, L. and HOFFMAN, I. (1979) A three-dimensional theory of teachers' personality. *Journal of Education Measurement*, 73, 1, 21–25.

KREMER, L. and PERLBERG, A. (1979) Training of teachers in strategies that develop independent learning skills in their pupils. *British Journal of Teacher Education*, 5, 1, 35–48.

KREMER-HAYON, L. (1986) Supervisors' inner world: Professional perspectives. *European Journal of Teacher Education*, 9, 2, 181–187.

KREMER-HAYON, L. and BEN-PERETZ, M. (1986) Becoming a teacher: The transition from teachers' college to classroom life. *International Review of Education*, 32, 4, 413–422.

KREMER-HAYON, L. and MOORE, M. (1985) Dogmatism in teacher education practices: Aptitude treatment interaction effects. *Research in Education*, 36, 19–26.

LAZAROWITZ, R. and TAMIR, P. (1980) How do high school science teachers, student-teachers and university professors relate to teaching science by inquiry. *Studies in Education*, 27, October, 95–104.

LAZAROWITZ, R., DREYFUS, A. and JUNGWIRTH, E. (1986) Consonances and dissonances between student teachers and co-operative teachers in secondary school biology. *Research in Education*, 36, 27–35.

LORTIE, D.C. (1975) *Schoolteacher: A Sociological Study*, Chicago and London: University of Chicago Press.

MAHLER, S. and BENOR, D. (1984) Short and long term effects of a teacher training workshop in medical school. *Higher Education*, 13, 265–273.

MARMER, M. (1980) Incentives for choice of teaching profession. Summary of MA thesis, University of Tel-Aviv, School of Education.

MILGRAM, M. and MILGRAM, N. (1976) Self concept differences in student-teachers in primary, elementary, secondary and special education. *Psychology in the Schools*, 13, 4, 439–441.

MILGRAM, M. and MILGRAM, N. (1978) Cognitive and personal social variables in the performance of Israeli student teachers. *Megamot* (Behavioral Sciences Quarterly), 24, 1, 39–45.

NEVAT, R. (1984) Teacher education with regard to individual differences. Thesis submitted for MA degree, Haifa University, School of Education.

NEVO, B. (1984) Selection of candidates for teachers' colleges in Israel. *Studies in Education*, 39, 17–36.

SHAFIR, E. (1979) Vocational identification of students in teacher training program. Thesis submitted for MA Degree, Haifa University, School of Education.

SHULMAN, L.S. (1984) The practical and the eclectic: A deliberation on teaching and educational research. *Curriculum Inquiry*, 14, 2, 183–200.

SILBERSTEIN, M. (1984) Teacher educators and their views about the use of curriculum materials in teacher education programs. *Newsletter*, Ministry of Education and Culture, Department of Curriculum Development, 47, 1, 13–15.

SILBERSTEIN, M. (Ed.) (1985) *Teacher Education for Curriculum Issues*. Jerusalem: Ministry of Education and Culture, Department of Curriculum Development.

SILBERSTEIN, N. and TAMIR, P. (1986) Curriculum development and implementation as a component of teacher education in Israel. *Teaching and Teacher Education*, 2, 3, 251–261.

TAMIR, P. and BEN-PERETZ, M. (1981) Learning materials in teacher education courses in Israel. *Studies in Education*, 31, 85–98.

TAMIR, P. and BEN-PERETZ, M. (1983) Evaluation practices in teacher education in Israel. *Singapore Journal of Education*, 16, 6–13.

ULLMAN, H. (1979) Students' expectations from their professional training in a university of teacher education. Thesis submitted for MA degree, Haifa University, School of Education.

ZAK, I. (1976) *Personality Characteristics of Students in Teacher Education Colleges*. Tel-Aviv: Tel-Aviv University, School of Education.

ZAK, I. (1981) Continuous self-selection processes in teacher education: The way for survival. *Journal of Education for Teaching*, 7, 3, 263–273.

ZAK, I. and HOROWITZ, T. (1985) *The School Is Also the Teacher's World.* Tel-Aviv: Ramot.

ZMORA, D. (1979) Belief system of student teachers as a factor in the change of educational orientations. MA thesis, University of Haifa, School of Education.

Chapter 13

Education Reforms and Research on Teacher Education in China

Zhaoyi Wu and Jean Chang

Introduction

During the last decade China has been confronted with the task of all-round social reform aimed at modernization to transform it into a great and powerful socialist country with modern agriculture, industry, national defence, and science and technology. Consequently, education has been geared towards new objectives, where teachers are the key to educating people to meet the needs of the economic development of the country (Deng, 1984, p. 119). But teachers require more social support for teacher education, better living conditions and financial returns.

The educational reforms include, among other things, decentralization of the administration of education, implementation of nine-year compulsory education, reform of the procedure of enrolment, development of vocational and technical schools and a steady increase in the education budget. As far as teacher education is concerned, it is recognized that the qualifications of teachers should be evaluated and in-service education of various kinds be provided to ensure that the overwhelming majority of primary and secondary school teachers are properly qualified for their work by the end of 1990. Quality and qualifications of teachers are vital issues which determine the basic requirements of teachers and the kind of training and education that should be provided.

What is the general quality expected of teachers in China? According to Wang (1987),

> There are different interpretations and definitions for the 'quality of teachers'. According to our understanding, the 'quality of teachers' means the basic conditions under which teachers are able to play their dynamic role. In other words, the 'quality of teachers' refers to teachers' various inner elements, such as their

political quality, their cultural quality, their intellectual quality and their physical quality. (p. 31)

By 'political quality', Wang means political consciousness, devotion to education and moral integrity. 'Cultural quality' refers to 'to be knowledgeable on a wide range of subjects and to specialize in the knowledge and skills of the subject he teaches' (p. 38). 'Intellectual quality' means 'the ability to organize his educational work and teaching...to apply educational theories to practice' (p. 39). 'Physical quality' refers to teachers' health conditions, which, according to Wang, are far from satisfactory. In fact, these qualities boil down to *political orientation, professional competence,* and *health conditions.*

The traditional view of a good teacher in China involves 'competence in subject matter, teaching ability and moral character' (Hayhoe, 1984), and a post-1949 criterion from the new Communist regime, 'dedication to communist ideology and willingness to serve the people' (p. 156). While still adhering to political goals and moral integrity, current reforms seem to emphasize professional competence, which includes the ability to apply pedagogical principles and appropriate methods to the teaching of relevant subjects at school, and *academic qualifications.*

What are these basic qualifications for teachers in China? Although China has not adopted a consistent system of teacher certification, the basic requirements are that primary school teachers must attain the qualification of graduates from secondary teacher training schools, junior middle school teachers must attain the qualification of graduates from *zhuanke* (two- or three-year) colleges, and senior middle school teachers must attain the qualification of graduates from *benke* (four-year) colleges or universities (Yu, 1987, pp. 119–120). Efforts are now being made to ensure prospective teachers fulfil these basic requirements. As mentioned earlier, teacher education in China must be viewed in the context of nation-wide social reforms for achieving the ultimate goal of modernization.

This chapter provides an overview of teacher education in China with regard to the impact of current reforms on teacher education. Then the scope and areas of research that have been and are being done in pre-service and in-service education, and the problems involved, are discussed.

Teacher Education in China: An Overview

In China, a country with a population of over one billion, the number of primary and secondary school students is ever increasing. Today primary school pupils total 145,000,000 and the number of secondary school students has surpassed 50,000,000. To match such astronomical figures, there are 5,600,000 teachers engaged in primary education and 2,800,000 in secondary education. It is estimated that at least another 1,000,000 teachers are needed for primary schools and 750,000 for junior secondary schools in order to implement the nine-year compulsory education during the period 1985–1990.

The majority of teachers proceed through teacher training institutions at different levels. The institutions are:

1 national teacher training institutions, namely, the two 'key' teacher training universities: *Beijing Shifan Daxue* (Beijing Teachers University) and *Huadong Shifan Daxue* (East-China Teachers University); both are funded by the Central Government through the National Education Commission;

2 one hundred and eighty six teachers' universities and teachers' colleges, funded by municipal or provincial governments; for example, Beijing Teachers College obtains funds from the municipality of Beijing through the Municipal Bureau of Higher Education, and Shanxi Teachers University is funded by the provincial government of Shanxi;

3 teacher training schools, or secondary professional schools, which provide teachers for primary schools and kindergartens; they are funded by governments at municipal, provincial or county levels;

4 education institutes, which, like teacher training schools, are government-funded at municipal, provincial or county levels; they are mainly concerned with in-service education and provide short-term refresher courses.

Teacher colleges (tertiary institutions) are divided into two types:

a *benke* or four-year system: graduates from these colleges obtain a bachelor's degree as well as a diploma of education, which qualifies them to teach in both junior and senior secondary schools;

b *zhuanke* or two- or three-year system: those who complete the two- or three-year courses are awarded a diploma of education, which qualifies them to teach in junior secondary schools.

The tertiary teachers' universities or colleges are composed of departments of different disciplines to match the subjects taught in secondary schools, such as mathematics, history, Chinese, English, etc. Undergraduates major in one area which takes up more than 50 per cent of their total coursework. A second compulsory area consists of pedagogy (history, theories and principles of education), psychology and methodology for about 10 per cent of the total number of credits. In four-year universities and colleges a 'pre-practicum' is usually arranged in the second year, and a 'practicum' in either the second semester of the third academic year, or the first semester of the fourth year. These vary in length from six to twelve weeks. The two- or three-year colleges have a similar curriculum except that the courses tend to be more practically than theoretically oriented due to shorter time available.

Research on Teacher Education

In recent years research on teacher education has concentrated on human resources, and at the national and local levels surveys have evaluated the quantity and quality of teacher education. They are conducted by *administrative organizations*, e.g., the Central Institute of Educational Research, and institutes of educational research in teachers' universities and teachers' colleges. Usually, administrative bodies provide statistics, and academic institutes evaluate the qualifications of teachers. Sociological data are collected through national or local surveys, observation of micro-teaching, interviews and questionnaires, case studies and examinations to determine the effectiveness of teacher education. Nation-wide projects are funded by the state through the National Education Commission, and regional projects are funded by local governments or research institutions.

Four types of research have been reported recently:

1 research on general issues;
2 national and regional surveys on conditions and needs;
3 micro-observation of teaching processes and research on practicum and teacher supervision;
4 case studies of exemplary teaching.

Research on General Issues

Yu (1987) identifies the problems and weaknesses in China's teacher education, namely, an inadequate number of primary and secondary school teachers; a large proportion of teachers who do not meet the basic qualifications; a shortage of teachers in particular subject areas such as history, geography, biology, music, fine arts and physical education; an outflow of talented teachers from the teaching force; and unsatisfactory material conditions (low income, housing shortage, etc.) for teachers.

He also proposes reforms in teacher education using teachers' colleges and other institutions to prepare qualified teachers. Teachers' colleges, he says, should be engaged in research on educational theories and evaluation.

Wang (1987) has provided an overview of teacher education in China and emphasized the role of in-service education in upgrading teachers. He reported on 290 institutions at the provincial and municipal levels and 2174 at the county level which organize programs for school administrators and teachers. The teachers were either

a unqualified or had failed in qualifying examinations set by local authorities, or
b basically qualified, but without the corresponding educational background, or
c qualified, with required academic background, or
d required, as 'core teachers' to be qualified in different subject areas.

He documented the in-service education provided to train the unqualified and those who lacked adequate educational background.

National and Regional Surveys on Conditions and Needs

Since the late 1970s, nation-wide surveys have reported on the conditions of teachers and the numbers needed for the period 1980–1990. For example, a document issued by the Ministry of Education on 22 August 1980 indicated:

> Of 667,000 senior secondary school teachers, only 338,000 graduated from 4-year universities or colleges; of 2,410,000 junior secondary school teachers, 250,000 had diplomas from 2-year or 3-year colleges; of 5,380,000 primary school teachers, 2,530,000 graduated from secondary teacher training schools or senior secondary schools.

In other words, 50 per cent of the senior secondary school teachers, 90 per cent of junior secondary school teachers and 53 per cent of primary school teachers had to receive in-sevice education to meet basic teaching qualifications.

According to some 1984 statistics, nearly 2,400,000 teachers engaged in primary and secondary education require induction or continuing education. They are distributed as follows:

primary school teachers: 1,450,000

junior secondary school teachers: 750,000
senior secondary school teachers: 140,000
agricultural and other technical school teachers: 60,000.

Continuing or in-service education is provided by:

a   teacher training institutions at tertiary and secondary levels (with comprehensive or single subject courses ranging from three months to two years);
b   education institutes at provincial, municipal or county (district) levels (with short-term refresher courses);
c   television universities at the national and local levels;
d   correspondence courses in universities, teachers' colleges and education institutes;
e   self-education programs from the National Commission of Examination of Self-Taught Students; and
f   special institutional teams: for example, in 1985 the Central Government of China organized an instructional team of 3250 employees from different departments to assist local authorities in twenty-two provinces and autonomous regions to set up one-year teacher training courses; subsequently, from the experience gained, provincial governments assigned their own employees to in-service education in different local areas.

There are many more teachers involved in in-service education in China than in pre-service education. In 1979, for example, 24,331 trainees graduated from tertiary teacher training institutions, and 102,341 graduated from secondary teacher training schools, compared with more than 1,000,000 secondary school teachers and more than 1,300,000 primary school teachers engaged in different in-service programs. The emphasis is for in-service education to upgrade the qualifications to teachers.

Research on in-service education has taken several forms. One is surveys of teachers who need in-service education. For example, surveys of English language teachers in secondary schools of Beijing reported that of the total 4554 secondary English teachers nearly 40 per cent required in-service education to reach basic teaching qualifications. A second form of research on in-service education is the assessment of teaching materials and teaching conditions in educational institutions.

Research on these issues has implications for teacher education and teacher supply. For example, in certain instances it has been shown that teaching materials for English are out-of-date, with a consequent effect on the nature of that teaching in secondary schools. An implication is that in-service education through refresher and correspondence courses is needed to reform the curriculum and teaching methods. Other surveys (He Bin, 1987; Wang, Zhang and Wang, 1987) have shown that school conditions, such as heavy workload, ineffective administration and few opportunities for further education, stunt professional growth. These findings imply that more attention must be given to induction practices in schools, and in-service activities that foster professional growth and lead to more collaborative and democratic practices in running schools. It is appropriate to note that although there is an acute shortage of competent teachers, a proportion of the top graduates from teachers' colleges are assigned to places other than high schools (Wang, Zhang and Wang, 1987).

Micro-observation of Teaching Processes and Research on the Practicum and Teacher Supervision

Pre-practicum and practicum are an inseparable part of pre-service education, required of all students in teacher training institutes. Pre-practicum usually takes place in the second academic year and the length ranges from two to four weeks. It is sometimes part of a methodology course in a particular area of study such as the teaching of mathematics and the teaching of English. The practicum, which lasts between four and twelve weeks, is required of all students who wish to obtain a diploma of education. It consists of two parts: observation of 'demonstration classes', and teaching practice.

Many institutions produce 'in-house' reports and descriptions of successful cases in their own college journals. Publication is usually preceded by a symposium where the successful cases are reported. Included in these reports are attitudinal analyses indicating how a student views teaching as a career, and professional competencies to illustrate how successful a student is in presenting a subject.

Case Studies of Exemplary Teaching

It is generally acknowledged in China that the effectiveness of pre-service education is reflected in the degree of success a teacher achieves in a secondary or primary school. Therefore, one of the chief methods of research on teacher education is a case study, and typical cases are publicized for discussion. The following is an illustration.

In the national examination for entrance to tertiary institutions, applicants for an English major have to pass an additional oral English test.

Students from remote rural secondary schools are at a disadvantage, as the majority have never heard English spoken by native speakers, nor have their teachers the ability, or desire, to teach spoken English. Generally, the students who obtain the highest scores in oral as well as written English examinations come from big cities and, most likely, from 'key schools' with experienced English language teachers and good audiovisual facilities. However, in the entrance examination for the 1984–1985 academic year, the only student to obtain the full score (100) in the written English examination came from a distant county north of Beijing. Several other top scorers came from the same secondary school. But, what was more surprising, was that they all spoke English with a good accent.

As this news spread, education administrators, researchers and journalists went to the rural school to investigate. They found that top scorers in the English examination were taught by a teacher named Meng Yen-jun, who had been an undergraduate at Beijing Teachers College. When her studies were interrupted by the 'Cultural Revolution', she was assigned, in 1969, to teach in the mountainous county of Huairou. Although, later, most of the former 'Red Guards' returned to the cities, she was one of the few to remain, in spite of the fact that her family were in Beijing. Devoted as she was to the teaching of English, a subject considered 'useless' by most people in the distant rural areas, she tried her best to motivate the students. Her method of teaching was different from that adopted by many English language teachers in secondary schools. She emphasized practice in spoken English. By using pictures, objects, charts and other visual aids, she encouraged the students to use the language in class. One year before the 1984 college entrance examination, she set up an English group interested in practising spoken English outside the class. For a whole summer the group received voluntary, individual tutoring from Meng Yenjun. They listened to tapes, corrected each other's pronunciation, and spoke to each other in English about their daily lives. Those who were preparing to apply for an English major in universities and colleges completed additional assignments in written English, vocabulary, grammar and translation, which are the components of the written English examination. An investigation on her teaching, organized jointly by the Education Bureau of Huairou County and the Education Institute of Beijing, reported as follows:

A   A teacher's motivation — his or her attitude to the teaching profession, correlates with his or her success.... Meng Yenjun's success was due to her devotion to the teaching of English and her persistence in working in a remote area. She spared no effort to give voluntary tutoring to her students outside the class, not for any personal gain, but out of love for her students and her sense of responsibility.

B   A good teacher-student relationship and cooperation generally yield positive results in teaching. There are many moving stories about how Meng Yenjun visited the parents of those who had difficulty in their study, and worked out plans for remedial lessons. As a result, her work was supported by both parents and students, and there were fewer discipline problems in class, and the drop-out rate was very low.

C   Continuing education plays an important role in raising the professional competence of teachers. Meng Yenjun studied English for only two years at Beijing Teachers' College before the 'Cultural Revolution' broke out in 1966. In fact, she did not have much English at her disposal, to say nothing of her teaching experience. When she started teaching English in a secondary school in the county of Huairou, she aimed to catch up in language proficiency and methods of teaching. She observed 'demonstration classes', attended refresher courses at the Education Institute and applied new principles and methods to her teaching. She familiarized herself with the requirements of the university entrance examination, and helped her students to prepare for both the oral and written tests.

We have taught a former student of Meng Yenjun at Beijing Teachers College and we found that she was highly motivated and was more active in class than other students. She finished as one of the top students in the class. Comparable case studies have occurred and are reported regularly, especially those of teachers awarded special honors.

Considerations for Further Research

Rosen (1987) states that within the past several years survey research has emerged as a major source of information on Chinese society, and one striking aspect is the sheer volume of that research. There are attendant problems. In the cases of teacher supply and demand the general estimates are given but there are no clear indications as to how the figures are obtained to help assess their reliability. In the cases of interview information it is clear that informants are cautious about providing unreserved comments or criticisms about the nature of teacher education. Furthermore, needs analyses only touch upon general or surface issues, such as social status and pay rises. More detailed, in-depth studies are rare. We believe these methodological concerns must be addressed in future projects on human resources in teacher education. In addition, we believe future research must build upon the vast amount of human resource survey information, take a broader perspective and consider the following issues.

The Goals of Teacher Education

In retrospect, we can distinguish three major goals of teacher education in different phases of Chinese history. Traditionally, teacher education was regarded as a social force with a view to disseminating knowledge, solving puzzles and maintaining moral integrity. Under the socialist regime, especially from the 1950s to 1970s, teacher education served as a political force: teachers were supposed to be loyal to 'the Party's educational cause' — to educate people to be socialist-minded. The current social reforms seem to emphasize teacher education as an economic factor with the pragmatic approach aiming at providing technocrats and professionals for modernization.

While teacher education in China is constrained by its special social contexts, its goal for the future will inevitably be affected by global issues such as war and peace, ecological concerns and psychological and psychophysical problems confronting the next few generations. Therefore, research on teacher education, we suggest, should be concerned with teachers' preparedness for those fundamental issues of common interest to all groups of people in the world. This should be reflected in the policy and content of teacher education.

Awareness of Teacher Demand and Education Legislation

Recent surveys in teacher education in China have indicated a nationwide demand for increasing the number of teachers, improving their quality and expanding their roles in society. One crucial area of research involves the necessary laws concerning teacher education. For example, as Chen (1987) points out, there should be a 'teaching staff law' which will 'stipulate the standards, positions, examinations, rewards and penalties, rights and obligations, and the conditions of the teaching staff' (p. 213). The significance of such a law is to affirm the legal rights of teachers and assure their position in society. An equally important law will be the education budget law, which will 'provide stipulation in regard to the raising and use of education funds' (p. 213), especially the budget for the preparation of teachers. At the national level there should be a steady increase in the budget for teacher education. However, because of limited central government revenues, funds from different sources such as local taxes should be included for the preparation of teachers, improvement of the facilities of teacher education institutes at different levels and teachers' regular pay rises.

Teacher Credentials and Certification

It is laid down as a basic policy in the 'Decision of the CCP Central Committee on the Reform of the Education System' that measures should be taken to insure that the overwhelming majority of high school and elementary school teachers qualify for teaching in the next five years, or in a little longer period of time. 'After that, only those with a qualified record of formal schooling or certificate of examination can teach' (Hu and Seifman, 1987, p. 197). Who, then, will decide the qualifications of teachers? Who will issue credentials, and on what basis? Research will have to be done to determine the basic qualifications for teachers and set standards for the nation as well as for different localities (rural versus urban, majority versus minority education, etc.).

Evaluation of the Effectiveness of Existing Teacher Education Institutions, Systems of Selection and Placement, In-service Programs, Curriculum, Methods of Teaching and Examinations

Evaluation of teacher education, for example, is a crucial problem in our country and associated with that is the controversial issue of whether teachers' colleges should have an independent existence. Some educators argue that colleges should be integrated with universities, while others say they have special characteristics and are fulfilling an important role. There is, however, no convincing information to indicate which training institution produces the best graduates.

In short, further research on teacher education in China should consider social (such as status of teachers), economic (such as financial resources) and educational (such as goals, approaches, etc.) factors. In the Chinese context both macro-type research and detailed micro-studies on individual issues should be combined to draw implications to improve teacher education.

Furthermore, a network must be established for gathering and disseminating data and information. According to Rosen (1987),

> Thus far, there has been little attempt to build an academic literature on any of the social issues being investigated.... The methodological information provided is commonly not detailed enough to enable other researchers to replicate the study...there appears to be little interest in following up, or even referring to, studies done by others. (p. 198)

We hope that in the process of research and educational reform a national clearing house will be set up, new methods of research will be introduced and adopted for better results in teacher education in China.

References

CHEN, YUNSHENG (1987) What is education legislation and why is it necessary to have education legislation? in HU and SEIFMAN (Eds) *Education and Socialist Modernisation*. New York: AMS Press.

DENG, ZIAOPING (1984) *Selected Works (1975–1985)*. Beijing: Foreign Language Press.

HAYHOE, RUTH (1984) *Contemporary Chinese education*, New York: M.E. Sharpe.

HE, BIN (1987) Troubles and needs of school teachers: Survey and analysis. *Chinese Education*, 20, 1, pp. 43–63.

HU, SHI-MING and SEIFMAN, ELI (Eds) (1987) *Education and Socialist Modernization*. New York: AMS Press.

ROSEN, STANLEY (1987) Survey research in the People's Republic of China: Some methodological problems. *Canadian and International Education*, 16, 1, pp. 190–197.

WANG, CONGFANG (1987) Pre-service and in-service teacher education in China. *Canadian and International Education*, 16, 1, pp. 133–143.

WANG, HUI, ZHANG, C. and WANG, H. (1987) On the importance of improving the essential quality of teachers. *Chinese Education*, 20, 1, pp. 31–63.

YU QINGLIAN (1987) The strategic position and prospects of teachers' education. *Canadian and International Education*, 16, 1, pp. 114–122.

Additional Sources on Education and Teacher Education in China

CHAN, SYLVIA and PRICE, R.F. (1978) Teacher training China: A case study of the Foreign Languages Department of Peking Teachers' Training College. *Comparative Education*, 14, 3, pp. 243–252.

CHEN, THEODORE HAI-EN (1981) *Chinese Education since 1949: Academic and Revolutionary Models*. New York: Pergamon Press.

Gu, Mingyuan (1981) Teacher training in China. *Journal of Education for Teaching*, 7, 3.

Hu, Shi-ming and Seifman, Eli (Eds) (1976) *Toward a New World Outlook: A Documentary History of Education in the People's Republic of China, 1949–1976.* New York: AMS Press.

Ji, Xiaofeng (1986) Teacher education: Past and present, in *China Educational Research.* Beijing: Central Institute of Educational Research.

Leung, C.K. and Chin, S. (Eds) (1983) *China in Readjustment.* Hong Kong: Center of Asian Studies.

Talor, Robert (1981) *China's Intellectual Dilemma: Politics and University Enrollment 1949–1978,* Vancouver and London: University of British Colombia Press.

UNESCO Regional Office for Education in Asia and Pacific (Ed.) (1984) *Diagnostic Studies on Educational Management: Country Studies; China.* Bangkok: UNESCO Regional Office for Education in Asia and Pacific.

White, G. *Party and Professionals: The Political Role of Teacher in Contemporary China.* New York: M.E. Sharpe.

World Bank (1985) *China: Issues and Prospectives in Education.* Washington, DC: World Bank.

Chapter 14

A Framework for Research on Teacher Education Programs

Lilian G. Katz and James D. Raths

Introduction

This chapter draws upon a conceptual framework to summarize research in the field of teacher education. The framework was originally proposed by Katz and Raths (1985) as a heuristic device with which to examine, classify and synthesize research on all aspects of teacher education programs. Using this framework we examine the research on teacher education from the twelve countries reviewed in the preceding chapters.

Definition

To begin with, a teacher education program is defined as 'a set of phenomena deliberately intended to help candidates acquire the knowledge, skills, dispositions, and norms of the occupation of teaching.' The phenomena constituting teacher education programs are numerous and varied. They include lecture classes, seminars, field trips, practice of various kinds, modules on specific topics, micro-teaching, observation in schools and elsewhere, tutoring individual children, peer tutoring, examinations, screening procedures, social events, meetings of student educational associations and so forth. Though this definition emphasizes deliberately planned phenomena, we acknowledge that many unplanned or incidental factors impinge upon them that may contribute substantially to the nature and consequence of candidates' experiences.

Parameters of Teacher Education Programs

The varied phenomena constituting a teacher education program are characterized, defined, influenced and circumscribed by broad classes of variables we refer to as 'parameters'. The term 'parameter' is used here to indicate a category of variables that applies to every teacher education program.

The parameters proposed for the framework are not parallel levels of abstraction. Nor are they assumed to be operating on the constituent phenomena of teacher education programs merely as external 'forces'. Furthermore, for heuristic purposes the parameters are discussed as though they were discrete classes of variables, even though our experience suggests that the parameters encompass complex interacting and confounding collections of variables. Inasmuch as the relative contribution of each parameter to the ultimate nature of teacher education is unknown, we list them without implication as to their importance.

Each parameter is defined briefly below by indicating a few of the variables that might be included within it.

I   Goals
Variables such as the content of the goals, the extent to which they are explicit, realistic, shared, specific, practical, theoretical, political, coherent, compatible, thematic, technical, humanistic and so forth.

II   Characteristics of the Candidates
Variations among candidates such as age, sex, socio-economic status, ethnicity, academic aptitude, intellectual ability, creativity, motivation, commitment, understandings of teaching and learning, competence in the language of instruction or any other attributes potentially related to other parameters of the program.

III   Characteristics of the Staff
Staff members are those whose assignments include activities deliberately intended to prepare candidates for the occupation of teaching. Among them are professors, instructors, graduate teaching assistants, adjunct professors, cooperating teachers, advisers and counsellors, supervisors of student teaching and perhaps others. These individuals may vary in age, experience, knowledge, skills, dispositions, qualifications, ideology, ethnicity, morale, commitment, reputation, etc.

IV   Content
Variations in the information, facts, knowledge, skills, techniques, competencies, ideas, philosophical tenets, texts, curriculum materials, topics the programs present to candidates. Variables in this parameter include the emphasis given to specific topics, including zero emphasis for those not taught.

V   Methods

Variables for describing the types of activities by which the content of the program is presented and exposed to candidates, e.g., observation in schools, fieldwork, practice or student teaching, micro-teaching, modelling simulation, direct instruction, discussion groups and seminars.

VI   Time/Timing

Variables of duration, e.g., two, three, five years; variables of timing and sequencing, e.g., temporal order and simultaneity and constituent events and activities of the program, time of candidates' entry into the program.

VII   Ethos

Variables include characteristics of the affective quality or tone of the relationships between and among program participants, as well as the content of the relationships between and among candidates and staff members, aspects of the ambience of the program such as whether it is offered on an urban commuter campus, 'Ivy League', parochial, land–grant or rural campus.

VIII   Regulations

Variables include characteristics of graduation requirements; certification and licence requirements and examinations; laws, regulations, legal restrictions and constraints related to teacher education and certification, accreditation and the stipulations of labour unions, school district regulations, local education authorities, governing boards, etc.

IX   Resources

Variations in the availability of laboratory or demonstration schools, micro–teaching laboratory, teachers' centre, curriculum library and so forth. Variables related to budgets, costs and expenditures and other financial or funding variables and size of the program and its institution are included in this parameter.

X   Evaluation Practices

Variables describing the frequency, objectivity and degree of formality in the ways candidates progress in academic work and student teaching are assessed; departmental and college evaluations of various aspects of the program, follow–up studies of graduates, licence examinations, etc.

XI   Impacts of the Program

Various effects of the program, from immediate to long-term, proximate to ultimate; they may include candidates' learning, competence,

> sentiments and evaluations of their experiences; proportion of graduates employed, superintendents'/principals' evaluations of the teaching effectiveness of graduates; graduates' pupils' achievements and so forth.

We assume that every instance of a teacher education program has entries within each of the eleven parameters defined above. Furthermore, the 'values' entered for different programs in most of the parameter variables will vary, and many of the variations — but not all — are of scholarly, theoretical and/or practical interest.

Even though the countries represented in the chapters in this collection differ along many dimensions, we assume that all teacher education programs within them have 'values' in the variables within all of the parameters in the matrix. We illustrate the use of the matrix with citations from the chapters in which parameter values have been mentioned.

A Matrix of Parameters of Teacher Education Programs

Uses of the Matrix. As shown in Figure 1, the eleven parameters can be displayed as a matrix of rows and columns. The cells created by the matrix provide a framework for summarizing research.

Diagonal cells. Summaries of research on within-parameter cells are 'located' in the shaded cells on the diagonal created by the matrix. For example, the first cell in the upper left-hand corner of the matrix would 'contain' studies of aims, goals and objectives of teacher education, or summaries of the available literature about them. In this way, each cell on the diagonal could include the findings of research on within-parameter topics, or any of the subtopics within it. The diagonal cells may also suggest new questions on within-parameter variables.

Off-diagonal cells. All other cells in the matrix depict the interactions of variables in the row parameter on variables in the column parameter, and vice versa. For example, in the second cell in the top row, research concerning the effects of variables in parameter *I: Goals*, on variables in parameter *II: Candidates*, is addressed. In this way, each cell can be used to examine the influence of variables in the row on variables in the column as well as ways in which they may be interactive. The cells can also be taken several at a time, in small or large blocks. We realize, however, that the chances of being able to ascertain the direction of

Parameters

	I	II	III	IV	V	VI	VII	VIII	IX	X	XI
I Goals	■										
II Candidates		■									
III Staff			■								
IV Content				■							
V Methods					■						
VI Time						■					
VII Ethos							■				
VIII Regulations								■			
IX Resources									■		
X Evaluation										■	
XI Impact											■

Figure 1. A Matrix of Eleven Parameters of Teacher Education Programs

245

effects or to discern cause-effect relationships and sequences are very small. It seems most likely that the majority of variables of interest will be interactive and/or confounded.

New Questions. Displaying the parameters as a matrix has the advantage of stimulating fresh questions about the relationships between parameters and the variables they include. For example, in looking at the second cell in the third row, *III* × *II*, questions concerning the effects of characteristics of staff on candidates come readily to mind in much the same tradition as the teacher effectiveness literature looks at teachers' effects on pupils. But the third cell in the *second* row: *II* × *III* (*Candidates* × *Staff*) gives rise to questions about the way candidates might influence staff, and raises potentially interesting issues concerning the direction and types of effects.

Types of Research

In most of the chapters in this volume authors have commented on the types of research methods used within their own countries. It should be noted here that the proposed matrix is methodologically neutral in that research 'prompted' by it need not be limited to any particular research method or tradition. Studies may be historical, descriptive, experimental, naturalistic, longitudinal, case studies or any other approach appropriate to the problems to be examined.

Katz and Raths (1985) presented the original formulation of this matrix with illustrations of research under three headings: within-parameter research, inter-parameter research, and new questions raised by examining the matrix. However, because the present chapter is based on reviews of research rather than on direct examination of primary sources, the matrix is used to categorize the research cited in the twelve chapters according to the parameters of the matrix. Furthermore, since these chapters do not include detailed discussions of the individual studies reviewed, the appropriate classification of a particular citation into a parameter is not always possible to determine. It should also be noted that in some chapters some parameters were not discussed at all, presumably because research within them is not available. In addition, some chapters take up issues and research related to in-service education; since the matrix is specifically designed to address pre-service teacher education programs, discussions of the research on in-service education are not included here.

Using the Matrix for an International Perspective

I. Research on Goals. The first cell in the upper left-hand corner of the matrix locates summaries, analyses and syntheses of the literature pertaining to goals and objectives. Direct studies of goals and other subtopics in the parameter also belong in this cell. The data might come from surveys of colleges and departments and could be analyzed in terms of explicitness, practically, coherence, ideological assumptions, sources, changes over time, within-program consistency or compatibility or any other within-parameter variables of interest.

Ho Wah Kam describes a 1981 study in Singapore on teacher education objectives which concluded, 'An effective teacher education program in the eyes of pre-service students is... one that prepares them to cope with the many and varied day-to-day problems they will encounter within the four walls of the classroom.' Zimpher and Howey point out that in the U.S. pressure exists from students and the critics of teacher education to focus the goals of teacher education programs on more practical preparation for the realities of the schools. The same theme appears in Sato's discussion of teacher education in Japan. Similarly, McNamara points out that in Britain strengthening teacher education candidates' awareness of discriminatory practices in the classroom should be incorporated into the goals of the program. One study cited by Govinda and Buch indicates that the goals of teacher education programs in India are quite diverse.

A series of significant studies in Sweden of the goals of teacher education reported by Gran suggested that there were discrepancies between what sort of candidates the teacher preparation institutes were graduating and what the 'field' expected, and led to some implications for reform in Swedish teacher education.

According to Wu and Chang, in the People's Republic of China the goals of education at every level, including teacher education, have recently been redirected toward the country's need for economic development; the goals of teacher education are to produce graduates of high political, cultural, intellectual and physical quality. The remaining chapters did not include references to issues related to the goals of teacher education programs.

II. Research on Candidates. The next diagonal cell summarizes studies of characteristics of candidates. Studies of the characteristics of candidates appear to be common in most countries, and the kinds of variables explored in these studies are similar.

Studies of the characteristics of candidates have been reported in most of the twelve countries included in this collection. For example, Klinzing states that West German scholars conducted a large number of studies of such candidate characteristics as expectations, motivation, values, interests, attitudes, abilities, self-concept, personality attributes and opinions of teacher education, among others. Findings from these studies indicate that most teacher education candidates had idealistic and altruistic motives for becoming teachers, and saw teaching as a distinct 'calling'. Ho Wa Kam reports that a study of the motives for entering teaching was the first major project of the Research Unit of Singapore's Institute of Education. The data showed that, like the West German studies, Singapore's teachers typically are motivated by altruism to enter teaching. Research in Singapore addressed the ethno–linguistic character-istics of candidates because competence in the language of instruction is important in Singapore. Fondness for children was frequently given as a reason for choosing a teaching career in Singapore.

McNamara, in his discussion on Britain, notes the development of procedures for the selection of candidates. Zimpher and Howey discuss concerns with recruitment of ethnic minority group candidates into teaching, and the possible inhibiting effects of recent emphasis on teacher testing on these efforts in the United States.

Wu and Chang state that a large proportion of teachers in the People's Republic of China do not meet basic educational qualifications themselves. The authors point to poor qualifications of candidates and teachers as one of the reasons why in-service education continues to receive a great deal of attention in the People's Republic of China.

Ben-Peretz notes that many studies of the backgrounds, motives, attitudes and expectations of candidates have been conducted in Israel. Like other countries, altruistic motives such as 'service to society' are ranked the most important reasons for entering teaching in Israel. Other Israeli studies investigated the personality traits assumed to be related to competence in teachers.

III. Research on Staff. The twelve chapters in this collection discuss little research on the characteristics of the staff of teacher education programs. Zimpher and Howey suggest that some preliminary studies of the charac-teristics of teacher educators have stimulated interest in this area. The Canadian concern with special workshops and seminars for cooperating teachers, included here as members of staff, suggests that their compe-tence as supervisors of candidates' practicum experiences attracts the attention of researchers. One study in Israel replicated a U.S. study of the professional reputation of teacher educators. Ben-Peretz points out that, unlike the U.S. results, teacher educators in Israel appear to enjoy the same high reputation as university faculty members in other disciplines.

Reasons for the dearth of research on characteristics of teacher educators remain unclear. Neglect of this topic seems unlikely to be due to the failure to perceive staff as major contributors to the quality of the teacher education program.

IV.   Research on Content. Ho Wah Kam traces the shifts in the content of teacher education in Singapore since 1972. A survey of candidates indicated that they gave highest priority to content focused on effective classroom teaching. Zimpher and Howey report that the U.S. reform reports have urged strengthening the rigour of the academic instruction of candidates, especially in subjects they will be expected to teach. At the same time strong pressure exists within the field of education to improve and strengthen the clinical content of teacher education.

In the People's Republic of China the relatively limited time available for teacher education is allocated to practical rather than theoretical content. Sato and Ushiwata report research in Japan indicating that candidates fault their teacher education on the grounds that a big gap exists between the content of the examination used to select teachers and the content of their university courses. A similar theme appears in the review of Canadian research by Wideen and Holborn which reveals discrepancies between the content of courses and school practices expected of graduates of the courses. Tisher's summary of research in Australia suggests that candidates value most the practical part of their teacher education. However, his review indicates that some increase in just the knowledge of science can strengthen teachers' confidence and effectiveness in teaching that subject.

V.   Research on Methods. Klinzing reports that research has been conducted in West Germany on the reactions of candidates to videotapes of classroom experiences designed to minimize the need to observe classrooms directly. Candidates gave a mixed response with some favourable, and others being critical. In Singapore one study found that a clinical supervision model worked well with mature candidates, but less well with candidates who felt uncomfortable in the non-judgmental, indirect approach characteristic of the model. Zimpher and Howey's review points out that in the U.S. great interest exists in the use of laboratory studies and intensive coaching in particular teaching skills. McNamara describes research in the United Kingdom in which candidates in teacher education were provided with the opportunity to select different approaches to their learning, viz. the authoritarian expert, the authoritarian consultant, and a democratic approach, and concludes that the students did not regret having chosen the democratic mode. An experiment on Radio Assisted Practice (RAP) in which college tutors communicated directly with candidates during their classroom practice via miniature radio equipment received favourable reactions from the candidates.

Gran's review includes a report of studies having to do with methods of micro-teaching and self-confrontation. According to Gran, these studies and others were influential in changing the ways in which Swedish teachers were prepared for practice.

In India positive results came from a large-scale experiment that explored the efficacy of micro-teaching as a tool for developing teaching skills. Canadian researchers assessed the efficacy of two different instructional techniques within a mathematics methods course. A seminar/workshop group showed greater improvement in their attitude toward mathematics than the group in the lecture method treatment. Australian research includes a study showing the successful integration of micro-teaching techniques in such a way as to produce changes in trainees' verbal behaviours.

VI. Research on Time and Timing. The most frequently mentioned time factor in most of the chapters is the amount of time allocated to practice teaching. The emerging theme indicates that the time available is generally insufficient.

Teacher preparation for West German candidates occurs in two phases: the first emphasizing subject matter and educational studies, and a second consisting of a two-year supervised practice teaching experience in special state institutions separate from universities. It appears that students complain in both phases; the first phase is faulted as too impractical, the second phase as too stressful because of the demands of working directly with children.

One of the variables in this parameter attracting attention in the U.S. involves the developmental progress, transformations or stages that occur in candidates as experience accrues. Variables examined within a developmental paradigm are candidates' 'concerns', conceptual stages, and adaptation to the social role of teacher in a socialization framework. Zimpher and Howey assert that these developmental approaches might suggest shifts in the design of teacher education programs that better take into account the developmental changes candidates experience.

In many countries practicum experiences have frequently been offered as penultimate or ultimate phases of candidates' experiences. The obverse of this pattern is a trend during the last two decades to provide early field experience. For example, in Canada more than half of forty-two institutions surveyed indicated that they provided some kind of early field experience, in some cases to enable the screening of candidates, and in others designed to strengthen the link between theory and practice.

VII.   Research on Ethos. We define ethos as a combination of the affective quality and content of the relationships among all participants. Together these attributes of a program constitute an ambience through which candidates' values, attitudes, norms and dispositions may be affected. While no research bearing directly on these variables has been reported, some studies mentioned in this collection may be relevant. Zimpher and Howey report on their own intensive case study analysis of various teacher education programs in the middle west of the U.S. which may capture some aspect of the ethos of the programs; however, no details are given. McNamara cites a British report of research on teacher training institutions that concludes by proposing that Anglican colleges are distinguishable from other training institutions by the nature of their sponsorship and the expectation that they display certain Christian qualities — a part of the ethos of the program.

Although no studies on variables in this parameter are cited by Ben-Peretz, she suggests that methods of teaching and evaluation of the teacher education program may contribute to its ethos. Further explication of the theoretical basis of the assumption that ethos is a significant parameter is required before the potential interactions of the ethos variables and other parameter variables can be fruitfully studied.

VIII.   Research on Regulations. Although most of the reviews in this collection mention patterns of governance and regulations such as examinations and various course requirements for certificates, diplomas and degrees, no research concerning their possible effects has been reported. At least two exceptions follow. A great deal of concern existed in Sweden about the impacts of massive change in the governance of teacher education brought about by the higher education reforms of 1977. Askling studied the question and judged that the impacts were close to zero. Her findings were supported by a number of other studies cited by Gran. Teacher education in Sweden seemed unchanged by the implementation of the reforms. Wu and Chang draw attention to the consequences of uniform regulations in a very large and diverse country like the People's Republic of China. For example, data showed that the oral English part of a national examination for entrance into tertiary institutions puts rural students at a great disadvantage because they have fewer opportunities to speak or to hear English spoken than urban students. Sato and Ushiwata also note that the effect of the exams used in Japan to select teachers is that students must 'cram' for them; graduates complain about the big gap between the content of the examination for selection and the pre-service education offered in the universities and colleges. In many countries staff complain that the content of the examinations shapes the content of the curriculum; however, no reports of studies of this problem are mentioned.

IX. Research on Resources. As already suggested, variables in the resources parameter might include a wide range of instructional, technical and physical material and financial support for any aspects of the program. None of the twelve chapters cites research focusing on the effects on teacher education of the supply of such resources. One explanation for this omission may be that the need for more resources is typically so obvious that it seems unnecessary to engage in systematic empirical studies of the issue. One hardly needs an empirical study to become convinced that the shortage of all kinds of resources in countries affects the quality of the teacher education they are able to provide; the sheer number of teachers needed to staff primary schools in countries like India and the People's Republic of China is stunning in itself. It may also be that meaningful, precise and realistic estimates of costs are difficult to obtain. Furthermore, analysis of relationships between the availability of such resources as micro-teaching laboratories, library books, curriculum guides, etc. and the quality of a teacher education program would require more consensus concerning an appropriate criterion measure of quality.

X. Research on Evaluation. Many countries note the use of formal examinations to assess candidates' progress through the components of their teacher education programs. As Ben Peretz notes, written examinations and papers are the most widely used forms of evaluation of candidates during training in Israel. While issues concerning the nature and function of supervision of practice teaching are mentioned in most of the chapters, relatively little is said about the difficulties of evaluating the practicum. Wideen and Holborn cite a Canadian survey indicating that the predominant criteria for the evaluation of student teaching were candidates' relationships with pupils, their ability to arouse and sustain interest, and their energy and enthusiasm. Another Canadian study of student teaching experiences indicated that among several suggestions for improving the practicum was that candidates have more 'evaluation-free' time. The report did not indicate what benefits would accrue from having more time free from evaluation. Perhaps candidates would benefit from a greater sense of freedom to concentrate on the task at hand rather than on making favourable impressions on the supervisor. It may be also that candidates were making a plea to be left alone in the classroom more often so that they could make their mistakes unobserved, and perhaps learn more from them. As Tisher notes in the review of Australian research, candidates' anxiety during practice teaching is one of the variables of interest to researchers in this field.

XI. Research on the Impact of Teacher Education. One of the strongest motives prompting research efforts in the field of teacher education is to strengthen its impact on candidates' ultimate professional competence. The impact of a teacher education program might be reflected in its very specific teaching techniques, or in the candidates' knowledge of schooling and society, or their professional dispositions and attitudes toward their work. Klinzing cites a West German study indicating that teacher education programs that use predominantly 'direct' methods of instruction are highly recommended for teacher education since they lead to desirable changes in candidates' behaviour.

Zimpher and Howey describe a review of U.S. studies comparing provisionally certified and regularly certified teachers as a way of assessing the general impact of teacher education. They concluded that graduates of teacher education programs were perceived, at least in the short term, to be more effective than those teachers with little or no formal teacher training. McNamara refers to a British study that suggests teachers tend to absorb messages on the job which undermine the training program's attempts to encourage acceptance and non-discrimination in candidates.

Govinda and Buch report that a study was conducted in India of the effectiveness of pre-service teacher training at the elementary level by comparing the performance of 363 trained and 187 untrained teachers. A variety of techniques including observation was adopted for collecting the relevant data. It was concluded that trained teachers were superior to untrained ones in almost all aspects of their professional work. In particular, untrained teachers were more prone to purely content-oriented interactions in their approach to teaching.

Wu and Chang attest that the effectiveness of pre-service education in China is often reflected in the degree of success a teacher with a diploma from a teachers' college achieves in a secondary or primary school in China. Therefore, they argue, one of the chief methods of research on teacher education should be case studies. They describe an exceptional teacher (mentioned above) in a rural school whose students were more successful on oral English tests than normally expected, and whose case provoked the study of her teaching by the local county bureau of education and education institute. They reported that the teacher's motivation, good student-teacher relationships and continuing self-education seemed to be major factors accounting for her extraordinary success as a teacher. It is not clear how her teacher training might have had an impact on these qualities and competencies.

Sato and Ushiwata cite research in Japan on the impact of teacher education on candidates' desires to remain in teaching. They report that 90 per cent of the candidates under study increased their desire to be teachers. However, 60 per cent came away from their training experiences with a poor impression of the teacher's role and with little confidence in their ability to teach. Canadian studies of the impact of teacher education compared a program that combined campus and practicum activities with another regular, more traditional program. Based on the candidates' reactions to the programs, the combined campus plus field-based program was perceived more positively than the regular campus-based program.

Summary

We have proposed that teacher education programs are circumscribed, affected and determined by eleven interacting parameters containing a wide range of variables. The parameters were displayed in a matrix which provides a device for ordering, summarizing and synthesizing available literature in the field and for generating new questions for research.

The number of variables that can be generated in each parameter is almost limitless. The remaining problem is to select those research questions which can be expected to have the greatest power to improve our understandings of teacher education, and to guide the kind of research and development which may further that end. In order to select from among this vast potential set of variables, some persuasive theories concerning which ones might be related to which others are required. We hope that the ordering of available literature and the generation of new questions suggested by the framework presented above will aid in the development of useful theories to guide the next steps in the field.

Reference

KATZ, L.G. and RATHS, J.D. (1985) A framework for research on teacher education programs. *Journal of Teacher Education, 36*, 6, 9–15.

Chapter 15

Review, Reflections and Recommendations

Richard P. Tisher and Marvin F. Wideen

This book emerged from an examination of research in teacher education using the perspectives of researchers from different cultures to determine what we know about teacher education and its research. In our view reform about the process of teacher preparation and its research must be guided by conscious critical analysis of what has been learned. Both are complex in that both are affected by political, economic and sociological factors. The twelve international contributions, which we hope provide the flavour of the research in the respective countries, attest to this complexity. In this chapter we take stock of what we have learned and present proposals for future research.

What Do We Conclude about Teacher Education and Its Research?

On the one hand, the preceding chapters provide a frustrating, despairing picture but, on the other, we find much room for optimism in that a base has been built for future research and for the revision of teacher education programs.

A first reading of the chapters provides a pessimistic picture of teacher education. The reviews show a lack of balance between theory and practice: teacher educators do not always practise what they preach; in-service education is often unrelated to school issues and inefficiently carried out; pre-service programs do not always produce effective teachers; the socializing effects of schools militate against what is done in college pre-service training courses; trainees emerge from programs with negative attitudes to pupils; practice-teaching supervisors have no clear idea as to their role; and practice teaching is less effective than we generally believe. National and local governments provide inadequate finances for teacher education, hinder the process, have no clear commitment to in-service education, attempt to interfere with the content of training programs and jettison criteria for teacher certification in order to meet shortfalls in teacher recruitment. It appears that more exhortation about what teacher education should do occurs than do changes to produce more efficient and effective programs.

Similarly, a disconcerting picture of research into teacher education emerges. We see a disconnected set of studies with no coherent objectives and a lack of balance; poor anchoring to the practical, day-to-day problems in teacher education; a predominance of surveys with minimal experimentation on new ways of delivering teacher education; unwarranted overkill with sophisticated statistical analyses; studies designed and driven by persons who are often not involved in educating teachers; little or no compelling effect on policy and practice; a lack of national research priorities; and, in a number of cases, projects of dubious rigour. Researchers appear to pursue their own interests, with little or no attempt to refer to or replicate the work of others; investigatory samples draw on captive groups of teacher trainees with no relevant theoretical frameworks serving as substantive scaffolding for studies. The adjectives 'exciting', 'stimulating', 'barrier-breaking', 'trend-setting', 'knowledge-expanding' and 'innovative' can hardly be used to describe research of this nature.

A closer look at the preceding reviews reveals a more encouraging picture, at least in some countries. More qualified and committed people now enter teacher training; students benefit often from their pre-service programs; some college and university pre-service programs have a liberalizing effect; pre-service trainees' competencies increase throughout their training and they develop more realistic ideas of what they can do as teachers; teaching skills are enhanced during pre-service and in-service activities; and in-service is found to be especially effective in those instances where teachers have some ownership of their professional development activities. Finally, teacher educators enjoy a relatively high reputation in some countries.

The research too conveys a positive note. As the preceding chapters show, it is alive, well and on the increase in most countries. We find studies of teacher education reported more often in the international literature and discussed by national and international groups. The number of studies now available in several areas provides a basis for replication and international comparison. Research has begun to document some of the positive features of what we do in teacher education such as skill training, the models that are effective for delivering teacher education, and the improvements to come from the supervisory process in student teaching. The more pluralistic approach to methodology that has developed in the last decade seems better suited to address the complexity of teacher education. The critical mass of research in certain areas now raises issues that policy-makers and course designers can no longer ignore. We also find moves to develop coherent frameworks to guide future research programs.

What other things can be said about the research? It provides an impressive foundation on which to build. It tells us about successes and disappointments in teacher education programs, thereby providing information as to where consolidation, adaptation, reform or modification should occur. It shows what kinds of pay-offs result from different research approaches, indicates areas where more understanding is required, and has the potential to inform practice and policy. If we take a long-term view of building and consolidation, then there is much to be gleaned from the foregoing chapters about the methods for conducting the research, the appropriate people to do it, the impact it might have on practice and policy, and the contribution it can make to our understandings of the process of teacher education as well as the effects of the contexts in which it occurs. We shall address each of these matters in turn and then conclude with recommendations as to directions future research might take.

Methods for Conducting the Research

The twelve review chapters illustrate what we outlined in Chapter 1, that the use of qualitative research methodologies has been increasing, which has broadened the scope of research considerably. In places where the empirical-analytical orientation appears to be the preferred approach, e.g., China, India, Japan and Singapore, increasingly there are calls for situational-interpretive procedures.

We contend that world-wide a better mix of methodologies exists, that pluralism of methods should be retained, and that clear benefits emerge when studies use qualitative approaches such as case study and action research in order to understand better and to improve practice teaching, supervision and in-service education. We have been greatly encouraged by reports from the USA, Britain and Australia where trainees and teachers appear to favour and respond to these approaches as ones that indicate to them what works.

The People Who Do the Research

The questions of who does the research and how those doing it conceptualize their work provide important points of departure for assessing both the worth of the research and its potential for influencing policy and practice. The chapters reveal that those occupying university positions, or posts in special research institutes do the bulk of the research in teacher education. In some countries, for example, the Netherlands, India, Sweden and West Germany, it is well-nigh impossible to undertake research if you are not an employee in one of these places. Because these people are relatively independent, we might take this as a positive factor for the research. They are free from governmental or political constraints to focus on those issues they deem to be important. Some of the research reported in this volume has, as we have seen, been determined by the researchers' own curiosity and interests, and their responses to local issues, but this has resulted in an ad hoc character to the research, with little attention to an overarching national or international plan or purpose.

The Canadian and British chapters raise an issue here that bears note. Both draw our attention to the fact that other players also conduct research in teacher education. In Britain governmental agencies engage in inquiry-oriented activity; in Canada districts provide a source for research. In this work we have relied primarily upon studies cited in refereed journals, books and dissertations and read by a certain audience. That may pose a limitation to this review. Future efforts should attempt to be inclusive of other players.

In some countries the university researchers also teach in teacher preparation programs. That fact carries with it a number of implications. Depending on how close the researchers are to the actual practice of teacher education, and to policy decisions made about it, there will be variations in the impact the research has on practice and policy. Clearly the situation varies from country to country, but in those where the researchers are also involved in teacher education we might expect the results of the research to be felt in an immediate kind of way. Where they are also members of national policy-making committees the impact can be even greater.

It has been suggested in the preceding chapters that researchers who are not teacher educators may be less sensitive to the complexities and problems of teacher education and may, at times, have inappropriate frames guiding their research. Narrowing the gap between those who do the research and those who deliver teacher education can, to some extent, allay these criticisms. Our considered opinion is that more teacher educators should be involved in research in teacher education for the research to have greater salience in the teacher education community. A corollary to this belief is that in those places where teacher educators have restricted research funds they should now be given greater access to funding agencies.

Given the complexity of teacher education and its research, and the fact that in each of the countries reviewed the proportion of researchers devoting their attention to teacher education is small, there is a case for increasing the 'critical mass' of research groups, thereby moving away from the present individualistic nature of conducting the research. There are trends in this direction in the USA and pleas for it to occur at national and international levels from the Netherlands and Israel. We return to this issue in a subsequent section.

Impact on Practice and Policy

As we indicated, who does the research bears a relationship to practice and policy changes. Research by graduate students in India, for example, rarely impinges upon policy-makers. But even when research is commissioned by national policy groups, policies may, as instanced in the Netherlands, be determined during the lifetime of the commissioned study or before it commences. Even our expectation of a more immediate impact on practice when teacher educators or persons close to the practice of teacher education are the researchers can be thwarted when other teacher educators, as shown in India, reject the research because it told them what they already knew, or because, as has occurred in Australia, the training context for the study differed from their own.

To expect that research results can be immediately applied to policy and practice is to adopt a naive attitude towards educational change. Policy and practice changes are processes conditioned by the cultural, social and political environment and are the result of negotiations and compromise among various interest groups, including groups of teacher educators who tend to tread warily with respect to change. From experiences in our own national contexts, however, we believe that research has produced changes, especially in those situations where teacher educators have been researchers. Evidence for this belief can be found in committee papers and other in-house documents, but not adequately in published papers. Publication is a task for the future. Lessons can also be learned from experiences in places like Sweden where researchers have been members of policy-making committees.

It is evident that research in teacher education is on the increase: more people in many countries are involved in it; greater dialogue, of which this book is evidence, is occurring at national and international forums; dissemination of the findings has been increasingly widespread; governments are more favourably disposed to research in teacher education; and networks for sharing the accumulating wisdom are increasing. All these activities point to a favourable climate for research in teacher education, including an acceptance of that research, which augurs well for the future impact of research on practice and policy.

Contribution to a Theory of Teacher Education

What contribution has the research made to basic theories about education? Very little, if the review chapters are any guide. The authors are generally disappointed about the theoretical underpinnings of much of the research and regard it as inadequate, but not non-existent. The research has been affected by theoretical conceptualizations. Psychological constructs about anxiety, for example, have been invoked in studies of trainees' characteristics in Australia; conceptualizations about modelling, practice and feedback have influenced teaching skills studies in West Germany; and socialization theories have shaped induction studies in Britain and the USA. But there are no dramatic advances in how we conceptualize the process of teacher education. Our earlier suggestion that research does not simply and easily develop basic theory appears to be attested to by the contributions to this volume. There are, however, some intriguing developments in the USA and Australia where researchers are studying the process of teacher education and how it unfolds for teacher trainees. These developments appear to have the potential to contribute to conceptualizations about the process.

We are of the considered opinion that for research to contribute more to our conceptualizations about the process of teacher education more information is required about how the process unfolds for pre-service, beginning and experienced teachers. They are, after all, constantly learning new ways of being themselves in different teaching-learning contexts.

Understanding the Context

We argued in Chapter 1 that different contexts for teacher education frame and influence research in each country. For example, studies in Japan about the process of teacher selection, preparations for that selection and alternative selection criteria have been prompted by the strong competitive climate for entering teaching. This same phenomenon gave rise to studies in Israel and Singapore, where individuals with high academic and personal qualities are desired for the teaching profession. In the Netherlands policy changes with respect to school management, autonomy and innovation have spawned many studies on the role of in-service. In China and India studies of teachers' in-service needs and academic and skill deficiences are driven by manpower issues, inadequately qualified teachers, and associated national necessities to upgrade their academic knowledge and teaching skills. The mode of delivering in-service education is not a major research priority in these countries. In contrast, in Australia and Canada, where teachers play significant roles in in-service activities, modes of delivery are investigated, often through collaborative action research and case study.

Geographical proximity, and economic and political interdependence are other contextual factors affecting educational research and desires to undertake collaborative cross-national studies in teacher education. Our European authors, who are very cognizant of the likely developments and educational issues associated with the establishment of a European Government and Community, naturally propose more collaborative international research in teacher education.

Institutional context variables such as administrative structures, financing, staff establishments and staff deployment frame and influence the delivery of teacher education. Research has occurred on these variables in Britain, Sweden, the Netherlands and the USA and to a lesser extent in Australia and Canada. However, not all of the countries with traditions of research in educational administration have focused on the effect of these variables in teacher education. Why is this so? And why the apparent paucity of reported research on institutional variables in teacher education? Is it due to lack of enthusiasm or theoretical knowledge about teacher education organizations? Is the research so sensitive that those who venture into it fear becoming social or occupational outcasts in their country? Whatever the reasons, a gap exists in our understanding and a consequent need arises to invest some effort to learn more.

Where to from Here?

Given the preceding scenarios, where do we go from here? We believe, as we said earlier, that much room for optimism exists and much can be gleaned to provide direction for future research. We can learn from our mistakes as well as our successes to improve the quality, quantity and impact of research in teacher education. To stimulate discussion and action, we present four recommendations arising from the reviews and interpretations in this volume. They are not mutually exclusive; they deal with: building upon what we have; developing collaborative teams, links and networks; conceptualizing teacher education; and fostering ownership of in-service education.

Building upon What We Have

It is easy to denigrate what has been done, especially if we ignore the complexities associated with research in teacher education. One can argue that even inadequate research can heighten our awareness of issues and increase our understanding. It is more difficult to capitalize on previous endeavours and consolidate. We believe we must strive to build on existing work and offer *two* proposals for consolidation and *four* for extending what we know.

With respect to consolidation a first step could be to undertake meta-analyses across nations in selected areas such as those defined in the Katz and Raths' framework in the previous chapter. A large research literature exists for this purpose in English-speaking countries, and cross-national collaboration could include many reports in other languages. The time appears ripe to emulate the useful meta-analyses that have occurred in other areas in education.

Another consolidating step involves the replication of many of the qualitative as well as quantitative studies so that (1) subsequent findings will reaffirm a previous result rather than merely complement it; (2) outcomes will be more relevant to teacher educators since some projects are likely to occur in contexts approximating their own; and (3) our understanding of the teacher education process will grow in an iterative manner. But knowledge does not simply grow by accretion; it must also be linked to conceptualization about teacher education — a point we take up later.

The majority of the authors have pointed to research lacunae. Four steps, at least, can be taken to fill the gaps and extend our knowledge. First, the Katz and Raths' framework in Chapter 14 can be used to identify topics to be tackled using qualitative or quantitative approaches. Ben-Peretz, in Chapter 12, refers to this possibility by highlighting the neglected issues of goals, time and finances (i.e., resources) in the Israeli context. Wu and Chang (Chapter 13) also refer to goals and finances and add the teacher education curriculum. A variety of intersecting or interacting issues may also be deemed worthy of study, such as the effects of interactions between teacher educators' value systems and the modes of delivering teacher education programs.

Second, we can take up issues deemed by a majority of the authors to be neglected areas. They are aware of and understand the critical issues in teacher education; their pooled wisdom provides direction for future research. The following summary lists some of the neglected research areas with cross-referencing to some of the chapters where they are mentioned.

Some proposals for

further research on	*by authors from*
Selection, including, when it occurs, characteristics of entrants and their relation to subsequent pre-service programs	Israel, India, Japan, Singapore and West Germany
The curriculum of pre-service, including the knowledge base for teacher education and the sequencing and timing of components	Australia, China, Israel, India, Japan, Sweden, USA and West Germany
Development of teaching skills	Singapore and West Germany
Practice teaching and its supervision, including limitations to be overcome, models of teaching and training of supervisors	Australia, India, Sweden and the Netherlands
The participants (trainees, teachers, teacher educators), including their characteristics and cognitive structures	Australia, Israel, Japan and the Netherlands
In-service education; needs for, and mode of delivery; bearing in mind impact of national curricula, school reforms, role of delivery agencies, school-based activities, and up-grading requirements	Britain, Canada, China, India, Israel, Japan, Singapore, Sweden and the Netherlands
Institutional contexts for teacher education including goals, finances, faculties of education and staff deployment	Australia, Canada, China, Israel, Japan, Sweden and USA
Entry to teaching including socializing effects of schools, hiring	Canada, China, Sweden, Netherlands and West

| policies and profiles of teachers and teacher educators | Germany |
| Future of teacher education | Canada |

Two lacunae are singled out for brief comment. First, the recommendation that studies of selection for teacher education be continued must be coupled with another that research on entrants' characteristics be put to better use by developing programs matched to and capitalizing on these characteristics. Second, there is the recommendation that the teacher education curriculum, especially that of pre-service, be subject to greater scrutiny in order to provide information about the relevance and effectiveness of the content and timing of program components. The suggestion to examine content is associated with Shulman's (1986) arguments about the kinds of knowledge — subject matter, pedagogical, content, curricular, propositional, case and strategic — that must be part of a teacher's repertoire. It also highlights the need to understand trainees' and teacher educators' cognitive frameworks to discover how trainees learn about teaching and how teacher educators teach about it.

The third and fourth steps for extending our knowledge deal with research procedures more than research topics. Our third recommendation is for more detailed, published evaluations of pre-service, induction and in-service education than have occurred in the past in order to document the nature and benefits accruing from the various components of teacher education. Several authors mention evaluations in their list of lacunae, but we single them out as special process features to highlight the lack of reporting of systematic evaluations.

The final procedural recommendation is to follow the process of teacher education as it unfolds for the pre-service, beginning and experienced teacher. We have already mentioned that this approach is being adopted in some places with pre-service trainees and has the potential to inform our conceptualizations about the teacher training process. We refer to this again in a subsequent section.

Developing Collaborative Teams, Links and Networks

How to cope with the complexity of the teacher education process in order to understand, master and deliver it, and how to influence policy and practice are crucial, not easily resolvable issues for researchers. Some encouraging ways in which resolution might proceed have been reported, including adopting a more pluralistic approach to methodology, and narrowing the gap between those who do the research and those who deliver teacher education and those who make policy about it. For these procedures to continue and be more widely adopted, it is necessary, we believe, for more individual researchers to band together in larger collaborative teams to share physical resources, personnel, expertise and theoretical conceptualizations in order more efficiently to tackle the tasks of unravelling the mysteries of the teacher education process. We recommend increasing the critical mass of persons in research teams in most countries. Collaboration in teams, as occurs in the USA and is beginning in Singapore, has the potential of reducing the idiosyncratic, ad hoc nature of the research, of fostering long-term studies which centre on coherent themes, of providing more insights with respect to matters for study, and making available knowledge about a wide range of research methodologies.

As already mentioned, influencing policy and practice becomes complicated, as social, political and organizational realities come into play, and outcomes are the result of negotiations and compromises. The contrasting lessons learned from Sweden and Britain about the influence researchers can have when they are members of policy-making groups, or the way biased individuals isolate, extract and use research results to support preconceived policies, suggest that if researchers eschew membership in policy groups, research will continue to have a low impact. If this occurs, the more favourable climate for research and the more widespread knowledge about the successes and deficiencies in teacher education may not be significantly sufficient to bring about desired changes. We advocate networking and linking with policy-making groups as a sine qua non if research is to have an impact. Educational researchers must become more politically wise, not naive, as now is the case.

In addition to more collaborative approaches with policy-makers and other researchers, we should, as was mentioned earlier, seek to remove the gap between those who do the research and those who deliver teacher education. Our considered opinion is that when that gap is narrowed research can have a greater impact on local teacher education practices.

Developing Conceptualizations or Theories about Teacher Education

A general dissatisfaction can be discerned about the way in which teacher education research has been conceptualized, and the contribution that the research has made to explanations about the process of teacher education. We contend that more appropriate conceptualizations/explanations are required. The need for this can be illustrated by considering early research on micro-teaching which was predicated on concepts about the role of modelling, practice and feedback, but neglected considerations of the cognitive and affective stages trainees had reached in their teacher education process, trainees' conceptual readiness for micro-teaching, the timeliness and salience of the training activities, and the congruence between these activities and what occurred in actual teaching situations. Disappointing training outcomes, such as negative self-evaluations, unwillingness to experiment with a wide range of strategies, and failure to persist with newly learned strategies, were explicable in terms of the neglected features, thereby demonstrating that theories about training must not only relate to, but be embedded in, the process of teacher education.

Innumerable difficulties face anyone who attempts to construct and validate hypotheses and theories about teacher education. These hypotheses and theories may, or may not, be complex, plausible or convincing; and may, or may not, concern causal relations. But it is clear from the preceding reviews that more adequate theories dealing with the process are desired. What they will look like is left to others to determine. We have only scratched the surface of this challenging task by suggesting that investigations of, and accounts about, the process of teacher education as it unfolds for pre-service, beginning and experienced teachers can contribute. We believe it is now imperative that others accept the challenge to develop theories about teacher education and thereby create more adequate frameworks and the potential for future research to inform those basic theories.

Foster Teacher Ownership of In-service Education

In-service education is important for continuing professional development, and for enhancing teachers' pedagogical and curricular knowledge. A lesson to be learned from the research reviews dealing with India, the Netherlands, China, Canada and Australia is that while there is no one preferred model for in-service education, the impact of its activities will be greater when teachers have major ownership in planning, organizing and delivering them. We recommend action research projects of school-based as well as centralized in-service education where teachers are the major 'owners' in order to comprehend better the range of effective modes by which in-service may be delivered. It is our belief that action research will also ensure that practical benefits accrue to teachers, schools and, in turn, to pupils at the same time as the activities are being evaluated.

Concluding Comment

The preceding descriptions, analyses, comparisons and contrasts about research in teacher education in different cultural contexts have created an awareness of successes and deficiencies in teacher education, lacunae in our understanding of the process, strengths and limitations of the research, and ways to improve teacher education, its future research and its impact on practice, policy and theory. What will happen in countries depends on local needs, priorities, finances, credibility of the researchers and the research, the political sensitivity of teacher education issues, and who is involved in making policy. We are confident, however, that researchers and their research can make a significant contribution to theory, policy and practice. The future for research in teacher education is challenging, arduous, requires persons with tenacity, creativeness and vision, and is bright and full of promise.

Reference

SHULMAN, L. (1986) Those who understand: Knowledge growth in teaching. *Educational Researcher*, 15, 2, 4–14.

Notes on Contributors

Miriam Ben-Peretz is Dean of the School of Education, University of Haifa where she has been a faculty member since 1965. She has been a biology teacher, director of a biology curriculum project, and chairperson (1977–1985) of the Department of Teacher Education, University of Haifa. Her research interests include the role of teachers in curriculum development and implementation, issues in teacher education, teacher thinking, and cross-cultural studies on teaching. She has been a visiting professor in universities in Australia, Canada, USA and West Germany, and has published numerous articles in scholarly journals and books.

M.B. Buch, a senior educationist in India, was a Director of the Centre of Advanced Study, University of Baroda. He has worked in the National Council of Educational Research and Training, numerous national committees on teacher education, educational administration and educational surveys. Professor Buch is also Chief Editor of four volumes of surveys of research in education in India, covering a period of 131 years (1857–1988) and incorporating 4700 research studies from 150 universities and research institutes. He is chairman of the Society for Educational Research and Development, and Chief Editor of its journal, *Perspectives in Education*.

Jean Chang is an Associate Professor at Beijing Teachers College. From 1981 to 1982 she was a visiting scholar at the New York State University at Oswego, USA. She now teaches English and educational psychology in the English Department of the College.

R. Govinda is the Senior Fellow and Head of the Unit on School Education and Non-Formal Education in the National Institute of Educational Planning and Administration. He has authored and co-authored numerous research monographs and books, and a chapter in the *Third Survey of Research in Education*, an overview of research in education in India during the last fifty years. He is editor of *Perspectives in Education*, the journal of the Society for Educational Research and Development of which he is founder Secretary.

Bertil Gran is an Associate Professor of Education, University of Lund, Sweden. For the past five years he has been responsible for research and research studies, Department of Educational and Psychological Research, School of Education, Malmo. He has served as an expert member of government committees dealing with reforms in teacher education, and chairman of educational research committees in the Council of Europe. He is now responsible for planning follow-up and evaluation of teacher education reforms in Sweden. His publications include numerous reports, books and articles on teacher education, innovation and school development and documentation systems in education.

Ho Wah Kam is currently Head of the Educational Research Unit at the Institute of Education, Singapore. He received his PhD from the University of Chicago in 1981. His research interests are in teacher education, teacher socialization, language acquisition and language testing.

Patricia Holborn is a teacher educator based at Simon Fraser University. She conducts courses in primary education, teaching for thinking and supervision of teaching, and works with school districts as an in-service consultant and classroom coach. Recent publications include *Becoming a Teacher*, an edited book of readings and seminar activities for student teachers (with Marvin Wideen and Ian Andrews) and 'Cooperative Group Development: Strategies for Success', in the journal *Prime Areas*.

Kenneth R. Howey is a Professor of Education, College of Education, Ohio State University with research, development and instructional interests in the education of teachers. He has researched and written extensively on all phases of teacher education; served as adviser to numerous institutions and agencies (e.g., National Institute of Education, Far West Laboratory for Educational Research and Development, and Research and Development Center for Teacher Education at Michigan State University); been active in numerous professional teacher education organizations; and consulted on teacher issues with the Forum of Educational Leaders. He is research editor for the *Journal of Teacher Education*, and consulting editor for two other international journals.

Gunter L. Huber is Professor of Educational Psychology at the University of Tübingen (FRG). He has three years of practical experience as a teacher in Hauptschule. He graduated in psychology at the University of Munich, received his Dr Phil from the same university in pedagogics. His interests are in learning and instruction, especially in the role of group processes and interpersonal differences, and with complementing quantitative methods with systematized qualitative approaches.

Lilian G. Katz is Professor of Early Childhood Education and Director of the ERIC Clearinghouse on Elementary and Early Childhood Education at the University of Illinois at Urbana-Champaign, Illinois, USA. She is also Editor of the *Early Childhood Research Quarterly* and Vice President of the National Association for the Education of Young Children. Professor Katz has been visiting professor in Australia, India, West Germany, Canada, the West Indies and Great Britain. Her principal interest is in early childhood education and teacher education. She co-authors the series *Advances in Teacher Education* with J.D. Raths.

Frans K. Kieviet after his education at a training college for primary schools worked for several years in various types of school while studying for some certificates and his master's degree in education. Since 1965 he has been working at the Department of Educational Sciences of the State University of Leiden. This department, of which he is head, is responsible for training different kinds of educationalists and for research in various areas of education. He was awarded his doctor's degree for the dissertation 'Micro-teaching as a method in teacher education', by which he introduced micro-teaching in the Netherlands. In 1973 he was appointed as a full Professor of Education, especially in didactics. His main domains of interest are teaching and teacher education.

Hans Gerhard Klinzing is Ausserplanmassiger Professor (adjunct professor/personal chair) of the School of Education at the University of Tübingen (FRG) and Honorary Professor at the University of Stuttgart (FRG). After graduating in literature, linguistics and history, and teaching at secondary schools, he studied education and received his Dr.rer.soc. (1975) and his Dr. habil. (1983) from the University of Tübingen. His teaching and research interests are in the areas of instructional research, teaching-learning models, and in the development and evaluation of teacher training methods.

Gisela Klinzing-Eurich is Lehrbeauftragte at the Department of Education II at the University of Tübingen (FRG). After graduating in literature, linguistics and history, she studied Education and received her D.rer.soc. (1981) from the University of Tübingen. Her teaching and research interests are in the areas of the development and evaluation of teacher training methods.

David McNamara BSc PhD began his educational career as a primary school teacher. Most of his research and published work has been in the field of teacher education and evaluation. He is now Professor of Primary Education and Chairman of the School of Education, University of Durham.

James D. Raths is currently Dean of the College of Education and Social Services at the University of Vermont in Burlington, Vermont, USA. He serves as an executive editor of the *Journal of Educational Research*. In the past he was an Associate Dean for Teacher Education at the University of Illinois and Director of the Bureau of Educational Research and Field Services at the University of Maryland. His research interests include evaluation issues and questions concerning teacher education. He was educated at Yale College, BS mathematics, 1954; Yale University, MAT, 1955; and New York University, PhD evaluation and statistics, 1960.

Akira Sato is Chief of the Teaching Profession Division at the National Institute for Educational Research of Japan. He was Associate Professor at a national university for teacher education. Before that he was a senior high school English teacher. He holds a PhD in education from Tohoku University. He is the author of articles on various aspects of teacher education and has served as executive editor of the *Bulletin of Japan Educational Administration Society*. His current research interests are in the improvement of teacher education programs and of educational personnel administration including teacher selection.

Richard P. Tisher is a Professor of Education and head of a group concerned with professional development, curriculum, teaching effectiveness, evaluation, and science, mathematics and computer education in the Faculty of Education, Monash University. He has held posts as a science teacher, lecturer in teachers' colleges and University Reader in Education. His publications include articles on teacher induction, teacher education, classroom interaction, higher cognitive questioning, non-verbal behaviour and research on science teacher education. He is also co-author, with R.T. White, of 'Research in the Natural Sciences' in *The Third Handbook of Research on Teaching*.

Jun Ushiwata is Dean at Sendai Shirayuri Junior College. He completed the course for PhD at Tohoku University in 1982. He has served as a visiting researcher at the National Institute for Educational Research of Japan and as a member of the Board of Directors of the Japanese Association for the Study of Educational Administration. He has published articles on teacher education in the United States of America in order to compare it with counterparts in Japan. His current interests are in developing the curriculum for in-service education of teachers.

Marvin F. Wideen is Professor in the Faculty of Education at Simon Fraser University. Prior to his becoming involved in teacher education, he worked both as a teacher and as a principal in public schools. He writes and conducts research in the areas of teacher education, science education and school improvement. His recent works include *Staff Development for School Improvement* (Falmer Press) and *Becoming a Teacher* (Kagan and Woo).

Zhaoyi Wu is an Associate Professor at Beijing Teachers College. He obtained his BA (Hons) from the English Department of Victoria University of Wellington and an MA (Hons) from the Anthropology Department of Auckland University. He has been a researcher and visiting scholar at the School of Education of the University of Massachusetts at Amherst, USA, from which he obtained his doctorate in education.

Nancy L. Zimpher is an Associate Professor of Education in the area of curriculum, instruction and professional development, College of Education, Ohio State University. Her scholarly interests are in selection and professional development of teachers, and she has conducted research on student teaching and field experiences, nature of leadership in schools and colleges, program evaluation and assessment, and the design and development of teacher education programs. Currently she is principal investigator for a grant to utilize research on teacher education to assist in beginning teacher programs. She has published widely on the preceding topics in books and international journals.

Index